Behind the Membership

Callie Willows
& Mike Morrison

Behind the Membership

First published in 2019 by We Do Digital Ltd t/a The Membership Guys, Darras Hall, Northumberland, UK.

This edition published in 2019 by The Membership Guys.
www.themembershipguys.com

ISBN 978-0-244-21324-4

Contents

Introduction

"There's a lot of beauty in ordinary things. Isn't that kind of the point?"
Pam Halpert, Dunder Mifflin.

One of my favourite things as a membership site owner is talking with other membership site owners.

What's working for them?
What isn't working for them?
What would they do differently if they were starting again?
What challenges have they had along the way and how did they overcome them?
What tips do they have?

I'm not alone in this inquisitiveness I know, and in 2017 I started the podcast Behind the Membership, out of a desire to share the everyday experiences of being a membership site owner with the wider public.

My aim was that it would serve as inspiration for those thinking about creating a membership site, without glossing over some of the harder details, but also that it would provide insights and ideas for those who already had membership sites too.

There's a lot to be learned from those who are actually in the trenches, day after day, working on their membership site, rather than just gurus and experts after all.

After 3 seasons and 32 episodes, a lot of great information has been shared on Behind the Membership, too much to just be relegated to podcast archives!

And so this book was born, taking the greatest insights from each episode so that my guests experiences can be spread far and wide, inspiring even more membership site owners to think differently about how they run their membership sites.

I hope you find it useful!

Callie (& Mike)

Stacey Harris: Hit the Mic Backstage

Membership Details:

Name: Hit the Mic Backstage

Topic: Social Media

Launched: August 2015

Website: hitthemicbackstage.com

Interview Date: June 2017

Stacey Harris runs Hit the Mic Backstage, a membership site which helps online entrepreneurs get their message out to their audience, by keeping them up-to-date with the latest social media developments.

The membership is closely linked to Stacey's podcast, Hit the Mic, and is the natural next step for her listeners. Stacey also runs a done for you social media agency alongside the membership.

"My membership is really positioned and structured to be essentially an upgrade to my podcast. **We talk a lot about the same things in the podcast and in the training community. However, usually the training community gets stuff first.** *One of the episodes we do every month on the show is '3 things you must know right now' - that's network updates and things like that. All that stuff goes on as I hear about it in the membership community.*

We have a library of 60 plus trainings as of right now. And we also have three full structured courses in there. Which is how I used to deliver trainings and content like this.

And then we also have a VIP lounge which is a private community forum right on the site. And that's where people can ask me questions."

The membership is open all the time, something which suits Stacey and her audience.

"Selfishly I don't super love launches, they're just not my favourite thing to execute in my business. So there's times when we go to a higher promo period for the membership. But I really enjoy being open and accessible all of the time…

… Because it is positioned as an upgrade to the podcast it doesn't super make sense to have it closed. I mean there's a reason the show was called Hit the Mic with The Stacey Harris and the membership community is called Hit the Mic Backstage. ***It is the next logical step for listeners. And so to structure it as something that closes and opens, sort of hinders my ability to have it positioned that way."***

From Courses to Membership

Stacey started out creating and selling stand alone online courses to teach business owners about social media. But as the industry is constantly changing, Stacey found herself needing to regularly update the course material - an activity she wasn't getting paid for.

"So I have always always really liked the training library kind of model. I wanted one for a really long time. I built four courses before I launched Backstage. And the struggle in my area is that, when you build a course and they buy it you have to keep updating it. But you're no longer getting paid.

The first course I ever created was called The Rockstar Guide to Facebook and I sold it for like $97, it was a six module program. It is current and exists inside Backstage. But here's the deal - I made the $97 per head, and three months after it launched it was outdated. And so I found myself sort of every time it would get completed, I was starting over again....

It was feeling like I was rolling this rock uphill but I kept convincing myself that my audience wasn't big enough for a membership site. *My audience wasn't there I needed to have this massive list of like a hundred thousand people before I got a membership site.*

...at the time I did a brand new webinar every month. And I had been doing it for about a year and a half. But I always take my webinar down three days after they were run live. So I had this library of great webinars that were totally current and ready to use just sitting in my Google Drive. So I packaged them up and made them something called the Rockstar Resource Pack. And it was awesome because I could sell that real quick and hit my income goal"

After Stacey had success with selling the bundle of her webinar recordings and resources, a friend suggested she turn the materials into a membership.

"A friend of mine goes 'why don't you just put them in a membership site?'. And I was like 'I just don't have the audience, I just don't have the audience for that'. And she was like 'well just try it, if it doesn't work then just turn it back into the pack give everybody lifetime access and stop charging them'.

So we launched Hit the Mic Backstage which started with that training library which is essentially the Rockstar Resource Pack.

And it took off and it's been two, almost two years now, and it's hands down one of my favourite parts of my business. We add new trainings every month, or update old trainings, one of the two. But yeah it all started with a bunch of webinars that I had done nothing with."

Because Stacey was able to make use of existing content, once the idea of the membership site was formed she was able to take action and launch her membership site very quickly.

"I was able to go from yeah I'm going to do this to launching in about two weeks...

Once I decided to do it, it was able to evolve really quickly because I had that stuff in place already that I could repurpose. And I think sometimes we get so distracted by all the things we're going to have to do that we don't take the time to look at what we have. I know a lot of people who listen to my show have entire courses sitting on Google Drive or Dropbox that they've built and written and created and they've just never released, they've never sold.

So look at those things that you have, looking at the webinars you've done, the opt-in training funnels you've created before that maybe you're not using anymore or you are using and you can add a little bit more to to extend the experience. And then that can become your membership. **I think we get distracted on everything that we have to create from scratch and that becomes an obstacle to doing anything.***"*

A Pricing Sweet Spot

Stacey pre-sold the membership before launch with an early bird pricing offer, and many of these early adopters are still with her. She has since changed the price several times before finding her 'sweet spot'.

"Before I had built the site, we were selling spots in it. And so we sold to, without any real launch, just to my email list and to my social community, a price of $50 a year for the lifetime of their membership.

We still have members set at that rate which I find to be just super fun. I know a lot of membership owners sort of rub up against having that early bird members still there and they're not paying as much. But I find it fantastic. I feel like they stuck with me and that's really cool.

That was available only until the doors actually opened. And then we adjusted the price to $9 a month or $99 a year. That only lasted about three months. Then we went to $25 per month or $250 a year and that lasted probably eight months. And then at the one year anniversary, so maybe it was a little less than eight months. At the one year anniversary we raised it to $40 per month or $400 per year and I don't see it going up any time soon to be honest with you. I like the price point especially for who I'm serving and the value that's there."

The Marketing Challenge

The ongoing marketing of the membership has been an unexpected challenge for Stacey, despite her expertise in this area.

*"We always have some new sales funnel that's going out or some new piece of content. I mean, in full transparency, **everything I do that's at a free level is structured to drive traffic to this thing that's paid**. I don't think that I'm revealing any major marketing secrets here.*

I didn't anticipate it being constant. Maybe it's not that I didn't anticipate it because I would be a bit naive of me but I didn't think about it. I didn't consider it. But it is a constant sales process…

*…I'm always - 'so what can we try now? Okay what can we test now? What about this can we tweak? What about this ad? How can we tweak how we're delivering the message in the podcast? How can we make it easier for them to get from the podcast to the sales page? Should we run a special offer?'… you know all of those things. **I didn't anticipate the amount of time I would spend selling the membership site versus serving the membership site.**"*

Despite this challenge, Stacey has found what works for her when it comes to marketing the membership and attracting new members, although this is something that she is constantly tweaking and testing.

*"One thing we really do a ton of is having a really solid sales funnel that's kicked off by Facebook ads and drives traffic to either content or straight to an opt-in depending on the audience. Those funnels are again trainings with me. **We do a webinar and a challenge within one opt-in,** so they sign up for what's technically a challenge, or a three day training series as we call it."*

In Stacey's current funnel, when subscribers sign-up for a three day training series, a recorded webinar is delivered in the first email as a surprise bonus. Effectively the first email with the webinar covers all of the training content, and over the next few days the follow-up email walks them through it step-by-step. The email series closes with an offer for a 7-day $1 trial.

"That has been the best thing I implemented because when people can try something on like that, it's an easy yes to say okay it's a buck it's fine. And for me I learned very early if I can get a member in I can keep them. It was just about getting them in the door.

And when we pitch them the trial we also tell them exactly how to cancel it. So there's no hidden way out...Because I want it to be a no brainer yes."

Another way that Stacey gives members a taste of what to expect in the membership is through regular public Q&A sessions.

"We do a weekly Facebook Live, that helps a lot. It actually, it drives a surprisingly high amount of people because they get a feel for what it's like [to be a member]. Once a month we do something called Ask Me Anything, in the Backstage area. So it's essentially a live video call. People ask me questions. And so with the Facebook Live they kind of get a feel for what that's like. It's an even more tangible 'what it's like to learn from Stacey' kind of experience."

Engagement Through Participation

While Stacey is clearly the leader in her membership, her keys to member engagement are focusing her engagement efforts on those who are engaging back, and actually being a participant in her community, rather than trying to be seen as superior.

"For me it goes back to treat people like people. I think a lot of times as memberships grow it's easier to get stuck in the idea that 'I can't connect with everybody individually so I'm not going to worry about it.' **But in the reality of running a membership site a very small percentage of your members are actually going to try and engage with you.**

… There's definitely a section of people who are your biggest adapters and who who are going to be engaged and wanting to have conversations…And so I focus on them. I talk to them, I answer questions.

We've got office hours for two hours a week. But I'm in backstage every single day checking in, seeing what's going on. Sharing news, sharing wins, sharing podcast episodes, whatever it is that day. **I act as if I'm part of the community and not above the community."**

Stacey also offers a variety of ways to access her help throughout the month.

"We do weekly office hours. From 10:00 a.m. to 12:00 p.m. Pacific Time on Wednesdays I'm actually guaranteed to be in the forum so we can go back and forth and a lot of times I'll do profile reviews for people then. I'm guaranteed to be there so if you want a question answered fast that's the best time to ask it.

And then once a month we do our 'Ask Me Anything' which is usually somewhere between 15 minutes and an hour depending on how many questions I get. And that's actually a video. You can ask me questions, I'll answer it. I like doing that too because I can do a quick screen share.

But even during office hours if it's something that's easier for me to share with a video, I'll open up, I use a tool called Loom in Google Chrome as an extension, and I'll record a quick video and share a link in the forum…

…It's definitely something you have to care about what's happening to your members. You have to care about the experience they're having, the results they're having. It just makes it easier to stay with it."

The Power of Connection

While the recurring revenue provided by the membership is great for her business, the bigger impact for Stacy has been the connection that she has been able to create with her members.

*"It's changed my income from a business perspective but from a personal perspective **it's allowed me to connect every single day with my community in a really direct way** that I don't necessarily get anywhere else….*

…I love my people in my community. They're strong and amazing and wanting to make this world a really cool place in whatever way they're approaching that. And they tend to be very passionate about what they're doing. And I really enjoy being around people like that, who have that urge to support their little corner of the world. And I feel like, especially as online businesses, we're able to really make a much bigger impact than we initially think we're making because it is easier to make an impact on the other corner of the world. And so it's fun to get to connect with those kind of people everyday."

Keeping It Simple

For Stacey, success lies in doing one or two marketing activities really well, rather than trying to do everything.

*"I'm a big believer in there's not a lot you have to do with your online marketing. There are things that you should do to best connect with your right people. **Trying to know all the things, be all the places and execute everything at a super high level, is probably not the best use of your time.** So let's instead focus on the things that are the best use of your time - showing up in the right place at the right time with the right message."*

Setting Boundaries

When you run your own membership site, you're responsible for setting boundaries, and you shouldn't be too easily swayed by the many requests you'll get from your audience.

*"I still have members that ask if we can have a Facebook group and I still say no because again it's all about balancing your boundaries and their requests...If you were teaching in a classroom your students are going to ask for certain things that you know are not necessarily for their highest good...**So as the teacher, which is essentially what we are when we're running a membership, we have to make sure that we are protecting their learning environment.**"*

Updating vs Creating

When it comes to producing regular member content, Stacey recommends looking at what you can update, rather than always creating training from scratch - especially if the industry you're working in changes quickly.

*"When we first started we did two brand new trainings every month. Now we do a recorded training and a live training. Sometimes they're brand new but a lot of times they are updated versions of old trainings. So you know earlier this year we redid completely a Rockstar Guide to Facebook. And so instead of having a new training that month they got basically a brand new six module course, because all that content was updated. So that's evolved a little bit **because there's almost more value in updating than there is creating new for the sake of creating new.**"*

A Reality Check

One of the reasons many people launch a membership site is to enjoy the benefit of 'passive' recurring income. When the reality of the ongoing work sets in though, it can be tempting to give up.

For Stacey, being realistic about what running a membership actually involved is one of the reasons that her membership is still going strong while others have closed.

"...a month after I launched my membership site everyone in the world launched a membership site. But I would say probably 80 percent of people who I know of who launched membership sites in the three months after I launched mine have closed the doors and are done with it. Because I think people think it's going to be this awesome recurring passive revenue and it's not. It's awesome recurring revenue. It is not entirely passive."

That said, Stacey is also a believer that if you have an idea for a membership it is better to simply get started and see where it leads rather than waiting for things to be perfect.

"I think a membership, like anything in business, is about starting before you feel a hundred percent ready, which is probably true outside of business too, I'm just I'm a very business focused person. So if you're thinking about it or if you are hesitant about it, I think do it.

Nothing in life is permanent. If you do it for a year and you hate it stop doing it. No big deal."

Focusing Your Time

Enlisting the help of a team will free up your time and energy to focus on the member-facing activities, so you are working on the areas that matter the most.

For Stacey, a pivotal member of her team has become her husband, Charles, who takes cares of the logistics so that Stacey can focus on being the face of the business.

*"[Having a team] allows me to focus content forward, all the forward facing stuff so the podcasts, the Facebook Lives, the membership trainings, the office hours, the coaching call to consulting. **We joke about this but essentially my husband Charles runs the business and I'm the deliverable.***

So anything where you're engaging with the business, you're generally engaging with me. We do have a team that helps us execute some of those things ... but generally if you're engaging with any of the marketing materials or any of the trainings or the consulting or the coaching that's where you're going to get me. That's front end stuff."

What's Next For Hit The Mic Backstage

With the pricing and the content set at a level she is currently comfortable with, Stacey is looking for a new way to develop her membership site further, and is considering adding a premium level.

"So instead of just a monthly and the annual membership there'd be a VIP level that had a little more access to me. A little more focused on people who want the membership plus maybe a one on one call a month. I could see us doing that at some point maybe, versus and instead of raising the price across the board. Sort of adding an extra incentive."

In addition to this, Stacey wants to continue to grow her membership so that she can help even more entrepreneurs succeed with social media for their business.

"It's still growing and it's definitely something that we work on every single day. I have massive goals for this community, as you know. I want this thing to take over the world because I know for me the biggest frustration in my life is people telling me they're stupid, because it drives me crazy because just because you don't know something yet does not make you stupid it means you have a hole in your knowledge…And so I want the membership to eradicate people telling me they are stupid about online marketing and social media."

Colin Gray: Podcast Host Academy

Membership Details:

Name: The Podcast Host Academy

Topic: Podcasting

Launched: December 2016

Website: thepodcasthost.com

Interview Date: June 2017

Colin Gray has run his website, ThePodcastHost.com, for over seven years, writing about how to run a podcast and giving reviews of equipment, from mics to mixers to digital recorders.

The site grew up around the tech side of things and expanded into the wider world of podcasting, including how to launch your show, build a website around it, monetize it and grow an audience.

The site developed a large audience, and Colin was initially able to monetize it with affiliate and sponsorship income. Wishing to diversify his income though, Colin began looking into developing a membership site.

"It's always a bit dodgy relying on things like sponsorship and affiliate income. It relies pretty heavily on your Google rankings and jitters up and down and you get months where it's like down by 20 percent and you're like 'urgh' is this the start of a big decline or something? So that was really what got me into thinking about the more long term income strategies, and memberships always came up as a big part of this.

There were a few other people I knew at the time starting up memberships too and I **was actually initially really reluctant to get into the whole membership game** *because I have to admit I quite like the whole affiliate type approach because it's so little work. I'm lazy I don't like any work. Whereas a membership really there's a lot of work has to go into it.* **It is not half as passive but I do like the idea of helping people.** *I'm a teacher by background so I enjoy the teaching side of things.*

We created a lot of online courses and it just became natural that we did it, so we started The Podcast Host Academy which is really, I see it as almost a premium upgrade to our free content."

The Podcast Host Academy includes courses which lead on from the free content, but which go into more depth, with specific set-ups, and how-to tutorials to get members taking action. There are also live support opportunities available through group calls.

A Less Than Perfect Start

It hasn't all been plain sailing for Colin though, and the current membership site is actually a pivot from his first membership attempt, FanFission, which was created as a stand alone brand, separate from his blog.

When Colin saw disappointing results with his first membership, including lower than hoped for signups and a time-consuming forum, he realised that something needed to change if the membership model was going to work for him.

"So the first iteration of the of the membership there were a few problems with it. One of which was the fact that there's good competition out there for this type of

thing - there's a lot of memberships coming out now at the $40-$50 mark. And I thought one way we could differentiate actually was treating it like I said as a premium greater free content, and the way to do that would be more to have it as a lower cost higher volume membership approach."

The revamped and renamed Podcast Host Academy is now a thriving addition to his website.

"I was toying with the idea of trying to be able to expand out a little bit into video...a little bit around other types of content too. So kind of big media. Anyway that was the idea for the FanFission thing. We help people grow fans. But it was just a step too far. It was like the messaging just became really confused. The people that know us already didn't really know what it was about... It just didn't really make sense to people....I had just created it as a generic membership site. What we changed really, I brought the membership site into the Podcast Host so it went from fanfission.com to thepodcasthost.com/academy.

So it benefits a bit now because of the authority our site has in terms of search and all that kind of stuff. So that's good it means that it's much more congruent for people that visit our site already. So people who are already fans of The Podcast Host. They can find the Academy and go obviously this is for me because it's within this site that I already know and it's called podcast something which makes sense."

A key focus in Colin's changes to his membership was thinking about what he actually wanted and what would benefit his audience, not just what other membership sites do.

"When I relaunched I really thought 'what do I actually want to do?'. What do I want this membership to be, not just to help our audience, obviously that's the

biggest part of it is to help them. But also it needs to be fun and interesting for me and Matthew to run as well"

Content Over Community

Colin launched his membership site with an onsite forum, but has toyed with the idea of removing it completely due to a combination of low engagement and a desire to reduce management time. However recently engagement has started to take off.

"There is a forum there with the membership which may or may not be around forever. But actually right now it looks like I'm veering towards keeping it actually and starting to build that out again, because it's just doing really well it's almost maintaining itself right now."

As Colin's membership does rely more on content than on community though, keeping people coming back to the site again and again has been a challenge.

"I think the biggest challenge for me is trying to figure out ways to keep that continual value coming because...I'm not necessarily wanting to build a heavy community here. So how else can I bring in value?....I want to build in ways into this membership whereby people are getting something new every month, but it's not a huge amount of time to do, it's not a new course a month."

Drawing on his teaching background, Colin is considering a curriculum for his students to help guide them through the content more and emphasise that ongoing value.

"I think people rebel against the idea of structure and discipline and directive teaching because it's assumed that flexibility and choice is always the best. You should give everybody everything all at once. But actually in a lot of cases that really scares people. And to these people it's a big barrier because they see everything there and they don't know where to start…Whereas if you can actually break it up much smaller and either drip feed it or guide them through day by day or something like that. I think that makes it a lot more accessible and creates a lot more success and therefore a lot more satisfaction in your membership.

So that's the challenge …make sure that people are visiting us day by day not just like popping in every two weeks when they need a wee bit of help, but actually coming in every single day because there is something useful that they can do in just five or 10 minutes and they'll grow what they're doing just by a little increment."

Colin understands that the more he can help his members take action and get results, the more they will appreciate the membership, and market it for him.

*"That's not only what keeps them joined to your membership, it keeps them paying for your membership, it's what causes them to evangelize what you do. So they go out and sell it for you and I think that's what we're all looking for isn't it, **we want 100 fans that actually tell everyone else in their network about what you do.**"*

Thinking Outside the Box

Colin is aware of the fact that when he first launched his membership was quite generic and similar to many other membership sites, and since his rebrand particularly enjoys the challenge of figuring out how to make his membership different to what else is available.

"One of the most fun parts of it for me as well is figuring out something a bit different to do because I'm really conscious of the fact that I did create a kind of generic approach and I'm equally conscious of the fact that so many other people are doing exactly the same thing as well. I've got a list of about 30, 40 even 50 ideas that I've got that are just little things that I could add into the membership that I've not seen anywhere else. Bring in from completely different realms and different areas and nothing to do with membership. Nothing to do with business but they apply to the model that I have got here.

So I'm trying to put together ideas and plans for what we're going to put in over the next five, six months that I think will really surprise people, will really give them a whole lot of success and value and also will help them be really successful too and keep coming back like I say day by day."

Blogging vs Podcasting

Although the podcast is what Colin is most known for, new audience members usually actually find him via his blog posts, because they are returned in search engine results.

*"**Our blog is our biggest asset**. I know podcasting is what we do. And I would never stop podcasting because the way it works for us, and I think the way that it works for the vast majority of people who podcast, is that a blog acts as that kind of capture method. **So a blog is how people find you initially because text is still the biggest search out there.** Voice is supposedly catching up, thanks to smart speakers and the like, but still the return on a search is still almost certainly going*

*to be text for a long time... So text is that, that's the wide part of the funnel that's how people find you. **But podcasting is how you engage them basically**.*

People read one or two of our blog posts and then inevitably...find a reference to a full podcast that we do. And our job is to try and get them to listen to that because that's where I think we turn people from casual visitors of our blog, or even our videos, into massive fans because they end up listening, they get a bit of personality, they find out that much more about us, our values, our ethics, all that kind of stuff. And they listen for hours at a time. I mean that's the big power that podcasting has is that people listen for hours at a time because video can get personality across, it can do that kind of personality work, that engagement work. But attention is still really short - I mean three four or five minutes on YouTube max. But you can get people to listen for half an hour, an hour, or two hours on the podcast. So that's how it works for us. Blog is the kind of capture. And then the podcast is the kind of turn them into a super fan job.

Banner Ads and Contextual Mentions

In order to capitalise on the success of his blog and podcast, Colin has actually turned to more traditional marketing methods.

"I've got five or six banner ads on there. And they're basically injected into every single post on the site. So 400, 500 posts we've got on there currently have those banner ads in them... with a few thousand people seeing it every week, quite a few of them have converted into members for us..."

Colin has also embedded contextual mentions of the membership into his most popular blog posts.

"I went into analytics, looked through the top 20 posts, and I went into every single post...and put in contextual mentions in every single one. So still some of our most popular posts are equipment based, so for example our Best Mics article, I found two places within that article to mention in context: 'This mic is really good for this, this and this, and if you want to know how you set this up with a mixer so you can record Skype, we've got a course for that in our membership which is The Podcast Host Academy. So I've got a couple of mentions like that.

So a bit more subtle...they are actually really really interested in this type of thing and mentioning how the Academy can help with it. So that's our top 20 posts traffic wise have had that added in and its probably not solely due to this, but **our growth rate has jumped since doing that and I think we have gone from a new member every week to at least one a day, up to two a day right now.... It's funny what happens when you actually tell people about it.**"

Live Support Calls

As part of his engagement strategy Colin provides live group calls every two weeks, so that members can get their specific questions answered.

"We also do live support in there as well so people that have specific questions, which with podcasting particularly we get a lot of... 'So this is exactly where I sit and I have three people sitting around here and we have this recorder and those microphones, how does this all work together' and it's like it's no use to anyone apart from this one person so it's being able to help people like that as well because they come into our live support now and ask those questions.

I have a live events page on the membership site and it lists the upcoming four sessions, we do them every fortnight so every two weeks we do a live session. I alternate with Matthew, my sort of second in command at The Podcast Host. So we have them listed in there and it's always the same Zoom link so people just click on the Zoom link when the time comes along. They can join in and we just have a conversation."

To ensure members make use of the live calls Colin is pro-active about sending out reminders, using this as a good chance to mention other membership news too.

"I'm sending out an email every two weeks, a members update that invites them in to the live support, asks them if they have any questions in advance. But it also points out a couple of new things that we've added. So whether that's a live training that we've done, or a resource that me or Matthew have put in there like a checklist or a new course, something like that we'll mention too so that helps."

Building a Team

While the site started as a solo affair, Colin now has help both behind the scenes and with his member engagement and content creation, allowing him to focus on the bigger picture tasks.

"I started The Podcast Host years ago now but Matthew joined the team about two and a half years ago, back then he came on as an audio producer, when we still did a lot of client work helping people run their podcasts. But nowadays he creates more content than I do for the site. The two of us run most of our podcasts as co-hosts and he does lots of work in the academy too because his background is audio drama so he

knows audio editing, audio production equipment, inside out so he gives people tons of help on that.

...I took a journalism student on last year and he edits all of our posts. He's only part-time so maybe a couple of days a week just editing, writing up show notes, that kind of stuff for podcasts.
And I've got an admin assistant I work with as well. She does two or three days a week and helps us with all the admin, does a bit of my book-keeping but also does ... little changes to the website that type of stuff. And I've got a designer as well who does a lot of our graphics."

Low Cost, High Volume

One of the biggest changes with Colin's membership re-launch was the price, which was actually lowered in favour of a low cost, high volume membership approach.

"People automatically think cheaper, can't go cheap and there is a big mentality around just now isn't it like double your prices, double your prices. In some cases that's the right thing to do. But in other cases I think there's a lot of room for cheaper products as well. As long as you can make sure that the time you're spending on them is paid back you know you're not doing too much for too little income."

Reducing the price was a strategic move on Colin's part, based on changes to what the membership would be offering.

"I was cutting out the idea of the in-depth support and community in terms of the forum, that was the main thing that was going to drop and that was going to take it

down from what I saw as sort of 40 to 50 dollar membership down to 18 dollars a month basically. So I wanted it to be at a point where it was worthwhile for us and that's why I thought we had to take out the forum and make it less time intensive but it was still worthwhile for us profit wise, which I think 18 dollars a month is at volume. **But I wanted it to be low enough cost that people could see it almost as just that something they could have on hand just in case they need it**...*I wanted it cheap enough that if they don't use it for a month or two months they think 'well actually it's worthwhile keeping on just because next month I might need some help with that.'*

An unexpected side-effect of making the membership low cost was that some people joined not for the membership itself, but simply to support Colin and his free content.

"We've got a really big audience that come along and use our free content, that read a lot of blogs, that follow all the podcasts. Actually I discovered that a lot of them just wanted to support us a little bit for that free content. So we have people that have signed up for the membership that don't necessarily use the courses, the resources, they're just seeing it as a way to support the free stuff that we do. And I've put that in as a sales message I suppose on the sales page, it's one of the reasons you could sign up."

Taking Risks

The experience of building, re-inventing and re-launching his membership has helped Colin gain clarity over his business goals, while the recurring income has enabled him to take more risks with other aspects of his business.

"…when it didn't do so well in the early days, it kind of made me re-evaluate a lot of things around business. What we were aiming for. What kind of business we wanted to run. What I want my day to look like basically. What I want to spend the majority of my hours doing. And that's what made me sort of resculpt a little bit and go with the less supported and cheaper option.

*But now in the last month seeing the engagement starting in there, seeing one or two people joining every single day, having it confirmed that it could become a big popular thing has made a big difference to me. **It's helped me look more long term in the business in terms of that diversified income**, it's helped me see that my projections I put together last year, they could actually come true.*

*And therefore, I can take a bit more of a risk on the software [he's developing a SaaS product], for example, because that's costing us a lot of money to develop. And it was relying on the fact that membership was going to succeed. So now that it's starting to make a **difference it's given me a bit more room, a bit more breathing space to do more with the rest of the business that I wouldn't have been able to otherwise.***

It's the recurring income isn't it. As soon as you start to see people coming and staying for more than just a few months you start both relying on that and it lets you take more risks because you've got that back up."

Combining Membership and SaaS

Colin's team are currently building a software application to help people publish their podcasts more quickly, something the recurring revenue from the membership has allowed them to invest in. Being able to offer both a membership and a SaaS (software as a service) product to the same audience seems like it will be a natural fit.

"I think we're going to have a real strength here in that we can sell them as a package, we can sell them together or even if they're not a package they're a really strong partnership because we're teaching people how to podcast with the membership or showing them how to do it successfully, everything from the equipment to their monetization. But it still relies on them actually going away and doing the work. Now we're building a software application that will actually do a lot of the work for them...

So I think it's a natural upgrade for people who join the membership because we're going to show them how. And here's something that can help you do it. On the other hand with the SaaS application as well people come along thinking this is going to solve some of the problems with podcasting, but we can then say well by the way for an extra 10 20 30 whatever dollars a month we've got this community here which actually you get loads of courses, loads of resources around podcasting, live support all that kind of stuff. It will help you actually make the best use of this tool.

I feel like the two of them are going to be a really strong partnership together."

What's Next For Podcast Host Academy

As well as the upcoming SaaS product that Colin and his team are creating he is keen to create smaller tools that can be included within the membership, to aid members in their success and deliver more value and of course to increase engagement and retention too.

"I want to have a really active group of people, a few hundred folk in there, who are all helping each other out and I want to have built in a range of tools as well… I want to be able to help people organise their interviews, for example one of the biggest problems that people have podcasting is organising logistics around interviews and things like that. **If I can build little tools for them to do things like that I think that could be a really big value add that keeps people engaged.** So starting to think about much more customer stuff, and the advantage I have in that I suppose is that you know I've taken on a couple of developers to build our software our SaaS application so they can actually start to build little tools for the community as well. So I think in 12 months time I want to have done a lot more speaking to my members to figure out the real little problems that they have.

And we've done a lot of that already but do so much more and really try and create as many solutions as we can that just add these little incremental steps that makes it worth way more than the 18 dollars we're charging now. But that's probably another thing, we'll want to be charging a bit more at that point too. But offering enough value to justify it."

Avalon Yarnes: Avalon Cakes School

Membership Details:

Name: Avalon Cakes School

Topic: Cake Art/Decorating

Launched: September 2015

Website: avaloncakesschool.com

Interview Date: June 2017

Avalon Yarnes runs Avalon Cakes School, an online platform for creatives that enjoy making high end elaborate cake art.

"I don't even like to call it cake decorating because to me it's art. It's art all the way. It's something I like to drill into my students' or my members' heads that it's cake art.

We offer video tutorials, picture based tutorials, recipes, tools, community, at a monthly price so it's a recurring membership and it's geared towards just the creative side of the decorating. We're not really teaching people how to run a business or anything business based…my specialty is definitely the art."

While working in a bakery, Avalon started a cake decorating business on the side.

"I loved it and I was learning so much. And I was doing it at night after work and I was doing some client cakes on the weekends but it wasn't my full time job.

But I really got into just like exploring with it and perfecting it. And I really wanted to start sharing everything that I had learned... So I started selling individual tutorials on something really cool that I created or figured out and just really wanted to share with people. Me and my boyfriend Zach, we started filming and selling these."

At the time Avalon had worked at the bakery for 10 years, and had worked her way up to be the buyer of all of the corporate offices, but her side business wasn't a hit with the company.

"It was very obvious to them, and I knew, that my passion wasn't there for them. My passion and my focus was on Avalon Cakes and they could see that. And one day they demoted me.

I was in this position where I could either go back and work in the kitchen at the bakeries for them. Or I could maybe go a different direction because we had been selling these one off tutorials and I was starting to realize they were doing really well and people were liking them and I thought you know maybe we have something here."

Avalon and Zach talked over their plans that night, with Avalon determined not to return to the bakery.

"... I just really enjoy this teaching thing and I'd had a membership in the back of my head for a little while. There were a few other people in the industry doing it and I was like that's a recurring income that I can count on and that's kind of predictable. And we don't have to worry about 'is this tutorial going to do well this month'.

So that night we decided we were going to go all in. **We had enough money saved up to last us about six months. So we had this deadline, six months to get our butts in gear to get content created and a website out.** It actually ended up taking about eight months but we made the money work because him and I were both out of a job. So this was our whole thing like we put all of our eggs in one basket."

Jumping In

Avalon didn't have any experience with websites or online business when she first got started, but jumped straight in and learnt as she went, creating her own membership site from scratch.

She also chose to initially rely on her existing large Facebook audience, an approach that served her well but she is now venturing into other marketing avenues as well.

"When I first started the site I knew nothing about internet marketing. I didn't know. Like I just kind of jumped in head first started looking at membership plug ins and you know I had just made a WordPress website for my regular cake decorating company, I was like ooh this is fun, I can do this.

I made the whole thing from scratch and I didn't know anything about the marketing side and I kind of just went with my intuition. I had a really big following on Facebook already which is great and which is super helpful. But now you know I've kind of started to exhaust my Facebook following. I feel like you know I've tapped into that and now I'm starting to do other internet marketing type of things and I'm learning about lead magnets and funnels and all these other things you know."

Wearing All the Hats

Avalon finds running the membership time consuming, and she's expanding her team so she can hand over some of the workload.

*"The biggest challenge for me in general is the time constraints and the nurturing that the membership site requires...I think for me it's letting go of some of the control because I wear pretty much all the hats you know. I am the marketer. I am the website person. I'm the graphic designer. I'm the creative. I'm the person that comes up with all the tutorials. And there's just so many things to do and **I think my biggest challenge is actually letting go and maybe hiring some people in to help with that.** But yeah just being able to find that life business balance. That's my biggest challenge. Be able to find the time and I love my job that's the problem - I want to be doing it....*

I actually have a VA now so that's been lovely. But you know there's all that time that goes into training so there's like that transition period. And so the time is still not there."

Creative Marketing

Avalon connects with her audience mostly on Facebook and she's been attracting new members by showcasing her membership in videos with great success.

"Creating trailers of our video tutorials and creating hype around the tutorials themselves have worked really well for us.

…we want to have fun every once in a while so we do some fun little improv type introductions every time we have a guest instructor. So we'll just do some skits and just kind of wing it."

Avalon has also been experimenting with creating a sales funnel using a free lead magnet and paid Facebook advertising.

"I'm starting to go into the lead magnet and funnel realm which is fun but that's actually been doing really well too. So for me right now it would be advertising on social media and just getting them to visually see what the tutorial is all about and for my people that's what they need to do, they need to see what they're going to get. And then offering a little bit of the free tutorials through the lead magnets and, because right now we have just some free stuff out there that they can grab which is a video that is taken from a lesson that's already in the school so that you can kind of see the quality they're going to get. And all of that before they sign up and that's usually the thing that pushes them through the door."

…it's been amazing watching that convert so quickly. I didn't think it was going to convert as quickly as it did and it really has. So it's been rewarding."

A Member Points System

To increase retention, Avalon introduced a points currency system that enables her members to download and keep a certain number of tutorials.

"Basically our members get a certain amount of points every 30 days of membership and they can take these points and they can use them to purchase these tutorials to keep forever.

So even if they cancel they get to keep these tutorials. So the benefit of that I think is that they get to see these points stack up and it also takes that feeling of risk away. That risk of 'I'm just throwing my money away' because you're actually just throwing it back into purchasing a tutorial. And since all of this is digital for me it's not really a big loss or anything. But usually they end up staying for a long time because they realize that they're just getting a lot of value for their money anyway."

Members get a certain amount of points in return for their monthly payment, but they can also earn points in other ways too, many of which are great marketing opportunities for the membership

"They can earn points from sharing something on Pinterest, they can earn points from sharing something on Facebook. So it's also helping me move along sharing so I'm getting people to see more advertisements through just members sharing stuff."

The points system wasn't in place when the membership launched however and was actually introduced as a way to compete with something a competitor offered.

"One of my competitors gives her students the tutorial every month on one of her tiers. So one of her tiers you get the tutorial of that month [to keep]. And I had some students that were messaging me saying 'well what do we get' ...it's a small world kind of community...But that's what some of them said and I was like' OK well how do I combat this. How do I give them some kind of value where they can't argue that anymore?'.

And so that's when I came up with the whole points system. I wanted to be able to have something similar but different so they can get whatever they want. They're

not just going to get the tutorial that I'm putting out that month. They get to

choose and they get to earn the points."

Changing Communities

Avalon initially tried to keep her membership community on her membership site, but found that a forum wasn't the right fit for her audience and ended up switching to a Facebook group, which has been a huge success.

"We have a Facebook community, a private Facebook group and we do Facebook Lives in there which is really fun. And now I know that a lot of people do, we actually tried, to make the community work on the website itself. I used BuddyPress when we first started and I just, it just wasn't working it was too much work for me and my community lives on Facebook.

The Facebook cake community is big. It's huge, it's thriving. So that's where my people were. And it is very much a visual thing cake decorating obviously, you know we're constantly trying to share each other's work and get advice so Facebook was the perfect place for me to do that. So we decided to move over to a Facebook group and we love it. I love my Facebook group. They're like, they're the heart of Avalon Cakes for sure."

Community engagement is high, something Avalon attributes to the fact that Facebook Groups were already very common in her market, but she was able to provide a more intimate group.

"They take care of the community themselves. Because like I said there is so many people in the cake community on Facebook already. It was already all these groups. They kind of just like knew how to interact. And now you know it's a smaller group

because they have all these massive free groups on Facebook for cake decorating. **So I think a lot of them are really excited to have this smaller group where they could talk more on an intimate level.** *And then I was in there too. So they all talk to each other and I found it really surprising that they would ask a question in the group and I always felt like 'OK I need to go answer that question, I need to answer that question', but so many of them help each other. And like half the time I don't even have to answer the question because somebody already answered it perfectly. I was like, amazing."*

Single vs Multiple Tiers

From the start, Avalon launched with two membership tiers, 'Classic' and 'Premium'. In hindsight, starting with a single offering would've been easier to market, but once the two levels were setup, it was difficult to back out of that model.

"I offer a classic membership and I also offer a premium membership. I had just made it too complicated. I really just wish I would have had the one membership and that was just it. But I think that's the number one thing I would have changed. Because it's kind of been a pain.

The classic membership includes all classic tutorials. So these are more basic tutorials. We usually put out two of these a month. The premium membership, and it has some other tools and stuff right so we have the cake calculator and stuff like that. The premium membership you get a premium tutorial along with everything in the classic. So we do a premium tutorial every other month and that's usually like a really big impressive cake. So something that you really get excited about. And then you get some access to some extra tools and you get more download points and stuff like that.

It would have been much easier just to put it all together and do it that way instead of now I have this obligation to do a premium every other month. And it's confusing for people too."

Despite Avalon's regret at having two different membership levels, the higher cost tier is actually the more popular option.

"Actually the premium is more predominant. We've got about 70 percent on premium. And I think it's because the tutorial that they end up seeing and liking happens to be under the premium tier so that they need to get it. But they are happy to pay, it's only $10 more a month."

Freedom & Fulfilment

It's safe to say that Avalon made the right decision in leaving her job to start the membership, and the risk she and her boyfriend took has paid off well.

"[The membership] has had an amazing impact on my life and my business. I mean we're set financially, we're very happy financially.
We have freedom, even though we don't always allow it to ourselves, we have freedom. We could take a week off whenever we want really."

Aside from financial and lifestyle freedom, the membership has also provided Avalon with much more too.

"There's just a huge amount of pride in having something like this for myself. And you know there's a huge amount of pride in having your own business and not putting all your time and effort into someone else's dream, putting it into your own

dream...this is our baby. I don't have any kids or anything. This is my baby. And it's been the best decision I've ever made. I'm extremely happy with it."

And Avalon loves seeing the cakes her members make and knowing that she has been able to help them.

"My highlight has definitely been the members recreating the tutorials and being excited and thrilled in showing me their work because that is the most fulfilling part. Knowing that I'm doing my job right and that they're able to take what I showed them and actually recreate it. And they're super excited about it and happy about it and they're sharing it and they love it. That's just the most fulfilling thing for me with the type of membership site I have."

What's Next For Avalon Cakes School

As with many membership site owners, Avalon started out with dreams of a flexible lifestyle, but has ended up spending far more hours in front of a computer than she anticipated. Now the business is established and generating a recurring income, she's ready to reduce her working hours and increase her freedom.

"I think what's next is that life balance. I mean that's my goal. So that's always been my goal is to have some time for ourselves and to be able to dive into some other things that we enjoy doing. So for us it's just getting systems and everything else worked out so that we do have that time and fun."

John Tuggle: Learning Guitar Now

Membership Details:

Name: Learning Guitar Now

Topic: Blues & Slide Guitar

Launched: November 2014

Website: learningguitarnow.com

Interview Date: July 2017

John Tuggle runs Learning Guitar Now, a membership focused on teaching how to play blues and slide guitar.

When John launched his first eBook back in 2007, it flopped. He could've walked away from his idea of teaching guitar online, and gone back to his many day jobs. Instead, he used the failure as an opportunity to rethink his niche and business model and start over.

John initially focused on teaching guitar to beginners, because that's what he spent most of his time doing offline. However, he quickly realised that if he was going to the effort of building his own business, he may as well be teaching something he loves.

"When I started and I did the ebook it was all about beginner guitar, that's what the book was, it was only about beginners because I taught tons of beginner guitar lessons. That's what I thought people would want to see. And while that is true I've found that what I really had passion for was playing slide guitar. So when I decided to revamp the site and re put it out in January 2008 I said I'm just going to go all in for what exactly I want to do. And I didn't really see many people doing slide guitar

out there like Duane Allman, Derek Trucks. So I made a DVD of how to play like
Duane Allman, Derek Trucks style slide guitar. And that is what I'm really
passionate about and that so happens to be what was really successful.
And then after a while I was like well forget what people say, what people think I
should do. I'm just going to do what I want to do, what I feel I'm passionate about.
And that has led to me doing this thing for a living. Because if I would have stayed
with beginner guitar videos, I mean I probably wouldn't be doing this right now.
Because there's billions of guitar lessons for beginners and anyone can teach that.
It's not really that difficult. So I felt like I had a niche of how, or my specific method
of how, to teach slide and blues guitar and that's how it all came about."

Initially John was offering DVD based courses, however as technology
evolved he switched from offering DVDs to online downloads, and then in
November 2014 he launched his membership site, hoping to create a steady
recurring income.

"The thing about doing DVDs and downloads was I can have an amazing month if
I came out with a new DVD. And sales could be kind of slow the next month,
slower than what I need it to be. You always have ups and downs…

…So that was the idea with a membership site. It was the only way to really have a
steady income was to have recurring income that's guaranteed for the most part and
start working on getting subscribers. So that was one of the ideas, that was one of
the main ideas behind it. Also I felt like you could learn better if you have a
membership site. Because when you learn guitar there's so many things you have to
learn. So if you buy one DVD then how do you reference DVD 6 from DVD 3 and
DVD 3 to DVD 4 and 4 to 1 … you have to have all of them. But then the user
experience is awful. Because you have to pop in the DVD 3 then go to the DVD 6,

pop it in, fast forward. With a membership site you can go instantly to everything. And so that's kind of been my plan is to make the learning experience so awesome with online you just jump to any place any lesson anywhere. I thought that was a really sweet idea. I wanted to do it in 2008 but it really wasn't possible for me to put all that technology together it was just too much stuff to configure and it was kind of clunky back then."

Reducing Income Streams

John had multiple jobs when he first started his business and he was gradually able to quit all of them over the space of two years in order to go full time with the business.

"When I first started in 2008 I had a separate part time job but I was also teaching fifty kids a week - high schoolers, teenagers and some adults. So I had 50 private lessons and I also played in a wedding band. I played that every weekend. I mean I played in numerous bands at that time… and then I had this other part time job that, when I relaunched Learning Guitar Now the second time in January of 2008, I quit that other part time job and just did those three things. And then a year, lets say about six months into that I got rid of all the private lessons. And somewhere in 2010 I quit that wedding band. And so I've been doing this full time for seven years."

Once his business was established it was also hard for John to move from DVD sales to a membership model. John's DVD bundles sold for around $100 or more, which was at the higher end of prices for his industry, and so a low cost monthly membership fee was fear inducing. Despite that though, John actually wishes he had made the move earlier.

"I wish I would have started the membership site earlier instead of waiting until 2014....maybe 100 people would spend $100 on this one thing. A lot of people. And so to go from like a $100, $150, $200 DVD bundles to $19.95 a month...I spent this many years creating all this stuff and now people are going to get it for $19.95? They're not going to buy anything else? So that was always the fear to do it."

John no longer sells any DVD's at all, but does still have some popular courses available to purchase as individual downloads, as well as within the membership, which provides an additional income stream to the membership still.

"I'm pretty much focused on the membership site but I still sell the courses as individual downloads. Not all of them but some of them, the most popular ones. I've tested it to where I just went membership only for three weeks or so and didn't really have any more people sign up than normal...So I would say downloads are probably about 25 percent of my income now.

...If I need to make some quick money I can just release a download if I want. It's kind of nice having both options really right now. So until I get a certain amount of monthly members that I feel really really comfortable with I'll probably just keep selling downloads because right now like I tested it didn't have any impact in getting more members. I thought if I removed downloads that might be like double the members but it didn't really work like that. I got about the same amount so I was like well might as well keep selling the downloads and take the money."

The Creativity Challenge

For a musician, being able to spend time creating music every day is a dream, and it's something that John gets to do in the creation of his membership content, a big change from when he was working part time jobs.

"One of my favourite things is creating a lot of the material. Not really doing the video but I love to write music... I'm not writing my own songs or anything but I get up every day and create a drum pattern and play bass and play piano and play guitar and create some music. And that's what I really enjoy doing, that is putting stuff together that sounds cool... before I was doing all this for a living, I always worked like random jobs, played gigs and taught lessons but I never got the time to create music."

John loves it when he's feeling creative as not only does he enjoy the creative process itself, but he knows new content is key to both getting and keeping his members.

"Once you get into that mindset of creativity like I don't ever want to leave that because that's what brings in the most members I think. It's the new lessons and the new ideas about teaching that when I'm creating something I get really into it. If you go do something different then you can forget where you're at and it's hard to get back."

However, John needs to be in the right frame of mind to record his lessons, and he's been learning how to deal with low-creativity days.

*"Sometimes it can be hard to get creative sometimes and you can't figure out 'what shall I make.' And so you know that just happens. You know you can't be creative every day of the week. The biggest thing that's helped me is just not get frustrated and stop. **Because with creative stuff you're trying to teach someone something, you've got to create a lesson that's really good**. You don't want to put something out there that's worthless...Sometimes I'll just be like 'well I'm done*

I can't figure out anything more right now.' So I'll come back to it. And usually I'll take a day off, come back the next day, and have tons of creativity. So I think being creative, it's not really something that you can just do on demand."

Staying Motivated

Since launching his membership, John has also had sinus surgery and other medical issues which impacted on his ability to teach and create content for a time, however having the membership provided some stability and made the experience easier.

"Luckily I had the membership site already going so I was getting the recurring income. And that was really nice. The problem was, taking medication, being on random pills for getting over the surgeries... It's like wow this is really hard to create content. I was like am I ever going to be able to do this. I eventually got back into it but it was a challenge which you don't really think about. You always think I'm going to be healthy forever, until something happens."

John has also found he needed to be resilient when it comes to feedback and has developed ways to help himself stay motivated during the low times.

"... you're going to get negative feedback sometimes and just dealing with all that in one can be difficult. I remember y'all [The Membership Guys] talking about having this little sheet of paper with people that say good things about your membership site. That's what I found helps me as well.

Someone writes a good review, or has a good time, or has really learned something from the lessons and they'll post it in the forum and that gives me the mindset to be like 'oh yeah that's why I'm doing this'...If you have lower sales or you know things are just not going the way you want it to, looking back at that and saying 'the mission is to teach people how to play guitar. And that's what I'm doing so we have to move forward.' And having that kind of mindset really helps."

For John, being honest with members if you're having difficulties is the key to avoiding problems.

"And I think another thing is just being honest with members,' hey I've had some issues. I've been going to make some more content but you know things are a bit difficult right now.' I think people appreciate honesty about what's going on with everything rather than like silence."

Content Longevity

John discovered that a nice bonus to having a forum community as part of his membership site was the ability not just to answer questions but for those answers to then be permanently available for future members, reducing his email support.

"I have a forum available so when people have a question about a course you can instantly answer them. And that can be searchable. And that's huge for me because I have people ask a lot of questions about all these technical things and concepts about lessons and so I find I get less and less e-mail now that more people ask questions in the forum because then it's just searchable. People ask all these questions and then when anyone joins they search the forum and they can find everything. And that's happened in the last year.

In the future it'll make my life so much more easier when you know there's just so many questions have been answered. To me it's just more content in the membership site that people really want to see because if people see other people asking questions and it's answered that makes them feel good about what they purchased. It's like 'oh I'll probably get some attention.'"

Flexi-Time

John greatly appreciates the flexibility in his work patterns that his business affords him, although it didn't happen overnight and he's worked hard to get to this point.

"....having time to just take breaks during the day. I've been doing this for so long, 10 years, I like to have things go the way I like them to during the day. I don't want to be stuck doing nine to five Monday to Friday. I've never really got along well with doing that. So it's nice to just take a break to maybe go exercise in the middle of the day. Or you know go do something else or play guitar or whatever you want to do...

.... I mean it takes a lot of work to get to this point. You know that guy Dave Ramsey has a good quote. He says 'If you live like no one else soon you can live like no one else.' I think that's good for a membership site because in the beginning you're going to work all the time.

I've got to a certain point where I can do what I want within reason as long as I've got everything set up right. But it gives you a lot more freedom than I think you'll ever have with any other type of business."

High Quality Free Content

These days John focuses mainly on video content both within the membership and for his public audience too.

"I pretty much do all video stuff. I used to write blog posts a pretty good amount. These days I find that people enjoy the videos more. I do think that blog posts are helpful but people just want to see the video really and you can supplement it with a blog post. I usually just do a lot of free lessons instead of like writing a piece."

Around twice a month John creates free lessons for his audience, with upgrades available to members only. This keeps his audience engaged, and each lesson provides an opportunity to convert new members, as he demonstrates the high quality lessons they can expect to find in the membership area.

"You want to give out a free lesson that is really good. If you don't do one that's good then people are like 'who cares'...I record it the same way as I do my courses, three camera angles and all the audio setup, mic on the amp, lavalier, all the bells and whistles and what not. And it can take a whole day just to do one of those depending on how much I planned it out. But I think people really want to see quality. Even if it's free these days."

Promoting New Content

When John creates new courses he makes them available to buy separately, but also includes them in the membership, so the promotion he does for the standalone course pulls in new members.

"If I come out with a new course I usually sell it as a download. But you can also join the membership site. So when I sell as a download I'll sell a pretty good amount of them but also get a ton of new members. Some people like to download. Some like the membership. More these days people are just joining the membership. So consistently creating new content that can be accessed in the membership site and promoting that to people can really get members."

John drip-releases the content into his membership which helps keep members engaged, but also means he can mention the new course over several weeks of email newsletters.

"These days I've been creating courses that are say two maybe three hours long and then I'll release it section by section. So instead of taking the course and putting the whole thing out, I'll say week one we're going to learn part one. And then I'll promote it to the all-access, the members. And then maybe I'll promote it to the non members as well or I could also promote that it's coming out but that you can start learning now to our free members. so many different ways I can promote it. So then it'll last for like four to five weeks of just adding a new lesson. **I find it also helps with retention with current members because, well I don't want to quit now I'm not going to get that lessons that's coming out in three or four weeks.** *And so that can help that. And then at the end of it you know people that didn't really want to join I'll promote it to them to buy as a download and give them a discount. So that has really helped extremely. Just having that course that's just kind of drip fed over time over a month or so. I've been doing that for the last few months that's really worked really really well.*

John also actively targets past members when he releases new content. He uses ActiveCampaign to keep in touch with people who have cancelled their membership, and emails them when new content is available in the membership.

"So getting the old members to rejoin and promoting new stuff that I've created and then marketing to my previous members will get new members because if someone has joined they're probably not going to last forever but there might be something they want to see on down the line. And then having them on a newsletter, I use ActiveCampaign and have them as a tag that says these people are not active. It helps extremely because you can target all these people who are not active anymore because they're more likely going to join because they joined before. And I find that happens a lot."

Helping Members Learn

John's community is a big reason his members keep coming back to the site, as well as his extended onboarding sequence which provides regular action steps.

"I think most people just want to browse around and lurk for the most part on the forums. But there's certain people that want to get really involved. I think the more involved you get with something the more you get out of it. So if I get people involved then try to give them a plan to start with…I think it helps with retention if I've got an automation set up in Active Campaign for like two, two and a half months they're going to receive an email every couple of weeks or so that gives them like an action step to do. I want to extend that even further and right when they join there is like five steps you can do to start. You know the goal is for someone to learn something. And so there are a lot of things you can do to get people to learn better. A lot of times if people are just left alone they'll just browse everything and be like OK. I'm done.".

Some members need more help than others when it comes to knowing exactly what to do, so John makes use of action steps to try and help people learn better and make progress.

"Some people just don't know what to do. Or even if they have a lesson in front of them, they don't see exactly what they should be doing next. So laying out all of those actions steps if you learn this now what do you do and how do you implement it. There are certain things that I think helps people learn a lot better, so I just keep trying to get people to do those and I just have to keep saying it over and over and over again it seems like.

….And when people start seeing results they want to stay. When people get really into it they start having more fun with the guitar you know it's not as much fun to have a guitar if you can't play it. But the better you get, the better you want to get."

A Life Changing Result

After more than 10 years of running his own business, and 5 years of having his membership site, John can honestly say that his life has been completely changed.

"[The membership] completely changed my entire life. I mean I've never really worked a regular job ever. I did graduate with a business degree in college, but then after that I went and played gigs all the time and taught lessons. It's hard to make enough money when you're teaching lessons and doing part-time jobs. You just pretty much live pretty broke basically.

Starting the website completely changed my life to where everything was like wow,
I'm actually doing pretty well now. And then having the membership site gives me
even more free time...

You know you just have to have a lot of discipline. If you have the discipline to get
up every morning which I do and get things going and have things in place and
ready to roll you'll be fine. But if you find yourself getting up every morning and
being like 'I don't want to work on the membership site' you're probably in the
wrong business because I'm in a situation where I get up at 6:00 and I'm like I
can't wait to start working on it. So I like that feeling too.

I enjoy what I do more than any other thing I could ever want to do. ***To me that's***
one of the best things you ever have because you're going to have to make
money and you're going to have to work at something. So you might as well
try to find something that you enjoy the most *because you're going to spend*
years upon years working on something just forever."

What's Next For Learning Guitar Now

John currently has a system that works for him when it comes to getting and
keeping members, however he's still keen to test new things, like offering
one-to-one support.

"Well it is kind of more of the same because that's what's been working. But I'd also
like to take some chances with things. I would like to offer like only to members some
type of live one on one you know just very sparse. That if people just really have a
problem then they can go you know purchase a live lesson. I don't want to spend too

much time but some members really want that I make that option available to them."

In the 10 years John's been teaching guitar lessons online, he's created more than 130 hours worth of content. As he continues to add to that collection, and grow his membership numbers, his next big challenge is to interlink and restructure the learning materials.

"...What I've been doing is kind of restructuring the content where before it was like I made a course and that was it. Now I'm thinking about the whole site as one I'm not just thinking 'well okay maybe right now I will make this course.' But how does it fit together with everything else I already have on there. So basically it's just kind of restructuring everything to make it make a little bit more sense. It's like a step one two three four you know and on and on and on instead of just like course course course. ...basically just making it more concise putting things together in a more logical way."

Julie Christie: Togs in Business

Membership Details:

Name: Togs in Business

Topic: Business for Photographers

Launched: November 2016

Website: togsinbusiness.com

Interview Date: July 2017

Julie Christie runs Togs in Business, a membership site teaching business and marketing to photographers.

When Julie Christie moved across the country and needed to secure a source of income, she picked up her camera and started a photography business. She quickly became engrossed in learning about business and marketing so she could reach more of the right people.

After initially selling photography courses, Julie unlocked her real passion - teaching other professional photographers the marketing and business skills they need to succeed. But the course-launching lifestyle wasn't for her.

"Going back maybe two to three years ago, I had the idea to sell courses. I thought I would sell courses to beginner photographers, intermediate photographers. I didn't feel confident enough to sell photography courses to anyone above that level because I just didn't feel I was good enough. I was focusing on this beginner photography market and I was creating lighting courses for them and it was all about photography.

I was in this continuous launch mode. I was still running my photography business and I was trying to launch these photography courses. They were quite low price point as well, so they were like 50 dollars, 67 dollars, that kind of price. It actually did go quite well. I sold a lot of them, but what I was finding was I was exhausted with the thought of creating another course and launching it all over again.

I kept thinking, after the initial buzz and the initial high wore off, I thought, 'I can't do this forever. I can't just keep creating this content and launching it. I feel like a salesperson all the time.'

It was kind of killing my soul actually and I kept thinking, 'I'm not charging enough for this to work.' *I was having to reach far too many people to make it work. Then it was a one-time purchase. I was only getting like 67 dollars from this person and the more I started to understand the online business industry, I realised that I was getting it all wrong. I had started all wrong….*

It was actually advice from a peer mastermind that led Julie to first consider a membership site instead, as well as a change of topic. The idea took hold though and 2 months later Julie's membership site was launched.

"I was at one of my monthly Mastermind meetings and someone said to me, 'Julie, why on earth are you faffing around selling photography courses? You have a great business. You know all about that. Why do you not have a membership?'

Someone had mentioned it to me before and I'd said, 'I don't think I could cope with that commitment,' and it was only this time, when my friend said this to me, that I just thought, 'Actually, I could have a membership. I could do this,' and by the end

of that meeting, they'd all convinced me to start my membership. **That was in**
September and I launched in November...

...I literally just came home that night and I immediately joined Membership Academy because I knew I wanted to do this quickly, so I didn't want to make all those mistakes. I just wanted to learn from people who'd done it before and who'd made all the mistakes so that I could just fast-track it a little bit. That's the only reason I was able to launch so quickly."

Identifying Ideal Members

After initially welcoming any and all photography business owners to her new membership, Togs in Business, Julie refined her messaging to focus in on action-takers.

"My biggest challenge has been identifying my ideal member. I know it's still quite early days, but I did torture myself over this. When we first started, we were targeting any photography business owner and what we found was, we got lots of business owners who had been in business for a few years and then we got lots of photography business owners who had just begun or who were just thinking about starting.

I quickly realised we were getting a lot of the wrong people because our membership is very much based on you taking action. You have to take the action. You have to do the courses. You have to do the learning or you're not going to achieve anything. You're not going to get any results. We were getting a lot of people who were jumping in and they didn't have any time to do any of the learning. This was really frustrating for me."

Once Julie realised she was attracting some less than ideal members, she decided to make some changes to the membership to avoid this happening again.

"We actually closed down the membership to new members for a couple of months at least to really evaluate who was in there, who was logging in, who was actually doing stuff. Really, it doesn't mean that it was the people who had had their business for years. It was the people who had some time and who had reached a point where they needed this to work and they wanted it so much.

We then changed all of our messaging. We redid our landing page to really target people who were ready. We were very honest about the fact that it was not right for everyone. We have a section on our sales page which says that 'you are the right fit if you are this person' because we want to weed out those people who are not ready, because they are not good for us. They were joining. They were maybe logging in once and then they would leave two months later, having consumed no content. That was, I can't tell you how frustrating that was for me. I tortured myself, so that has been the big challenge, really identifying our ideal member and ... getting the messaging right so that she, because she is kind of a she, so that she believes that we are the perfect fit for her because we are."

Being more discerning about how she let into the membership did have a cost however.

"It was hard because obviously financially, you want as many members as possible. That is hard because right now, we only have ... I think we're at 130 active members at the moment. It's not enough to have this as my full-time gig with a staff member,

*but **I had to then just play that long game. I just couldn't cope with the low quality of members.***

*I think especially in the community as well because you can tell. If lots of people are jumping into the community and asking questions without doing any of the work or they're maybe having a moan all the time about how difficult it is to find the time, it's demoralising for everyone else. **You want people who are like-minded and who are action takers so that everyone's got everyone else's back and you're moving forward together**.*

It's definitely now a quality over quantity journey, which I'm not going to pretend is easy…"

An Application Process

In her quest to attract ideal members who are ready for what the membership offers, Julie has now introduced an application process rather than allowing people to join straight away.

"This was all part of finding our ideal member. What I've decided, and again I'm trying it so it might be that I change it again, but I decided that I would prefer to have members who are not put off by a small obstacle. I have got this hugely long sales page and that's still up because I want people who are willing to go and read through that whole thing and really watch the videos. I think if they've taken the time to read that, then they're really interested and they're ready.

If they then take the time to fill out the application form, then that's another sign that they are really ready to take action. I think those who are maybe put off by that or who put it aside for another time, they're probably not the right member for us. It's actually putting an obstacle in the way, but it's on purpose. Also, when they fill that in, there's questions in there that help me understand if they're going to be a good fit.

For example, someone got in touch just yesterday and I said no to them in a very nice way, but they had very little time to dedicate. One of the questions is, "How much time do you have to dedicate to your business?" They had next to none, but also they were interested in a type of photography business that is not really my area of expertise, so we will say no to people.

...what we will always say is, "If ever your circumstances do change and you have more time or you feel more ready, then we're here for you." At least they're on my email list."

Success with Webinars

When Julie first launched her membership, her initial members came from marketing to her email list. Now the majority of new members come via her value-packed, pitch-free webinars.

"The initial launch was via email, but since then the most members have come in via my webinars.

*I was doing webinars before I had a membership site, so I kind of cut my teeth already on photography webinars. I've shifted to photography business webinars using Easy Webinar. **I just love webinars. I think that's just such an amazing way to give your potential members a taste of what your education is like.***

A YouTube video is five minutes. A Facebook group is little interactions here and there. And a webinar is like an hour with you, where you can give them something really valuable to take away. **If they love it and they get something from that, then why would they not look into your membership?**

Julie makes use of both live and automated webinars, preferring to start with live so that she can test the response to the training first. Webinars are switched regularly to avoid a fatigue effect on the audience.

"I always do them live first to get an idea of the questions that come in and just to get that live response to them so that I can then make some tweaks and then they're automated after that using Easy Webinar.

We're on our second webinar, so our first one lasted a couple of months until it started to fatigue a little bit. We've just launched our second one, so it just runs in the background basically on its own after the initial live one. It just runs on its own, but I think what I'd like to do is have four webinars that just rotate. Maybe I'll do three months of one and then move to the next one and the next one, and then it just starts again because you're always going to reach a new audience with it, aren't you?

The new focus on only attracting ideal members does impact on the current webinar process however, and the fact there is no offer or time limit involved removes any immediate 'must buy now' urgency and need for heavy selling.

"...And because of my new focus, my new ideal member, these webinars going forward have very little sales in them because I'm not trying to snag everyone and anyone. **I really want that right person, so there's no offer. There's no time limit or countdown. It's just value and then at the end, 'By the way, we**

have a membership. It's by application only. If you've watched until the end of this webinar, then you're probably a really good fit for this membership,' so we invite people to apply, but there's not this big sales pitch, which I used to do with my old webinars."

Implementing a 'Success Month'

Julie's combined her new focus on finding the right members with an intensive first month for new members, which she calls Success Month.

*"This was another issue that I was getting frustrated with. **There were two courses in the membership that I felt were vital for everyone to do, but what was happening was members were joining and just picking the course that they wanted to do.** They would maybe jump right into the marketing course or they would jump right into the website course, but there were these two courses which were all about setting you up for success, thinking about your vision and recording it, really nailing down your ideal client, all that kind of stuff, which I think you can't not do that stuff and jump into a website course. You need to know where you're going and you need to have this really solid business foundation.*

***What we did was we refined the messaging and said that if you want to join, you have to commit to Success Month, which is 12 lessons over your first month as a member.** We tell them how long it's going to take. It's probably going to take about 18 hours of your time in one month and if you can't commit to 18 hours in one month, this membership is not for you so please don't join."*

Implementing the Success Month was as much for Julie's benefit as for her members, as she grew tired of fielding questions that were already answered in the courses.

"Success Month is vital and I had to introduce that or I was going to just get more and more frustrated because people were asking questions and I kept saying, 'You kind of really need to go back and do that course,' so now it's almost compulsory. I can't actually sit with them and make them do it, but I'm going to try my best."

The other benefit of Success Month is increased retention, with those who complete the intensive first month also likely to get better results from the other membership content.

"And if they do that [success month], if they actually do spend their first month doing that, then they're going to have lots of success with the other courses and they're going to be very likely to stick around because they will have had so many light bulb moments during that first month."

Mix & Match Communities

While Julie wanted to have an on-site forum so that the content would be searchable, her members wanted to interact on Facebook. She's reached a compromise so that most of the community action happens in a Facebook group, but any questions that require input from Julie must be asked on the forum.

"They are living there on Facebook and when we started, we decided to play around with a Facebook group and we opened that just for chat only. That was supposed to be where our members could hang out because what we found was they were going into the forum to ask a question, but they weren't hanging out there. They weren't getting to know each other there. They were just not doing that, and only a very select few were using it properly.

We thought, "We need a way for our members to get to know each other and bond," so we started the Facebook group. That initially was meant to be just to chill out, hang out, share wins, get to know each other, but actually we still have the forum"

While most engagement happens on Facebook now, Julie is still utilising the forum for both providing more indepth feedback (which isn't easy on Facebook) and for making sure any useful threads are archived so that they can be referred back to in the future.

"... if someone asks for feedback, we're still only giving that in the forum. If they're asking for something, if they're asking for a particular piece of advice that we would like to archive for others in the future, then we ask them to put it in the forum. I've been known sometimes to even just copy the question and put it into the forum and answer it there and then link back. Really, I've kind of relaxed about it as long as I'm archiving the stuff that I think is really important that I don't want to repeat over and over and over, then that is kind of working for us at the moment."

Julie particularly enjoys spending time in her community and can't imagine running a membership site without one.

*"**I don't think I could do this without a community. The community is everything to me.** That's my favourite part - watching the members themselves form relationships and bonds, becoming actual friends, not face-to-face friends, but real virtual, online friends who can't wait to meet up with each other, seeing their wins inside the community, really being able to help them with their challenges and their problems.*

...It's a real pick-me-up. Sometimes it's a bit overwhelming. You maybe log in and you think, 'Oh my God, I'm going to be here for two hours answering stuff,' but you feel great afterwards. You feel really on top of the world. I love that."

Creating Base Content

In addition to archiving answers in the forum, Julie has also dedicated time to creating a solid base of content to refer her members to when answering their questions.

"I've never created so much content in my life. It's content, content, content all the time. I'm willing to spend all this time creating content at the moment because I know that it's going to ease off in the future. Right now, I'm trying to get as many great courses in there as possible so that I have something to refer members to for almost every question they have."

Learning from Mistakes

For Julie, failures and flops are all part of the learning experience, especially when you're a membership site owner.

"I've reached a point with my business where I no longer worry about making mistakes and I want to make them because I just leap forward every single time, whereas if you'd asked me two years ago, I used to hate myself for every mistake I made. But now I'm just willing to make them because it just gets you so much further."

What's Next For Togs in Business

While Julie has an ambitious goal of reaching 600 members, she's not losing her focus on enrolling the right action-taking, committed people.

*"I would love to have 600 members. That would be amazing, but the future, the big vision is to have the right members. **It's definitely my absolute focus right now is the quality of the members, collecting as many of their stories as possible, the ones who are active and doing the work, and really just reaching that tipping point where we are unmissable in the industry,** but keeping that integrity so I just want to keep that vision of the right members doing the right work, taking the right action. **I don't want to take money from anyone who is not going to get anything from this membership,** so keeping that integrity, focusing on quality, not quantity, but even then, I still have to have a number that I'm striving towards."*

Christopher Sutton: Musical U

Membership Details:

Name: Musical U

Topic: Ear Training for Musicians

Launched: 2016

Website: musical-u.com

Interview Date: July 2017

Musical U, run by Christopher Sutton, is a membership that helps musicians develop the inner skills of music so they can play by ear, improvise, or write their own music.

"There's plenty of websites out there to learn how to play guitar or how to play piano. We don't teach the instrument technique. Instead we fill in what is often a missing piece for musicians which is how do you understand what you hear in music. We teach them the skills they need to play by ear or improvise or create their own music.

...This area which is traditionally called 'ear training' is something that's always been around, you know, literally for hundreds of years it's been a part of music education. But if you look around online it is relatively under-served and it is a niche where you don't find many membership sites or products or courses. There are some certainly but not that many...it was all very kind of heavily steeped in music theory and it was dry and repetitive and I found the process rewarding but very frustrating.

That was what really caused me to start my company and create the first products with the idea that this should be much more well known and much more enjoyable for musicians to do."

In 2009 Christopher launched his company, Easy Ear Training, which was later rebranded as Musical U.

Christopher actually began by selling iPhone apps, a very different proposition to a membership site, and even with 7 years experience as a business owner, there was still lots for Christopher to learn in the first couple of years running a membership.

"Marketing a subscription product is definitely more challenging than marketing a one time purchase product.

We got started in iPhone apps and you couldn't ask for an easier sell than getting someone to buy an iPhone app. Certainly you can do it badly. But in the comfy area of the App Store where everyone already has their credit card details in there, it's relatively easy to persuade them to spend a dollar and buy your app.

When we moved into info products, that became a bit harder. We were trying to sell through the website to sometimes cold visitors and **I learned the hard way that it takes a real skill to write good copy and to nurture a relationship to the point where someone is comfortable to buy**. *I don't think I'd really appreciated that, when it came to running a membership site, you were taking it much further.* **You were asking someone to sign up for recurring billing and that again just required a lot more persuasive copy and clearer value proposition and ongoing nurture to get them to the point of being ready to join your site.**

Certainly the first year of the site was heavily focused on that marketing and figuring out how to get new members to sign up. **We had a reasonably successful launch to our existing email list but after that there was a lot to figure out in terms of how to keep new members coming in."**

Going 'All In'

Having experienced the roller coaster of periodic launches when selling information products, Christopher was keen to create a more steady income stream, and focus his efforts on just one product.

"I'm not someone that thrives on that pressure and excitement [of launches] and I definitely am someone who gets frustrated when things drop off in between. **Definitely part of my motivation with starting the membership site was to create something more stable and sustainable and ongoing compared to that roller coaster of launches where each one might be a hit or a miss....**

...One of the major benefits for us of moving to the membership model - it allowed us to just put all of our efforts into one basket in a good way. Up until that point, I literally had more than a dozen products...it just became more and more complex. And that went for our customers too. If they came to know our brand, they'd still be faced with the decision of which product is right for me? How do I figure that out? **Moving into the membership site model and having what's sometimes called one hero product where this is the thing you recommend your audience sign up for, it just simplified things drastically both for our customers and for ourselves."**

The Commitment Challenge

For Christopher, his biggest challenge has actually come about as an unexpected side effect of his success.

*"I don't think this is something people warn you about but they should. **The downside of getting better at your marketing is that you start to acquire less committed customers.** Any business will have a mix of customers from the superfans to those who just kind of speculatively bought on impulse. But we found the more we dialed in our content marketing and email marketing and the better we got at converting people to that purchase, the less committed they were walking in the door.*

That was a big problem for us in particular because I was determined to provide a very flexible training system. Some membership sites are just community and people show up and there are things you can do to improve retention for sure but they basically are there for the forums.

Others are very course based so someone will come in knowing they want their SEO course or the how to build your own car course. They're gonna come in, they're gonna start that course, they're gonna plod along.

In our case, I knew from our experience developing these kinds of products that every musician's different and the skills they want to develop are different. While the training material we provide can be common across all of our members, people were gonna come in wanting a very different mix of that training and want to use it in a very different way.

What we built is a very flexible system and that's great, and for the first year or so that worked really well for our members.

As we moved into the second year after I'd done a lot of work on conversion optimization and improving the member acquisition, it became clearer and clearer that the people walking in the door were not the kind of motivated self-driven, self-guided learners we'd had to begin with who are gonna rock up and take charge of their learning. **We were starting to get people who really expected, with no disrespect, to be spoon-fed. They were people who wanted the teacher to tell them what to do and ... that's a very different user experience to try and design.**

The fact that Christopher offers a lot of personal guidance in the membership site meant that the change in member commitment level could be counteracted, as long as the member reached out to the team. However this wasn't a long term solution.

"We were kind of saved by the fact that we offer very personal help and support and guidance. When members did get stuck, as long as they were willing to say 'Hey I'm confused.' Or 'I need help.' We could jump in and help them and that kinda kept us going for year two but I didn't want that to be such a manual effort every time. And I wanted the new member experience to be really smooth and slick even if they were coming in requiring that kind of step-by-step handholding.

...We hired a great UX consultancy to help out recently. They came in and did a one week audit and really dug into what was it that was confusing new members and what we could do to change it. I have a fantastic laundry list of things to change and improve now that will hopefully help with that because it's not an impossible

problem. There's a lot of things that now need to be redesigned with a very different mindset of what we can expect from our new members."

A Win-Win

Christopher has seen two main benefits from running a membership: improved long-term results for his members; and predictable cash flow into his business.

"I'd been very happy with the products we developed and the results they got for people. But I had also been continually frustrated by knowing that it wasn't getting them all the way there. It would teach them this one skill but it wouldn't get them to the point of standing up at a jam session and improvising a solo.

I love that we are able to now take a new member, help them figure out their goals, help them plan their training and then be with them week after week, month after month until they get to that amazing, inspiring goal. I loved seeing that and I loved putting a team in place that can help support people in that way.

*The other aspect, the business side of things, it's been amazing to actually be able to project cash flow. When you're running an app business, you can only guess. And when you're running info products on a launch level, you can only hope. **So I think having the stability of income from the recurring revenue, it's really transformed how I can run my business and how I can plan for growth and in particular how I can hire a team** because if you're gonna say to someone 'Look I can pay you this much month-to-month,' you need to know you're gonna have the money to pay them. Yeah, it's been transformational for the business just to have that more predictable revenue stream."*

Combining Content & Email Marketing

Chris combines content marketing with a highly personalized approach to email marketing.

"In the big picture, what is working, what has always worked [for getting new members] is a combination of content marketing and email marketing....

...the vast majority will come across our website through organic search traffic or through our apps. We reach roughly 120,000 per month through those two media.

Then the step two is email marketing. Once they discover some of our content, we try hard to get them onto some kind of email sign up that provides more information for free and more value and helps to start that relationship nurture. Then we have offers in place to hopefully convert into membership if it's a good fit for them.

That's a very high level overview of our funnel. It's content discovery through organic means, email sign up, and then email nurture to the point of becoming a member."

A quiz on the website helps personalize the email marketing experience for each new subscriber, allowing marketing messages to be far more specific and effective.

"A few years ago, we started to experiment with something a bit more personalised. We had what we called the Course Finder where we took the six email courses we'd developed at that point and we put them into a Ryan Levesque style survey where people could answer a few questions and get told 'this is the email course for you.'

That was great because it made use of our existing email courses in a way that was much more effective for getting people to sign up and I think what I learned from that was that there's real value in that kind of diagnosis. **Psychologically if someone comes to your website and they feel like they've been understood and they feel like they're getting a recommendation that is personalised to them, that seemed to work really well in terms of getting them to enter their email address and get the value we were waiting to deliver.**

That was a great learning point but I was still a bit frustrated because they weren't really adapted to the person. We gave them the best of six options but it was clear from the answers people were giving that they weren't always the right match and I wasn't really happy with how each of those email courses matched up with pitching Musical U because most of them had been written before we launched the membership site...it was a bit awkward."

Christopher recently took the initial success of more personalised opt-ins and took it one step further.

"I guess about a year ago, we created the current opt-in which we call the Musicality Checklist. And the idea is to give people a self-assessment of where their musicality and their musicianship currently is and what they can do to improve it.

Again, this is kind of a survey based approach. If someone comes to this opt-in, it walks them through a series of questions and for each skill, they say I can do this or I want to do this or neither. The upshot is we then have a really in depth profile of them as a musician.

What that allows us to do is immediately deliver them a personalised PDF that gives them some next steps on each of those areas they're interested in

and then do a personalised email follow up that doesn't bombard them with irrelevant information but instead gives them just the emails, just the information that's relevant to them and allows us to kind of position Musical U in the most effective way.

It's really the automated version of what I would do in person if I met a musician and they were like "Well, why should I join Musical U?'... This email marketing funnel allows us to do that in a very personalised but automated way."

Reducing Barriers

To improve his marketing results further, Christopher also offers email subscribers a 7-day trial of the membership for $1. This works to reduce the barrier to entry and provide some risk reversal for joining the membership.

"I referenced before how it's a higher barrier to entry to try and make a sale online for a subscription product. **That trial definitely brings the barrier down a little bit because they are still signing for recurring billing but they feel like I've got this one week to try it out. If it doesn't work, I've only wasted a dollar....**

Even if you have a rock solid guarantee and you say 'Look, just sign up and if it doesn't work, you can get all of your money back' I found that wasn't enough and offering the trial I think just makes it one notch easier for people to be comfortable with taking that risk...they don't want to feel silly for having to ask for their money back and so making it just a dollar, for us that's the right balance.

If we let people in for free, our community would become a nightmare. You only need to look at YouTube comments to see the direction that would go but in terms of protecting our community's quality and also lowering that barrier to entry for people, a dollar for seven days seems to be the right balance for us in terms of offering a trial."

Retention through Excellence

When it comes to retention, Christopher believes the best approach is simply to ensure that your product is effective and delivers results.

*"It sounds like a bit of a cop out but my top tip is just to make the product really good. For us that means trying to make sure their training is as effective as possible because **ultimately if someone is getting the results they came for, and if they're seeing those results and getting the benefit of them, they're not gonna quit, right**?*

I think where a lot of membership sites struggle and certainly where we still struggle sometimes is if they're not getting those results, what can you do to keep them around long enough to get them back on track? That's a whole separate issue. But number one priority for us is just making sure if someone signs up to learn X, we do whatever we can to make sure they do learn X.

A Sense of Community

The other retention driver for Musical U is the community and ensuring that members feel like they belong and are supported there, even during times where they may not have been an active member.

"That's [community] making sure they feel part of something, they feel seen and respected and they're interacting. So that even if time gets tight and they don't have the opportunity to do their 10 minutes of training every day this week, they get our weekly update, they see one of their friends inside the site has posted a new discussion, they have a reason to come back and do something a bit lighter, something that keeps them engaged in the website, in the membership site, and keeps them feeling like they are a member. **They are part of something so that then when time does allow, when their enthusiasm returns, or when we are able to do something to reactivate them and get them training again, they're still with us rather than having hit cancel because they didn't find time this week."**

Being a Non-Expert

As he was building the membership, and still learning the skills, Christopher needed to take an alternative approach to developing his site content. So instead of being an expert teacher, he became the attentive student, and hired professionals to create the content he needed.

"I never hold myself up and say 'Look, I have perfect ears, you can have my ears.' I am not that hero character that is particularly prominent in the fitness world where you want to be just like that guy you see photos of."

The result is a membership site with a supportive community of musicians who are learning together and supporting each other, rather than a flock following one expert.

Rewarding Members

Christopher has used his technical expertise to build gamification into Musical U, rewarding members in a clear and visible way for their training results and efforts.

"I think any human, they want some acknowledgement when they accomplish something whether that's a progress bar or it's a little pop up or it's something in the community where other people can see they've achieved it or it's another badge on their profile page, some acknowledgement that you've put in the effort and you've accomplished that milestone I think is a really powerful thing in e-learning."

A Worthwhile Journey

While the journey to creating a successful membership site may not have always been smooth sailing, it's certainly been worthwhile and changed Christopher's business for the better in many different ways.

"This has not been an easy home run, no bumps along the way kind of journey. It is its own type of product, it is its own learning curve, both from the product development and from the marketing and from the ongoing customer support. It is a beast of its own so it's definitely something that has been interesting and challenging to do. But in terms of the results and the impact on the company, I couldn't really have asked for better.

At this point we're able to serve several hundred musicians in a very personal and in depth way. We're able to deliver much better results to the customers. We're able to plan much further ahead in terms of how to improve that product, how to market it better. *I've been able to grow the team because I actually know how much money we're likely to make next month and it's* *just ... I wouldn't say it's taken the pressure off and certainly hiring a team brings its own kind of pressure but it has taken a lot of the stress out of the day-to-day because things are more predictable, they're more stable, and you're able to take that longer term view on how to grow your company."*

What's Next For MusicalU

The growth of MusicalU has been in large part thanks to a successful combination of content marketing and email marketing - a strategy Christopher intends to keep employing.

In the future Christopher will also be building on existing industry relationships to launch Joint Ventures, and also looking outside his own niche, to learn the experiences of other membership site owners.

"I really love to hear from other member site owners, and I love the community (Membership Academy) for that opportunity just to get a peek inside some other membership sites and get the insights and tactics that can help you grow your own."

Holly Gillen: Business Cinema Academy

Membership Details:

Name: Business Cinema Academy

Topic: Video Marketing

Launched: 2015

Website: hollygstudios.com

Interview Date: July 2017

Holly Gillen runs Business Cinema Academy, a membership that helps online business owners with all things video, from production to marketing.

When Holly ran an impromptu 30 Day Challenge to help business owners be more confident about creating videos, she discovered a new passion: managing a community. She loved the experience so much, she launched her own membership site, Business Cinema Academy.

"It's basically all the stuff that you need once you overcome your fears of being on the camera and you're good, you're feeling confident, you're ready to go, and now you're like, 'Wow. How do I make my videos look better?' It serves all of that extra stuff at the end of that. Basically, it's for anybody who is ready to elevate their video creation and take it to the next level, grow, thrive, enjoy creating video content, but really need somebody to fill in those missing pieces for them...

... I focus on people who are running online businesses because video is just such an important aspect of running an online business.

When you're marketing and would like to work with people from all around the world, it's difficult to be in the same room with those people and establish like, 'Hey, I really do know what I'm talking about. You can look me in my eyes and I can shake your hand and you can see my body language and understand that I am an expert in what I'm talking about and I can help you and I do care.' The next best thing to that is by using video in your business to establish that know, like, and trust factor with your audience."

Back in 2014, Holly created a 30-day free video challenge for entrepreneurs. Her goal was to build her audience and attract new clients to her business, Holly G Studios, but the event had an unexpected, longer term impact.

*"...everybody created a brand new video based on a prompt that I provided for them. It was called 'Zero to Video Hero'. One of the things that was a game changer for me was the community... how everybody was so supportive of one another. I get the chills every time I think about how amazing and extraordinary and transformational it was, not only for the people who were participating, but also for me. **I fell in love with having a community and being able to help train and support people through their video journey at that moment.... that's what really planted the seed to start a membership community.**"*

Holly had experimented with a lot of different business models before running her free challenge, and feels that a membership community has been the best fit for her so far.

"I've been running this business since 2013, so I've experimented with a lot of different ways to launch things, run my business, tried courses and one off things or live things...I would say, by far, the membership and having that community and having a place where I can watch people grow has been amazing.

Back in 2014, when I did that first challenge... I loved being witness and being part of watching people grow and transform.

The biggest impact for running the membership community is just watching that happen. I didn't really enjoy like, 'Hey. Here's this course. Good luck with that. Don't report back. I don't really care what happened to your results.' It just felt empty to me and hollow.... This is really fulfilling for me and makes me feel really good."

A membership also was a better fit for Holly's industry, where technology and tactics move so fast that regular updates to training would be needed in order for people to have the most up-to-date knowledge.

"... I knew [the video industry] was going to be challenging for me and something that wouldn't get boring because there is always something new happening, whether it's new gear or new techniques or new tools or apps or platforms. The landscape is constantly evolving."

The One Regret

"I should have started this membership community after that original challenge back in January 2014. I wish I had. At the conclusion of this free challenge, which had, at the time, no conclusion, there was nowhere for anybody to go. I was frantically trying to build a course while the challenge was going because I was like, 'What am I going to do with these people at the end of this?' It was just an experiment that I was trying and it just turned out so well that people were like, 'We want to work with you more.'

I ended up creating a course, and the feedback I got was, 'This is so disconnected. We had so much interaction with you during the free challenge and so much connection and conversation and community that the course just didn't work.'

If I had created the community then and moved everybody from this free challenge into the community to continue that conversation, to continue that support and training and transformation and all of the things, that would have been boom, game changer."

Community Challenges

Finding the right platform for her community to connect on has proved difficult for Holly.

"I originally started with a Facebook group with the intention of moving that over into Kajabi, as Kajabi kind of branched out and had the ability to install forums and things like that to keep track of the community conversations.

In the interim, I opted to use something called Mightybell [now Mighty Networks]. I tested that out and I would say it was kind of not really ... It didn't really work out, but I would have never known if I hadn't tested it. I would say the challenge for me was just finding that sweet spot between not being complicated, being easy, being friendly, and something that people were actually going to use."

In the end, Holly decided to go back to using a Facebook group.

"I polled everybody. I asked. I was looking at all of the different angles. At the end of the day, I just went back to Facebook because that's where people were hanging out and that's where I was getting the most engagement."

Despite the initial challenges of finding the right home base for her members community, it is this aspect, along with seeing members progress, that is Holly's favourite aspect of being a membership site owner.

"The conversations, just watching people grow and blossom and succeed with what they're doing and continually putting in the time, the work, the effort to make their videos the best that they can possibly be and really enjoying it..... I just love it when somebody can take something that I've created, a system or tool or process, and really embrace that and then succeed with it and then even modify it and adjust it for how they want to use it. That just makes me so excited."

Holly also sees keeping her community lively as key to retaining her members.

"Constantly keeping the community flowing with lots of conversation and trying to ... I'm as engaged as possible just to keep everybody else as engaged as possible."

Free Challenges

To build and engage her audience, Holly runs a free video challenge called #oneminuteonetake. The aim is to create a video for use on social media, one minute long, in just one take. Whoever creates the most videos over a 5-day period wins a pass to the Business Cinema Academy.

"I have a limited amount of time that I can work on my videos every day, so I was like, 'I know. I'm going to create like a short version with no editing. I'll call it One Minute One Take.'...

...What I did was I upped the game and said, 'It's five days. You have five days. Whoever makes the most videos in five days wins a pass to the Business Cinema Academy, which is basically the sponsor for the #oneminuteonetake video challenge.'"

Ensuring a Good Fit

When visitors arrive on Holly's sales page they also find a quiz to see if they're a good fit for the membership.

"It's not going to be right for everybody. You have to be in a certain position. You have to be ready to work. I can provide you the tools and the information, but I can't do the work for you...

...if you're not ready, I don't want you in there because it's just going to be a waste of time and money for you if you aren't ready to start implementing some of these strategies and systems.

If you haven't even made your first video yet, this really isn't the place for you. It's really for somebody who's overcome their fears a little bit. You could be still kind of fearful, but you're ready to conquer that and move forward with your video journey and step your game up.

If you don't have time for video in your business, or video's not really a strategy you want to work on, or any of those things, it really isn't the place for you and I don't want you in there....

*...**It's really for me. I succeed when you succeed. If you're not ready to succeed, then I can't help you succeed**. I take so much pride in making sure that it's something that you're using and it's working and you're not just collecting dust."*

Themed Content

Themed months help Holly's members stay engaged with the content without getting overwhelmed by all the possibilities.

"Last month's theme was YouTube. I walked people through ... I have a course called 'The YouTube Channel Makeover Course' where I go through how to redesign your YouTube channel so that it's optimised for YouTube and what you're trying to do, so adding in playlists and optimising your metadata and custom thumbnails and stuff like that. Each week of the month, we went through a different aspect of that course, so it was like a walkthrough, a live walkthrough, version of The YouTube Channel Makeover Course for my members.

*....**I feel like people get confused about where to start and where to end, so going through these themed months was my way of just saying, 'Let's just focus on this one thing right now.'** Each of these things just kind of builds on each other and you just keep building your skills so that you're able to create better videos."*

What's Next For Business Cinema Academy

Holly is currently working on a pre-membership course - a course that will give the students the foundational knowledge they need to start using video more effectively in their business. Then once they graduate, they will be offered the opportunity to join the membership.

"I'm working on a new course that will lead into the membership group, which is basically the foundation you need for creating videos for YouTube. It's a full strategy from beginning to end. It's really everything that you need to know to get started.... How do you get those videos to be your sales person, your greeter, your everything while you're doing your own thing?"

2019 Update:

After taking a break from the membership world to have her first child, Holly has developed a number of products and services, and in the summer of 2019 launched a brand new membership programme, Video Made Easy.

Shannon Rogers: The Hand Tool School

Membership Details:

Name: The Hand Tool School

Topic: Wood Working

Launched: 2010

Website: handtoolschool.net

Interview Date: July 2017

The Hand Tool School, run by Shannon Rogers, is focused on wood working with hand tools and combines one-off courses with a newer membership product.

Shannon started his blog, renaissancewoodworker.com, back in 2008 as an online space to showcase the furniture he was building. It was initially a method to explain the value to customers, but quickly became a blog for other woodworking fans.

"The people that cared were the other woodworkers....'Well, how did you do that, or why did you execute that particular joint that way? How would you go about building this?'...I went heavily video focused about a year into it, and I just started building this community of people that really liked what I was doing..."

After his blog community started building, Shannon realised that he had found an underserved market and that there was a lot of potential for monetising.

"The more I began getting into this, the more I began really enjoying it, and realising there was a void of actual hand tool instruction. I said, 'I need to tap into

*that,' and **the membership site, the school model was really a way to kind of monetize that, because anybody who's run a YouTube channel knows that it's a heck of a lot of work to make a living on Adsense revenue.*...

...To me it made sense at the time to build a little walled garden, to build an actual school, to the point where I put school in the name of the site. And believe me I caught a lot of flack for that early on. 'Who is this jackass? Who is this guy who thinks that he can teach? He's only got like one more year of experience than I do.'

One of the things in the Internet, is all you need to know is just one more thing than the people you're talking to. That really carried me a long way, and here we are seven years later, and I can honestly say, I'm a much better woodworker than I was seven years ago....

...I've improved as a craftsman. I've also dramatically improved my teaching ability, my teaching skills, and I'm constantly getting feedback from members about you know, 'I've been struggling with this for years, 20 minutes you explained it in such a way. You're a great teacher.'"

A Unique Approach

Since its launch, similar memberships have come and gone, but so far Hand Tool School is unique in its curriculum-based approach.

In the Hand Tool School, Semesters are the equivalent of one-off courses, while the Apprenticeship is the recurring revenue of the site.

"Nobody has really tried to tackle the school mentality of a curriculum, of lessons, applied projects, another lesson, another applied project. So far I'm the only one doing that, so we'll see how long that lasts....

...*When I started the school the tagline was, 'The Hand Tool School, the world's first virtual apprenticeship'. That also got me in a lot of hot water, from the establishment. The established cabinet makers and the media they didn't like that, but it was always my intention to create an atmosphere of apprenticeship. The old-time guild systems, and master and apprentice, which over in the UK you guys actually still have that. We don't have that over here, not so much. There's only a shadow of what it used to be. I wanted to create that atmosphere, but that's really hard to do. You're talking one-to-one education at that point, so I had to scale back and just do more of a traditional course layout."*

As advances in technology and tools occurred, Shannon realised that advances in automation made offering an 'Apprenticeship' now a realistic and scalable possibility, in addition to his existing Semester courses.

"I started to look into some of the automation and the ability to tag users, and be able to speak to them based on what they just did. They just clicked on a video, a tag shows up on their profile, and now I can send them an email or send them an on-site message saying, 'What did you think of that video?' Or more importantly, 'Any questions after that video? Anything you're concerned about before you tackle the project in the next video?'.

Then I started to say, 'Okay. Well here's a way that I could actually make an apprenticeship relationship exist. It's scalable'...

I began to look at how could I structure a coaching programme, and a lot of it hinged around having a good community software that will allow everybody to have kind of their own little corner of the community, you guys call them progress logs, I call them apprentice logs. That was kind of the centre of communication.

I was then able to create videos that responded to whatever was going on there, and then do live broadcasts every month that specifically address questions that people have going on in there. All the while, this tagging and stuff is going on in the background, so every single apprentice ... it's ridiculous. Some of my guys had been with me a full year, they've got like 300 tags associated with their name. But I don't need to pay attention to that, I've got software that's paying attention to it, and suddenly the coaching becomes a matter of just responding...

It's less me asking you if you have questions, and more me responding when you have questions. Because the software, the automation, is asking the questions. **The software is touching base with them after every video they watch every week saying, 'What's new in your shop? What's going on? What can I help with?'** *And all I'm doing is just checking my inbox, and responding, and occasionally saying, 'You know what? That's a good idea for a video.'"*

The membership element is essentially an upsell to Shannon's existing Semester courses.

People who have enrolled on The Hand Tool School courses have the option to join Shannon's Apprenticeship, where they will benefit from personalized advice and guidance on their woodworking projects.

"The content that I create for apprenticeship is directly related to what is going on in the apprentices' shops. So whatever they're working on, whatever they're struggling with, that content is created to address that particular issue. It's coaching on mass if you will, scaled up coaching."

A Part-Time Membership

When Shannon first launched the school, he was working for a digital marketing agency, in a job he didn't enjoy. When he got laid-off, he was offered the perfect opportunity to combine a job with his side hustle.

"As I was walking to my car with the iconic cardboard box in hand, I got a phone call from a recruiter, for a lumber company, who wanted somebody that understood digital marketing and wood. I was like, 'You've got to be kidding me.'...

...I was offered the job the Monday after Thanksgiving, and I absolutely jumped all over it. It was an opportunity to run a marketing department, to build a website, and be an army of one marketer. Had it not been for that job, I probably would have tried to make The Hand Tool School full-time at that point. It would have been tough looking back on it and seeing what the revenue was in the first couple of years, although you know, if you can dedicate all your time to it, who knows what that revenue could be.

Because my day job is in the lumber industry, it directly relates to what I do at The Hand Tool School, so much so that my boss has actually offered to buy the renaissancewoodworker.com several times."

Running the membership part time alongside his full time job currently works well for Shannon because of how closely linked the two are and how much Shannon enjoys his job, but even so Shannon doesn't think this is sustainable in the long term.

"If it were a strict separation of day job and night job, I don't think I could do it. I don't think there's a way that I could possibly be able to manage it... it's a fantastic job to hang on to....

... In the end though, something's got to give. We're very close to a breaking point now. You know I have some very specific financial goals that I need The Hand Tool School to hit and sustain before I will turn one off, and turn the other one on full-time. It's a great situation to be in, don't get me wrong. If it were a bad job I would have dropped it long ago, but it's not. It still provides challenge and stimulation."

Utilising Live Video

"Get me on camera and throw questions at me, and you'll see that I know what I'm talking about..."

For Shannon, live video streaming is a quick and effective way for him to build an engaged audience and win their trust. He converts them into customers by offering an inexpensive standalone training video as a content upgrade.

*"**The authenticity of live really has driven a lot of traffic to the site, and a lot of people converting**. I do a live broadcast for the general public every single month, eventually I'll probably go to twice a month, probably very soon, because frankly it's a lot less work. There's no editing on the back end. It's fantastic. I generally will pick a topic, and I will dedicate an hour of a live stream to that particular topic. I'll do a demonstration and I'll open up for questions, and answer questions.*

*I've been pairing that for all intents and purposes with a content upgrade. I've been repurposing archived content in The Hand Tool School that has previously never been available...**I'm pulling content out of the archive and repackaging it as a standalone lesson, and selling it for $10, $15, kind of trip wire type prices.***

But it is directly related to that demonstration that I just did. It's kind of, 'If I were to go for another hour, this is what you would see.' That has generated a fair amount of revenue. I think in the total picture, I think it's about 6% of the total school revenue.

*It's not a huge amount, but in order to buy it, they have to create an account. **When they create an account, they go into the automation web, and then they get a series of five emails each with a video on it, that talks about the why**. Why is The Hand Tool School here? Why should you care? Why you should be a member, and how you're going to be a better woodworker when you become a member."*

Engagement with a Structured Curriculum

While Shannon has a structured step-by-step curriculum for each separately purchased semester course, he isn't simply dripping content on his schedule, instead everything is automated based on videos that the member actually watches, which helps keep engagement high.

"Because my semesters are a structured curriculum, I keep them engaged through the automations that are responding to the videos that they have watched.

...There's a semester one curation sequence, that waits for a tag to be applied when they've watched the first video. It sends them an email saying you know, 'In summary, this is what we talked about. Any questions on that,' with a link to the specific forum thread for that lesson. You know, 'Come over here. There's some other conversations going on about that.' Then kind of some pre-work for the applied project.

That's keeping them very engaged, because every time they're watching
something, they're getting a communication from me prompting them with
you know, 'Answer this question. Answer this question. Go and do this, or go and
download the parts list for the project you're about to build. Your next step is going
to be this project, so go do these things to help you get started on that.'...

...The open rates are through the roof on that stuff, because it is truly one-to-one
communication at that point."

Shannon keeps community engagement high by ensuring that every piece
of content encourages discussion and links to his community. Discussion
prompts are also tailored to what has just been viewed rather than generic,
which increases uptake.

"Every single bit of content, every video on my site, has a button at the bottom...
that says, 'Let's continue this conversation in the community.' Actually it says
something different for every page. It's usually related. If they just watched a lesson
on chisel techniques, you know, 'Let's talk some more about chisel techniques in the
community.' So it's all very, very related and focused, instead of it just being a
generic, 'Go to the community button.'

There's a call to action if you will at the bottom, which drives people from that
lesson, to a discussion in the community, and the rest of it just takes it from there.
Because people are talking up a storm about those chisel techniques, and that raises
other questions. More importantly it raises questions, which I can then turn around
and say, 'You know what? There's a lesson on that if you go over here and click on

that,' which drives them back into the lesson, which it's all a wicked ... web is a good term for it, now that I think about it. It traps them and sucks them in."

Real-Life Meetups

Shannon's also recently started hosting real-life meet-ups for his community, something he wishes he'd started earlier.

"Something that I've been doing lately is tapping into my community in real-life...

I just recently hosted, for lack of a better term, a tour of a local museum... I called them and I booked a custom furniture makers tour, and I got 15 members to show up, and it was... it cost money. They had to pay admission. It was only $37 for three hours of focused guided tour, but you know if you did a meet-up at a bar, you've got to buy your drinks and your appetisers, it's the same type of thing. It was phenomenal...

When I went to Membership Intensive with you [Callie] and Mike in San Diego, I did a meet-up after we adjourned, and we went to a local sandwich place, and then we went back to a member's shop, and we had like an impromptu guild meeting if you will. It was just incredible, and the relationships that I've built from those two meetups have been so strong since then, and gave me so much insight into what changes I need to make technically content wise, to the sites. Things that if you're ever in a face-to-face discussion with somebody and they're like you know, 'I've been meaning to write you about this. I've been meaning to email you about this,' and those little things that you forget, but when you're face-to-face with somebody, you get honest feedback. Very candid feedback. Man, the stuff that I learned from those two meetups, and I've done a third one since then, has just been invaluable...

...So whether it's a meet-up or conference or something, the in real life thing, it cannot be overstated how effective it can be. You want to talk about live-streaming breeding authenticity? How about live face-to-face? That's even more effective."

What's Next For The Hand Tool School

Membership sites often evolve to appeal to more advanced users, but Shannon is moving in the opposite direction. Recognising that there is a growing market of enthusiastic but inexperienced woodworkers, Shannon is creating material for entry-level beginners next.

"My demographic is squarely in their 30s. These people are young, and there are more and more young people, 20-somethings and teenagers coming into the craft, because the Internet has opened up this world...There's all these people coming into the craft that are so much less informed than my original customer base, my original target audience....This semester truly starts from nothing, to the point where I went to my in-laws place in Maine to film it, and will be going back in August to finish filming it, because they have a garage with nothing in it.....They get to see how it's done in a complete blank space. I think that will really attract a whole new demographic."

Lisa League: QPractice

Membership Details:

Name: QPractice

Topic: Interior Design Exam Prep

Launched: July 2012

Website: QPractice.com

Interview Date: August 2017

Lisa League helps interior designers in the United States and Canada pass a professional exam through her membership site, QPractice.

After finding the process of becoming a licensed interior designer herself stressful, Lisa and a friend had the idea of creating a website dedicated to helping people practice and prepare for their exams. Before building the course, she interviewed multiple potential customers, and created a sales page to float the idea with her email subscribers.

"I help interior designers in the United States and Canada pass a professional exam called the NCAIDQ. And that's where Q in QPractice comes from.

It's used for licensing and registration, so it's an important step in someone's career to go from junior to senior designer or to even be able to work on certain types of projects...

I offer test prep courses and practice tests and a study group, so it's like the paid community that supports the content and the courses, and the practice test."

There are three different courses, one for each of the different exams. These are available to buy separately, or in a bundle with access to the community.

Unlike most membership sites, there is an element of inbuilt churn in Lisa's site as once the exams are passed it is no longer needed.

"If you do a good job and somebody else does their part too, and they pass the exams, then you just have built-in churn. But I have people that stick around, they're still here from the beginning. Some people need more help than others. Then also there's an eligibility aspect to it. Not everyone is eligible to take all three exams at once. So there's one exam that people can take when they're out of school if they meet the educational requirements. And then the others they have to have a certain amount of work experience. So there's really like a five years period that they have to take and pass all three or they have to start again."

Lisa started the venture with a friend, after they both found passing their NCAIDQ stressful.

"I am a licensed interior designer. When I took this exam I just remember the whole process of registering and preparing for it, it was really very stressful...I had a friend who had gone through the process and it ultimately took her five times to pass the exams. She had the idea of creating practice problems for people and had someone else that she was interested in working on it and they came to me to help do the website.

I said, 'Well you couldn't afford me but I would like to participate.' I had been doing things for different people, I had built a membership site for a client, and I'd been building other people's businesses and I wanted to do something for myself.

...It grew into what really people wanted. They didn't want more practise problems but they wanted the support, they didn't understand when the testing organisation, NCIDQ released exam books with solutions and stuff, they didn't even understand that. They really needed somebody to teach them and help them understand, so it developed into something completely different than the original idea..."

Lisa spent a lot of time actually talking to her potential members before launching the site, in order to understand what it was that they really needed.

"Before we even had anything for sale, it was a lot of conversations with people one-on-one. I'd get on the phone, or on Skype with them and talk to them, and take all of the information and notes, to look at what the common thread is.

Then I put together a sales page for the first version of QPractice. I didn't even have the course built...sent out an email to all the people that we had gotten on our list and if we sold it, I was going to build it, if nobody was interested then I didn't really spend any time. We did this in December and then started in January so it was building it as we go."

Team Building Challenges

Despite having project management experience, Lisa has found building and managing a team for the membership difficult.

"The challenge has been getting the right people to help me. But then I have a really good team that work in my group who are past members who've gone through it and passed. The challenge there is that I get those good people... But everybody's like

a full-time designer so it's like a side thing for them and the people that are really good, the thing that makes me want them for the team also gets them a promotion in their job. So they either get promoted and move on, or they get pregnant and move on.. That's always a challenge - getting good people and keeping good people. Then customer support, it's always really important to have somebody that you can depend on. I've got somebody who's really great now and she's from outside the industry so it's super helpful to have somebody who has a beginner's eye to see and pick up on things. It's just that's a whole new thing for me... So the whole people aspect, and having 11 people, and then customer support, and then we have the online business manager, then working with 5 or 6 different developers... it's a lot more people than I ever planned on getting into. That has been a whole new experience for me."

Getting to Grips with Tech

Lisa has enjoyed getting involved with the technical challenges as her membership site build has evolved.

"I really have liked how [the site] has just grown and evolved over time.

The initial site was something that I built and I started with Paid Membership Pro, and no LMS. Then I added an LMS. Then I actually partnered with somebody and threw money at an LMS to try and build out some of my features and that didn't work.

Then I went along another year in and hired another developer who pulled in someone else, two top developers who developed more. And then I had a team of five out of Oregon, well they're all international but based out of Oregon that have taken me to the next level.

So being involved with that I've built my own plug-ins, even the codes on my site now, although this is the first time I've had a theme that somebody else has done I've been so much a part of it.

I've really, really enjoy the under the hood stuff as well as making the content."

Search Domination

Lisa pulls in traffic from organic search and referrals, then uses email marketing to convert visitors into customers.

"I have a lot of content and I've developed a lot over the years, and I rank it extremely well.

I've also been working with Team Yoast, they have a plan. I had done some site reviews and now they have an ongoing plan where they review a different aspect of your site every month and advise you, or make tweaks, and stuff like that, so I've been working with them on that. So that organic search is really good.

I do have somebody that's writing some ads for me now but it's just brand new this past month... So I haven't gotten my report back where we look and see how well it's done, and where we'd go from here."

*I'm going to be **building up more of my corporate plans** but I'm working with some companies that buy for their employees over and over, I have some professional association affiliates, so it's a variety of things.*

But I think having and developing a really strong content marketing strategy has helped me."

A Limited Audience

Currently the licensing exams are only available in North America, which limits the size of the market, although Lisa is still getting new members from overseas, and anticipates her international audience will grow over the next few years.

"The eventual plan is to take the exam worldwide, so there is some potential for that and I also have quite a number of people who are in other countries that come into the U.S. to take the exam, and so they're studying because otherwise they wouldn't have access to a study group. One of the first people I talked to back when I first started was a girl who was over in the United Arab Emirates and she came into the U.S. to take the exam. So somebody like her she wouldn't have access to anything else, as well people in the U.S. who are in Alaska or Hawaii, or something, just more remote parts where they don't have as many options in the design communities. It is becoming more international and we do have a number of international customers. I expect it to grow but the U.S. is the largest market."

The Double Guarantee

Lisa offers two guarantees when new members join. A 7-day guarantee will give them their money back if for whatever reason they decide the courses aren't right for them.

The passing guarantee on the other hand gives ongoing access to the materials if they have to resit the exam, provided they meet the participation requirements. This stipulation has encouraged new members to engage with the content quickly and keep coming back to it.

Although now the guarantee is causing some unexpected problems:

"One of the things that I have done in the past year is have a passing guarantee.

The requirements for that include participation, so it's participation in a study group, it's doing homework assignments, and emailing them in. We've had homework in the past for other exams so we have all the quizzes and stuff like that so it's actually keeping them moving through the process, so that has kept people pretty active.
The problem with that I'm seeing...is that people are so focused on the passing guarantee that I feel like some people are just rushing past and only going: 'What do I need to turn in this week so I keep the guarantee'. They're not really worried about learning or doing the lessons...

...I'm looking at changing some things a lot, drastically next year so that would be really less of an issue.

I give people a seven day guarantee so if they join and just for whatever reason they feel like it's not for them or it does not work on their computer, or we can't help them out, make something work for them, then I give that....

... The passing guarantee just allows for them to retake the course so depending on the plan that they purchase if it's a one season then they can take the course again for free.
Or if it's a one year course they can take whatever course, they have to turn in their test results, they have to do their homework, and participate.

All of those things that are part of the guarantee, if they actually do those they won't need the guarantee. Very likely that they won't need it. I want to help everybody pass the exam but I want people to do the work it takes. You can't pass it by buying a course, you have to actually do the work."

Creating Lifestyle Freedom

Running her membership gives Lisa the freedom to plan her day however she wants, and also gives her the flexibility and financial stability to cope when life happens.

"I like the whole freedom and flexibility of the schedule.
And for Scout, my cat, because she's older and she's had some health problems, I can be with her and give her the attention and care that she needs. I haven't had to worry about affording to spend money on a scan for a cat, or the things that she needs to get better, so that has been really helpful.

I haven't had to worry about certain things because both my husband and I we don't have traditional jobs and so we have a flexible schedule, we can do what we need to do when we need to do it and that makes life a lot easier.

My husband had an accident and somebody smashed his truck in and it was totaled, and I'm like, 'Just don't worry, we'll buy another truck.' And he was fine and it's like that's what you would worry about, but he's okay, we can get another truck. Those are the kinds of things that having the income and the freedom it really makes a big difference so I don't have that kind of worry like I would have if I had a job with a limited amount of income or restrictions on my hours to take care of things.

It's much, much better the way this is. I am totally unemployable now. I would never work for someone else."

What's Next For QPractice

At the moment Lisa charges a one-time fee for access to a course for a fixed period of time, but she's considering moving towards a more traditional membership model.

"I'm looking at moving everything to subscription. It will be beneficial to the people who get in and get out but it will also be I think very beneficial to me to have the ongoing recurring situation rather than a flat price for course, for a specific period of time. It will actually be very similar, so the pricing for a one year course and the pricing for one year's worth of subscriptions will be the same but having it in a way that I'm looking at things as a recurring ongoing and then covering recurring expenses for team, or recurring expenses for everything else. I think it just will be a better business for me, in the long haul it will also make it more affordable to people

to come in for one month. Not everybody can afford what the equivalent to the one year or even the sixth month, so it will allow more people in to get started, so offer them that type of scenario. That's what I'm looking at, I'm not 100% certain."

Laura Robinson: Worditude

Membership Details:

Name: Worditude

Topic: Copywriting

Launched: 2016

Website: writewitworditude.com

Interview Date: August 2017

Laura Robinson runs the Worditude Club, a copywriting based membership designed to help people create all the copy they need for their online business.

When Laura first launched Worditude, her digital copywriting business, she had no intention of creating a membership site. But as Laura's reputation as a digital copywriter grew, so did her audience, and she received more and more questions and requests for help. Laura decided to create an online space where she could share her copywriting know-how, answer questions and help entrepreneurs develop their copywriting skills.

"The membership club is a library of materials that will help people create the copy that they need for their website, and then also help them to write engaging emails to their email list, blog posts, guest posts. Alongside that, I'm providing feedback on what's been written and just guidance on what content might be needed. It's kind of a mixture between a hand-holding service, but also that pre-written training material for people to work through.

The biggest thing I have to help them with is, people really suck at selling themselves. They find it really difficult to write anything that might be even vaguely nice about themselves on their own website. That's the hardest thing. I keep looking at what they've written and sending it back and go, 'No, you can do better than that,' just to keep pushing them to own what they do and speak up with more pride about their work...

... To begin with I had in mind that it would be much more hands-off and a more traditional type membership model because I worked one-to-one with clients. I thought this would be more based on the platform and leave them to it, but I didn't find that very rewarding. I much prefer to get involved and be able to get to know each of the businesses. I find that just a few minutes of input here and there can make a really big difference and unstick people and get them moving again. I'm really happy to provide that input."

While Laura provides a lot of hands on support for her members, content is still the backbone of the membership, although her content strategy has changed since she first launched.

"In the early days, I was creating new content every month. Now I don't need to do that because I think that becomes overwhelming for people to try and keep up with. I didn't want to just create it for the sake of it, so now I'm working towards making that content much easier to navigate and helping people know where they need to dive in and what they need to do next."

Laura started the membership as a way to monetize the work she was doing for free, responding to help requests.

"I had a little band of followers who would ask me questions in other Facebook groups, or sometimes via email, and they weren't really in a position to work with

me one-to-one as a copywriter. But also it wasn't as simple as just needing one page of web copy or a couple of pages of web copy. It was more about the whole content marketing journey and the whole sales funnel. I was getting nudged by them too like, 'We'd like something. Is there some way we can pay you? Is there some sort of club where we can ask you for help and not feel guilty that you're doing it for free all the time?' **It was definitely demand-led….I knew I wasn't just working hard on something that was a shot in the dark and hoping that someone would want it in the end. I was trying to create something that I had already been asked for…"**

Juggling Priorities

Running a membership site alongside still running a service business, plus having a young family, has proven to be more challenging than Laura initially thought it would be.

"It's been quite hard to juggle alongside still doing one-to-one work. I think that's not how my brain is wired. My brain likes to have one job, not two. And this is already part-time. In addition, I've got two children. There are already quite a lot of jobs going on, and so if I have a big one-to-one copywriting job on, it's really hard to discipline myself to put the time aside to keep working on the membership site. And then, it's hard if I'm really involved in the membership site to remember I still need to be marketing myself for one-to-one work, as well. I would say juggling the two sides of the business has been quite a challenge…

…I have a VA, and she has a team. I know that there's a lot of the day-to-day stuff now that lands on my door and I can just go, 'Help me. Will you deal with this?'…

...I have a business coach, and she helps me not lose mind, or go and get a normal job. It's like her full-time job is to talk me down from the cliff edge when I'm going: 'That's it. I'm just going to go and work at a supermarket. This is too difficult. I don't want to do it anymore.'

It's about two or three times a year, and it'll always be something really stupid that sets me off like if a WordPress update goes wrong or I lose a piece of work, then decide it's just too much. It's too hard. Then I get over myself. I'll go and eat some ice cream and some crisps or something, then I'll be fine."

Creating Long Term Relationships

Laura's membership gives her longer term working relationships, something which had been missing from her copywriting work.

"I really, honestly love getting to see everybody's businesses and seeing the progression in them.

When I was working one-to-one with people, it's a smaller number of businesses that you get to see and you only get to see them for the tiniest snapshot in time.

Usually it was for a launch... It's exciting. I can see what the new thing is they've created and help them to launch it and see the results that they have.

But with the membership club, I've got people that have been there from the beginning, so about nine months in now, and I can see the progression of their business in that time.

I really love seeing the progression in their writing, as well, because people arrive and they're quite stiff and corporate in the way that they write their web copy and blog posts because that's how we're taught we're supposed to write, sound professional and grammatically correct and everything has to be done in a particular way. And then, you can see the progression of how they sound more and more like themselves in their web copy and in their blog posts, see their confidence grow that they'll post more frequently on their social media pages. I really love seeing that.'"

Growing Through Collaborations

Laura's built her online audience, and attracted new members, through regular collaborations with other business owners.

"One thing that's helped me to get in front of new people is when I collaborate with other business owners and also that's really cost efficient because I don't pay anything for it, or we pay some Facebook Ads, but the budget is nothing like what you need when you're trying to get something going on your own.

I've done collaborations where I've contributed to their programmes, where they run a programme and I'm like a guest speaker on it, or on a live event.

*...I've always got something like that on the go because **I like to team up with other business owners. It gets me in front of their audience and then we can usually grow, get more people in, just because you're doing something. Any amount of activity attracts attention, so I try to do something like that at least every other month."***

90 Day Member Plans

Creating a 90-day plan for new members is key to getting them engaged in the content early on for Laura.

"When they first join, we do a 20 minute Skype call where I just get to know where they are in their business and I get a feel for what would be the materials that are most going to help them.

I started doing that as an experiment, but I'm going to keep doing it because it's so helpful for me to know exactly where they are when I then give them feedback on other pieces of work they do further down the line.

From that point, we make a 90-day programme and these are your priorities for the next 90 days. And then, we just make sure every month we're rolling, keep updating that so we always know what the most important next steps are.

Usually people follow the same pattern. You need to get your website in order first because there's no point going out and getting a huge audience of people if your website's not ready to receive that big audience and to use that audience efficiently to convert into sales. Our first step is to get the website sorted out, and then we look into growing the audience.

And then once they're coming in onto your email list, what do you do to keep their sales going? I find that naturally a next step opens up. As soon as you've done one thing, you can add another thing to do the to-do list. It kind of naturally rolls on that they'll still need me the next month."

Reducing Client Work

Having a membership has created a smoother income, so Laura has flexibility over which copywriting projects she chooses to take on, and when.

"I haven't taken on one-to-one clients over the summer because I know I haven't got the mental space to deal with it. If I'm going to have a one-to-one client, I need the whole day to be really peaceful and not have any distractions. That's not possible over the summer holidays.

But with the membership club, it feels like it's a different part of my brain that's required to answer questions and give feedback... I can cope with doing that in much smaller chunks of time. It doesn't irritate me as much when I get interrupted because I find it easier to jump back in where I was. It's much better suited to family life.

It's definitely smoothed my income because like a lot of people who work one-to-one, especially copywriters, it's a bit of a feast or famine. *You're either begging people to leave you alone because you've got so much work on, and then turn around and they've all gone and there's nothing to do for three months."*

Laura also finds that the membership club is a great way to attract clients for her one-to-one services too, and the two go hand-in-hand when it comes to marketing.

"Having the membership club does naturally market my one-to-one services, because I'm constantly marketing the club but there's always going to be those people that look at that and go, 'No, I don't want to have to figure out this myself. I just want to pay you and you do it for me.' It's made it easier to get one-to-one

clients because there's always some sort of marketing noise going on around my business now, whereas before I would definitely go very quiet when I didn't want anymore clients because I was overbooked. And then, when those clients ran out, it would be too quiet and I didn't have anyone to work for."

Imperfect Action

Laura sat on her idea for a membership for a couple of years, so although she feels the launch may have been smoother with more planning, she's happy she took imperfect action anyway.

"When I was setting up my membership site, some of the materials that I'd written, that was coming out of documents that I wrote two years ago. I already knew that the structures that I used with my one-to-one clients, I was writing them down thinking, 'You know, I could teach people how to do this for themselves.' In the back of my mind I'd already had this plan, and so I was already gathering materials…

…I think I was just about getting to the point where it was the perfect time to just get on with it…at the point when I launched, I thought, 'I have sat on the idea for a while, but I've let it kind of ripen and mature. I've improved my skills and grown my audience, so now is the right time."

What's Next For Worditude

Now that the membership is well established, Laura is mainly looking forward to a quiet year of consistent growth and business as usual, rather than having any big plans for future products.

"I want a nice, stable year of consistent growth and just helping my members and nothing crazy, no big launches. I think sometimes you need a year like that to kind of regroup and to just feel like normal life for a little while. Nothing crazy. I'll probably end up launching something in about three months now I've said that, but my plan is nothing crazy for the next 12 months.

...That's what I'd like, just a year of business as usual and just see what that looks like. And then probably from that it will inspire new ideas or I will want to move in a particular direction. But I would like at least a few months of just consistent business as usual life. That would be lovely."

Scott Devine: Scott's Bass Lessons

Membership Details:

Name: Scott's Bass Lessons

Topic: Bass Guitar

Launched: 2012

Website: scottsbasslessons.com

Interview Date: April 2018

Scott Devine is the founder of scottsbasslessons.com, an online school for bass players and the world's leading bass education membership site.

Looking at Scott's current site, it would be easy to feel overwhelmed at the idea of creating something similar.

But Scott's Bass Lessons started in a much simpler format. Scott's first members were joining up for backing tracks to play along with, downloadable action notes, and an online community.

Initially Scott began creating YouTube videos to promote guitar lessons via Skype, until he decided to break free of the time-for-money model.

Scott created some standalone products, and also had a PayPal donate button for those wanting to support him for the free bass lessons he was providing on YouTube and his site.

After stumbling across online business membership site Fizzle, Scott stopped selling stand alone products and bundled everything into a membership site instead.

"I was selling products outside, so I had sort of rigged this membership thing and then I had some courses on the outside and I'm sure a load of people have been like that, where you're in limbo between 'Oh, should I go all in on the membership or should I go do this one foot in, one foot out thing.' At some point, I just decided to transition just into a membership so I can have all the educational content housed within it and just thinking backwards, I think that was based off really following that Fizzle model and seeing those guys are doing it, and have you seen how happy Corbett and Chase are? They're always really happy, aren't they? I thought, I want some happiness in my life."

Creating a Faculty

Initially Scott's Bass Lessons was purely focused around Scott and his teaching, however over the last couple of years that has changed.

*"Beforehand, it was really just me. And over the last two years...I've really transitioned into, I'm still there, obviously, it's called Scott's Bass Lessons. I'm in the videos every single week. But in terms of a lot of the content, other tutors come in because **I don't just want it to be me. I want to involve the entire bass community from a teacher or an educational point of view**, obviously from a business decision because I don't want to have all my eggs in one basket, which would be me.*

But also, I think that it's a nice way to dominate a market as well, having everybody involved in your one thing..."

Before other musicians could follow the model, Scott invited them to get involved with his membership.

"Thinking about the marketplace and what to do in terms of growth, that's when I started getting everybody else involved in what I was doing because they weren't doing anything. They were definitely gonna do something in time, given that that's what happens. So before that happened, I might as well get everybody involved in what I'm doing, making it good for them, good for us, good for the members. And that's moulded to what it is today."

Every Monday, SBL now host a live stream seminar from some of the best bass educators on the planet, including teachers from the Berkeley College of Music, and other heavy hitters. These live streams were the start of inviting outside experts to create membership content.

"The first involvement of anybody outside, like creating the educational content, was the livestream seminars, and that was me dipping my toe into the water thinking, "Is this gonna work? Are the members gonna go for it?" So we had them doing a live stream every week.

Then based off that and what was going on and the members were enjoying it. To be honest, I enjoyed not being the centre of attention all the time. I'm a real introvert and I don't really want to be the guy… I decided to start and other guys to create courses for the membership. That's actually been a real blast to do."

When the team batch recorded their first courses by guest experts back in 2017 though, Scott wasn't in the videos, which he later regretted, and remedied in 2018:

"I looked back and thought 'You know what? My name is on it. I feel like some of those courses would have benefited from me being in the courses so I can be like an

*ambassador for the students.'...so that's what we rolled with in 2018... So even though the guests are delivering the information, **I'm in the actual video on behalf of the students, drawing out some of the information from the artists that we're getting in to do the courses**. And sometimes that's a lot easier as well, because some of the guys that we work with have never taught in their lives. For instance, we've got Shaka Khan's bass player and musical director. He hasn't taught anybody in his entire life. He's just gigged forever. So he doesn't know what he does, where I can sit there in the course and say 'Hey, what's that you're doing there? Let's break this down. Let's break that down.'*

So it's given us the ability to work with artists that we wouldn't have been able to work with otherwise..."

Initially the courses contributed by guests were sporadic, but these days Scott has a much more organised approach to guest content and likes to batch things.

"We just go to New York, which is, in terms of where everybody is, all our tutors are, for the most part, in the states. We go to New York, hire a studio for like, 10 days or 12 days, fly everybody in that isn't in New York... and then each day we just create a new course and then leave New York and then we've got all this new content that's gonna stretch out for the entire year."

For Scott, the opportunity to collaborate with people who are as invested in the project as he is has made the last seven years worth it. He's created educational content with some of the world's best bass players in the world, resulting in a financially rewarding business, that is helping tens of thousands of people globally.

Implementing Quickly

One of the things that has contributed to Scott's success is his approach to testing out ideas. When inspiration strikes, he rolls with it and implements quickly in order to see if the idea is worth pursuing further.

This approach is how some of the memberships best features, such as the weekly live streams started.

"Each and every week on a Monday, we host a live stream seminar from some of the best bass educators on the planet…That was just, I had an idea on a Monday afternoon. It was in the summer time, I can remember standing outside the studio, having this idea, and then we rolled with it by the next week, and then that was it. Now that's what we do. And it's kind of like an amalgamation of a whole lot of random ideas like that and that's got us to where we are today."

30,000 Members and Counting

There's no denying that Scott's Bass Lessons is a huge success, with over 30,000 members and a solid 7 figures a year in revenue.

Scott didn't initially build the membership with those goals in mind however, and his success and what the site has become has evolved mostly organically.

"I didn't really know what I was building. And I think part of my issue is being that I kind of roll with it because I'm under experienced, to a certain extent, with building businesses. I've never really got the end goal in mind, which is a big mistake… The only thing I did consider is 'I'm on a roll, bigger is better, let's keep

pushing it as much as we can.' And I definitely still have that in me, but I do tend to think about my lifestyle as well at the same time.

So yeah, there was no point in the past that I really ever thought that it was gonna turn into this behemoth school with, I think on our sales budget it says 25000, but I think we have over 30000 people join up over the last few years. So it's been cool."

YouTube Success

Scott started growing his YouTube channel, uploading fresh content every week. Scott's consistency, combined with his early dominance in that niche, helped him attract more than 600,000 YouTube subscribers.

But that growth hasn't been linear over the last 6 years. In 2016 Scott's audience growth rate declined, for a surprising reason:

"When I started, I was one of the guys. I was sitting in my bedroom with a camera... I was playing the bass and people were learning from me. ...then over time we were fully DSLR'd up with cameras and the whole shebang. And what happened is that looking back on it, that actually killed engagement."

He discovered the source of the problem by chance on a trip to New York. Not wishing to load himself down with a heavy DSLR (that would probably get left in the bag unused), Scott bought a point and shoot Canon G7X to use for vlogging during the trip.

"When we started uploading the content... some of it was vloggy, some of it was just me sat in front of this camera teaching... the engagement went through the roof... If you're creating video content, what do your actual members want

to see and resonate with? It might not be what you think. It might not be really highly polished videos."

That uptick in engagement was back in 2017, and until recently Scott's channel was averaging 100,000 views a week on a brand new video. Recently this has dipped, which Scott takes as a signal that it's time to switch the style of content up a little:

"Audiences do fatigue with a similar type of content that comes over and over again."

Scott boosts his YouTube engagement by linking directly to the YouTube video when emailing subscribers about new content.

"YouTube values the views on YouTube itself way more than the views of an embedded video on your website. I want YouTube to be loving our channel and pushing our videos as much as possible."

Moving forward Scott plans to encourage more traffic back to his own site though by sending a couple of emails per week, one to YouTube and then one to an older lesson hosted on his website.

Prioritising Annual Subscriptions

Unlike most membership sites, the SBL academy is marketed at an easily affordable annual membership rate (currently $168 per year but started at $76), rather than a recurring monthly subscription, to get longer term commitment from their members.

"The reason it's low is so that we could get as many people through the door as possible and really... It was that and probably inexperience as well, because I bought

my first computer seven years ago. I struggle to use an iPhone. I am the most zero tech person ever. I'm just a bass player.

So definitely, I stumbled upon it, finger in the air, hey, that sounds cool for the price. And I really wanted to do it on an annual basis primarily because I wanted or I felt that I couldn't really make a difference to peoples' playing within a week or within a month or whatever. So that's why we went with the low pricing and why we went with an annual. And we've been annual only for six years."

After being annual-only for 6 years, Scott has recently added in the option for monthly payments, which has initially boosted sales of new memberships by 21%.

However, the impact of offering the monthly option is being carefully monitored, including retention rates beyond a free 14-day trial, and how well those choosing the monthly payment option integrate with the existing community.

"... you do get a different type of customer....to come up with 170 bucks as a hobby, can be a big spend. So you're getting people that are in it. They're committed to the fact that they want to progress and take their playing to the next level. Whereas a monthly guy might be just dipping their toe in the water. And I don't want the monthlies to spoil the experience for the annuals because I'm all about really keeping it super positive and a really great learning environment for everybody that wants to be a part of what we do."

Non 'Sleazy' Sales

Scott has found his audience respond better, in terms of sales, to less typical marketing and promotion videos.

"We split [test] a very typical marketing sales type video with a more relaxed sales video... These are actually exactly the same video, but I chopped out all of the marketing. Tell your story. You know aggravating the pain, all the marketer things that they tell you to do. I actually chopped all of that out and we split test those and the one with none of the marketing guff won by a mile. And all we did in the video was just say "Hey, here's what we got. Here's how it's gonna help you. Do you want to buy?" Whereas the other video was, you know, "Here's a little bit of my story and this thing that I discovered that I'm gonna teach you and it's amazing." You know, the whole thing. That whole marketing thing that everybody tells you to do.

...I think the more I go down this pathway the more I realise you can learn from all of the gurus in the world, but it might not apply to your specific market...your market might be completely different."

Managing a Team

Scott is still hugely hands on in the business but has gradually built up a team of around a dozen people helping him including Project Managers, Community Managers, Marketing specialists, Admin, a Social Media Manager and tech-specialists.

Managing a team doesn't come naturally to Scott however, and it's something he's found a challenge as the business has grown. The key has been hiring project managers to oversee other team members for him.

"I think for me, the one thing I've struggled with the most is that team building thing. I've found it really hard. It's definitely not my forte. I'm not a manager. I'm just, I'm scatty. One of the worst managers. Which is why I'm trying to put managers in place to do a job I find that I'm not really natural at."

Developing the support team, and using a faculty of guest experts to create new content, has enabled Scott to free up time to be a visible part of the membership, but in a very considered, managed way.

Community Managers

Scott has a very active and passionate onsite forum as part of the SBL membership, however he's not a natural forum user himself and so community managers have been integral to the success of the membership from day one.

"Right from the start, I had a community manager. That's always helped, in a huge way, the members feel like they're getting listened to and I don't feel like I'm getting absolutely bashed over the head with forum stuff...I'm not a forum person...I do not find it easy...So just getting people in place to do that for the students really helps."

Scott is still highly visible in the community, hosting an academy show every single week (200 episodes and counting), and recording a 90 minute student review video every single month, and makes time to comment and respond in the community on those threads.

"I think doing the weekly academy show really helps. I think that makes the members feel like I'm part of the community because it's just a video where I'm saying "Hey, here's what came last week, here's what's coming up for you to be

excited about." And I'll mess around a little bit in that video and my kids might be in the video or something. Whatever, to make it as informal as possible and fun to watch. And that's definitely made the members feel like I'm around for them, which is important."

What's Next For Scott's Bass Lessons

Scott's new website has just released, his first completely custom build outside of Wordpress - something Scott describes as a 'wild ride'.

He'll be taking advantage of the new design to cycle through different customer promotions.

"We're looking at changing up the promotional strategies and stuff that we use. Beforehand, we've predominantly focused on back end promotions. So for instance, we could be offering bonuses or whatever, discounts or whatever, in the background. But on the front of the site, you're gonna see nothing, nothing will ever change. It will be the same. So with this custom design, we've got more ability to have more front facing promotions that we can cycle through different months and all that type of thing.

So we'll definitely be looking at promotional strategies moving forward. Paid ads, I really need to nail that. I'm so weak on paid ads. We do Facebook Ads stuff like that, but really, we should be really spending a decent amount of money buying customers and getting them through the door and experimenting along with that. So that's on the cards."

His most exciting development is a new free app which provides a drum loop for people to play along with, and will be given away as part of a lead generation strategy.

And to boost customer retention (which is currently around 70% annually) his team have developed pathways for members to complete based on the UK's 1-8 music grading system.

Beyond the membership Scott is working with artists to create deep dive courses that would sell as standalone products. And he's also considering partnering with music bands to offer a white-labelled version of his site to their fans.

While many business owners take their foot off the pedal when they hit 7-figures, this hasn't been the case for Scott, who is constantly innovating to make his membership the best it can be.

Janet Murray: JanetMurray.co.uk

Membership Details:

Name: The Studio

Topic: PR & Marketing

Launched: 2015

Website: janetmurray.co.uk

Interview Date: April 2018

Janet Murray is a PR and marketing strategist, and founder of The Studio, a membership site helping business owners promote themselves using marketing and PR.

Janet spent 18 years writing and editing for fashion newspapers like the Guardian and during this time she received many poor quality pitches and press releases, which gave her a blog idea:

"…these pitches and press releases, often came from PR companies that have been hired by small business owners. I was kind of irked by this and I thought, 'You know, actually, I would really like to help these people and educate them on how to get press coverage and get in the press'."

Janet started a blog sharing information on how to write press releases, how to write pitches for journalists, and how to find journalists.

When Janet launched her membership a couple of years ago, it focused on helping people to get press coverage, how to get in national newspapers, magazines, radio, TV.

Later, she realised the membership content needed to expand into other areas though.

"Looking at my own business I realized that's really only part of the puzzle. So I started then to help my members with things like email marketing, with blogging content, podcasts, YouTube, social media."

Now in the third phase of her membership, Janet is restructuring the content to link marketing and promotion activities to income goals - something that's already working well for her members:

"That's really resonating with my members because suddenly it feels like there's a point and when you're teaching people about PR and marketing, I think sometimes people see it as a kind of activity or something else on their to do list that they have to do, but of course you and I both know that like marketing, PR is the lifeblood of your business. If you're not promoting your business then you're not making any money."

Building an Ecosystem

The Studio is at the centre of Janet's business, around which she's built a strong eco-system of products and services, including live events, public speaking, a printed content diary, one on one consultancy, a book and more.

"If I look at my media diary, and who buys it, my books, and my media diary owners club, and my events, then you know I'd say the majority of people who buy those products and services are all in my membership so that's really the heart of everything I do."

It also works in reverse, with Janet's other products and services providing a natural pathway to joining the membership site.

"Generally we get a really good conversion of people at live events as one example who will then join the membership and often I find that when I think about my sales funnel, like the book for lots of people might be their first step, their first paid product they buy from me, the media diary and the media diary owner's club might be the next one, then they might come into the membership and you know the way I'm sort of looking at it at the moment is ideally I'd like that to put people right through that journey...to take those people right through to my coaching and mentoring groups."

Janet is currently restructuring her membership and group program offers to allow an easier progression for members so that there is always a next step for them to take.

"What I'm really trying to do is create progression. I think one of the challenges with a membership is that if you get people in a membership, particularly people who are really keen, they're really motivated, they get through all the content and they start doing really well. Where do you take them next?

If I was going back in time and redoing things I think I would've thought that through more carefully and now I'm trying to create this kind of clear progression route through."

Open Days

Janet has found that running open days for her membership has been one of the most effective ways of promoting the site.

"One of the most successful marketing strategies that I use, I have these things called open days. So I used to do webinars, and I found that they didn't really convert that well so what we do now is we're actually still on an open close... we open and close maybe four or five times a year and what we'll do is we'll invite people who are on the waiting list to come in and to come to one of these open days where we'll show them in the back of the website, the membership site, show them what it looks like, show them the content.

And I'll actually get some of my existing members to come along on that call so we do it on a Zoom call. And I think there's something really powerful about that, you know I can say how brilliant the membership is and how helpful it is and I can put out blog posts and put out testimonials but actually to get on a call with people, to meet them in person who are actually members who can say yeah this is really working for me and these are the results I've had, you know that to me feels like a really powerful way to promote the membership."

You Are Not Your Member

"I think the one thing that I've learnt is, as a membership site owner, you can't run your membership site thinking that everybody's like you. And you have to really be sensitive and accept that everybody is very different. So I'm just learning things all the time about my members that are helping me to give them a better experience."

Janet has found that not everyone is as self-motivated and directed as she is.

"I'm somebody who's very much like I've joined it, I see it's my responsibility to just kind of get stuck in and go find what I need. If I've got a problem, I'll ask."

Upon realising that members didn't necessarily react to being in a membership the same way she does, and may need more direction and support, Janet made content to help them know what to expect.

"The more that I learn about my members and the things that they're struggling with, the more content I've created to support them."

Janet also creates blog posts helping members get the most from their membership and invites members onto 'reset' calls if they haven't been engaging with the membership.

Looking After Members

"The more you can support people to get the best experience then the more likely they are to stay, the more likely they are to tell their friends about the membership and feel good about it. "

Janet puts customer care at the heart of her membership management, focusing on helping members feel seen even though they're part of a big group.

"I've actually recently taken somebody on in the membership who I'm calling our membership care manager. And her job is literally to kind of hang out. We use a Facebook group for our community and her job is literally to hang out, when people ask a question that we know we've got content to help them answer that question, she'll just jump in and say hey have you looked at session four of the content course

or have you looked at this really great masterclass with Mike Morrison or
something that will help answer your question?"

Open vs Closed

Janet has always run her membership site on an closed basis, meaning that members can only join during certain launch periods throughout the year. While this has worked for Janet, it's something she's keen, but nervous, to change.

"I do want to kind of move to having it open all the time, however I don't know if it's something just about my audience and I think I do need to experiment with this, but they do seem to find it quite difficult to make decisions. And just having the membership open and saying look it's only going to be open for a week this time round then otherwise it's going to be closed again, it does encourage people to make a decision otherwise I think I might have a lot of fence sitters."

Low Maintenance

As Janet has many different services and products making the membership low maintenance by structuring her time well and outsourcing has been key. Other than community activity, Janet is able to manage her membership in just one day a week.

"So in terms of my membership I'll tend to go to my membership every afternoon, so I'll go and see what members have been posting, go in and help them with things, but the main day, it's just this one day a week so there's Wednesday that we tend to work on membership, we tend to put the newsletter together. Obviously we've

stepped things up like you know we have conversation starters everyday in our

Facebook group and I'll kind of like jumping in and looking at those as well.

But yeah it's mainly kind of like this one day a week that we're putting most of our

resources [into the membership]."

Induction Calls

While Janet keeps the membership as low maintenance as possible, she likes to do personal welcome calls with new members to get to know them better, something that is beneficial for both her members and Janet.

"One thing that I still do, which I do need to change, but actually it's so valuable, is

when we get new members in I do, if they want it, I give them a 20 minute

induction call where I will actually personally get on a call with them. I've had

some people say to me that I shouldn't do this, this is too much of my personal time,

too much access or whatever but actually for me I feel like it gives that member a

good start, they feel cared about because they get on a call with me and I talk to

them about their business.

I also feel I can direct them, I can say to them look I know there's a lot of content in

there but actually this is the best thing that I think for you to start with…I feel like I

learn so much from those conversations, I learn so much about what the members

need, I learn about what they don't need more of and for me it's been also really

good in terms of growing the mastermind and the coaching groups…

…And it helps me identify the people that might be ready for more, it helps me

identify people that might struggle, so I do think there's quite a lot of value in it.

But obviously that does take up a little bit more of my time…"

Exit Calls

In addition to offering members a personal call when they join, Janet also offers them this same opportunity when they leave.

"Another thing we've started doing as well is we've started offering exit calls so when somebody says that they want to leave the membership we say you know that's fine, but if you want you can book a call with me for 10, 15 minutes and I'll just have a chat with you… it's not even a 'I want to find out why you're leaving', it's just like would you like to have a chat with me before you leave? I'll give you a few pointers about some things you might want to think about…

…I think you can't get all heavy handed with people and start kind of interrogating them about why they're leaving. So I try and kind of just keep it positive and kind of say you know I just kind of wanted to have a chat with you about where you are with your business and you know give you a few pointers about a few things that you might want to think about and you know if you have got any feedback, great, but don't worry.

And that seems to be working. We're quite early on so you know in three months, six months I might be able to give you a bit more feedback as to how well it's working but I've certainly, a few people have decided not to leave as a result of that call."

Listening to Members

Janet accepts that some of the changes she's currently making to her membership may take some getting used to, but they've been made with the members in mind.

"The thing about being a membership site owner is that you're constantly learning from your members and they're showing you like where the gaps are, what they need help with and it can feel a bit frustrating because you kind of feel if you're getting somewhere and you get on top of something and then there's something new that you feel you need to create, but I guess that's part of the fun, part of the challenge."

Janet is also aware that while listening to members and feedback is important, she doesn't have to always act on it and sometimes you know what is best.

"I do listen to my members a lot but I think there's some decisions that you have to listen to your own gut and your experience as a business person."

She also prioritises her own well-being when making business decisions though, to keep her business and membership sustainable. For example, evening masterclasses and coaching calls aren't available because that is Janet's time for her family, socialising and running.

"I think that my wellbeing would suffer if I felt that I was tied to the membership in the evenings as well as during the days and I think I might start to feel resentful."

What's Next For The Studio

Big changes are coming to Janet's business, with the products, including the membership, being reorganised into monthly income goals: £1,000, £2,500, £5,000 and £10,000.

Members of the membership will have the option to progress onto smaller mastermind coaching groups for higher income goals.

"*I'm now starting to think a lot more strategically, when I first started out it was just like hey I've got this content and I'm just going to kind of create this membership and see what happens, but now I am very much thinking well I may well need to, hopefully might need to have seven figure group in the future, what might that look like and what I don't want to do with the membership, I guess there comes a point where maybe people will have done everything with you and you know there's no more to do.*

But I'd like you know the member journey to be at least a few years and you know one thing that I've said to the members already is that I don't really want to see them staying in the main membership for longer than a year or two because I want them to progress and I want them to really earn what they're worth. So I think that you know, sort of growing at the top end I think and the coaching and mentoring working with smaller groups as well that's something I'd really like to grow."

2019 Update:

In 2019 Janet closed down her existing membership site due to a change in direction and launched a new membership, the Build Your Audience Programme, instead.

Brandon Vogt: Claritas U

Membership Details:

Name: Claritas U

Topic: Catholicism

Launched: March 2017

Website: claritasu.com

Interview Date: April 2018

Brandon Vogt is the founder of Claritas U, a membership that helps Catholics to get clear on their faith.

While at college, Brandon began exploring religion, spirituality and faith, and eventually converted to Catholicism. To share his excitement for his faith he started a blog, and after a couple of years he was asked to write a book, The Church And New Media, about how Catholics could use things like blogs, podcasts and websites to spread their faith. That led to another book and public speaking opportunities.

After 5 years, and still only in his mid-twenties, Brandon had developed a reputation, an email list of more than 50,000 subscribers, and a large social media following, and was speaking all over the country. He was also still working as a mechanical engineer. And with a young family to take care of, Brandon was feeling stretched.

"I thought, I'm trying to do three things well, I'm trying to be a good engineer, I'm trying to be a good husband and father and I'm trying to build this platform and help a lot of people, but I can't do all three of those things well. So I need to figure

out a better way to do this, to get off the roller coaster of book launches and
travelling and speaking and all that kind of stuff.
That's when the membership idea first came on my radar."

With an email list of more than 50,000 subscribers, Brandon was able to directly ask his audience about what they needed, then build a membership site that gave them what they wanted.

"I spent a lot of time talking to my email subscribers, people who have
bought my books, asking them...what's the big pain point? What's the thing
you're struggling with most? You know, if me and you went out to coffee, what
sorts of questions would you like to ask me? And so I started pulling all that
information together over months so that by the time I launched, I was pretty
convinced that I'm creating something that I know is going to hit a hotspot for a lot
of people and I know it's really going to help, because I wasn't just launching it
arbitrarily on a whim. I had spent a lot of time trying to figure out and get very
clear on the offer. "

Exceeding Expectations

Combining a sizeable audience with indepth research, Brandon was confident that his membership would be a success, however even he was not prepared for quite how successful it would be, attracting over 1200 members in his first launch, and now with over 3000.

"I could give the false pride, the false humility answer and say, 'Oh, you know, I
had no idea that it would take off the way it has,' but to be honest, I had a hunch
that it would be mildly successful, only because I came into this with a significant
platform. I think I had 50 thousand email subscribers and I had a pretty big

Facebook following and all that kind of stuff. So I knew, I figured it at least would't be a flop.

But to be honest, I thought maybe it would top out at, you know, three, four or 500 members, which would have been amazing. It would have provided, you know, a steady, reliable side income stream. I would have been impacting the same number of people that I usually speak to. So it would have been great. I would've been thrilled with that.

I did not expect it to take it off at the magnitude it did."

Launch Anticipation

Brandon uses an open and closed doors model, meaning people can only join the membership at certain times, because he works full-time for a large Catholic ministry called Word on Fire.

Doors to the membership are open for one week in March, one week in September, and the other 50 weeks he's able to focus on creating content for the existing members.

During each launch Brandon rolls out a series of three or four videos in the week or two before the doors open, to generate anticipation for the launch.

*"Each of the times I've done this, I've focused on one topic or question in this prelaunch video series, but I only covered it in a shallow way. **I tried to give some good substance in the talks and the videos, but at the end of it I inevitably say, 'I wish we had so much more time to talk about this. This really deserves much fuller treatment. But that's why I created Claritas U**, because*

if you like this short video series on this topic, I've got a full series on that topic in here along with several other talks.' Those prelaunch video series work wonders during each of my launches."

Brandon has now run three launches for the membership site, each one bringing in over 1000 new members.

Removing Overwhelm

Heeding the experts' warnings that overwhelm leads to cancellation, Brandon keeps his churn rate down to a low 4-6% by delivering fewer, shorter pieces of content, that lead onto each other.

"The biggest mistake membership sites make is they overwhelm people with content and it's the number one reason people cancel...they just think: 'I can't keep up. You're sending me a new video every couple of days. I haven't watched any of the last 10 videos. I don't know why I'm going to stay on. I got to cancel.'

And so from the beginning I wanted to make this as low a commitment as possible for members."

Brandon releases just one new course, focused on a unique topic, every two months. Members receive one new video from the course each week. Six of these are lessons that last just 10 or 15 minutes, one video will be about recommended reading on the topic, and the last video is a one-hour live Q&A webinar.

The Claritas U promise is simple:
"..if you can watch one 15-minute video per week, then you can get clear about your faith."

A Complimentary Job

Brandon describes his current full-time role, managing the social media accounts and website for Bishop Robert Barron, as his 'dream job', which he has no intention of leaving.

As a result he has limited time to work on his membership, usually just an hour each morning, and some evenings when he batch-records videos.

".. you don't need to just drop everything, to drop your full time job and jump into this from the get go.

*In fact, **I think it makes a whole lot more sense to start out small, maybe you're devoting 10 or 15 hours a week to this**. Maybe you're attracting 20, 30, 40 members. You're getting your feet wet and seeing how it works. And then you could scale it up. And maybe one day this will be your full-time thing.*

But I think a lot of people are led to believe that a successful membership site has to be a full-time job...And at least in my case, and I know for a handful of others too, it's possible to do it kind of on the side....

*Anybody who maybe who feels like they're stuck in a day job but is working on a membership site on the side, I'd encourage them to think how can these two feed each other, **how can I use what I'm learning at my day job to help my membership site and vice versa**, how can I bring value to my day job based on, you know, now I've become fluent in membership sites or online marketing or that kind of stuff. So I encourage people not to see these two as competitive but as perhaps mutually enhancing."*

Price Anchoring

Claritas U has two levels of membership. The standard level launched at $17 per month. The VIP option started at $37 per month and included all the same digital lessons, plus shipments of physical products like books and a t-shirt.

"The main reason that I wanted to have those two tiers was to sort of price anchor, to make the student plan at $17 a month look like a bigger value because oh my gosh, the VIP plan's 37 bucks, this is less than half that. So instead of just having one option, which was $17 a month or nothing, I wanted to make the $17 a month one look more appealing by having it be a lesser priced option...

...I like keeping it at two tiers. Very simple, easy to understand. I think that that makes the offer pretty clear to the customers."

Overcoming Resistance

Brandon faces two challenges when selling his membership. His community are not at all familiar with membership sites. And they tend to expect religious content to be free.

"I think one analogy that helped get them over the hump was I very early on started comparing it to Netflix or a gym. You pay a monthly fee for Netflix and you get access to all these videos, but if you choose to stop paying the fee then you lose access. You can come back whenever you want. But that's sort of the model and I think that clicks with a lot of people in my audience, they're familiar with Netflix, they go to the gym, they understand how it works."

And to tackle the pricing issue:

"I tried to position Claritas U as something analogous to say a graduate level course or series of courses at a Catholic University. So if you went to go take a class at a Catholic university, the average annual tuition right now is $30,000 at a private Catholic University. And of course that comes with all the extra requirements of showing up at a particular place, at a particular time, and tests and homework and all that kind of stuff. And so I say Claritas U is $17 a month, which extrapolated annually is less than one percent of the cost of a traditional Catholic university."

Member Referrals

Brandon makes it very easy for members to share about Claritas U during his launch periods, and as a result finds that a large number of his signups come from member referrals.

"... it's my gut sense that I'd say probably at least half of the people who signed up for the third launch heard about it through somebody else who's an active member.

Because I fed my active members copy and paste announcements that they could put on their Facebook page, or Twitter or on email, all this kind of stuff. And I found myself constantly being tagged by all these people talking about it, and then seeing the comments below. Person A who's a member of Claritas U would post about it on their Facebook page and I'd see five people comment under there saying, 'I'm signing up now, you know, this is so great. I've been looking for something like this.'"

This is something Brandon finds easier to do with the open-closed model, because he's not asking his members to promote the membership very often, just twice a year.

"And to me that's the most valuable form of promotion. You know, when you can get somebody whose life has genuinely been transformed by your membership community and they want to tell others about it, what could be better?"

Influencer Marketing

Brandon chose to make his membership free for all those involved in the Catholic church, such as priests – the influencers in his market.

While he was initially motivated by wanting to say thank you and give something back, this decision actually had much greater results than he expected.

"From the very beginning of Claritas U, I made it totally free for priests, Catholic priests, religious brothers, or nuns, or sisters, and seminarians, so young men studying for the Catholic priesthood.

And initially my thought was I just wanted to give it to them for free, sort of a thank you for your service to the church, and most of these people make you know nothing or next to nothing in terms of money. So I didn't want to charge them for this stuff.

But what I came to discover unexpectedly was that these people became my most excited evangelists because they were receiving it for free, they liked it and they wanted to tell everybody else about it.

...in my little Catholic niche here, it had the added advantage of, these people tend to be the most respected voices in the church...this was all inadvertent. My original intention was just to give it to them for free as a thank you, but I sort of fell into this

tremendous blessing of finding these influencers, give it to them for free. And then I would say undoubtedly each of those people has brought in at least one or two or three people themselves through promoting it..."

What's Next For Claritas U

While the churn rate is just 4-6%, it still represents a significant drop in income, because few new members join between launches. So Brandon is exploring evergreen options to use in addition to his launches, or potentially switching to a doors open model.

He's also considering combining the travel he does for his full-time job with organising some in-person meet-ups with people from his community.

And as the membership continues to grow, he may bring on some team members.

"I'm on the fence about it because I think part of the allure of the site is that people are drawn to me. I had this personal brand or personal platform before launching this that helped draw in a lot of people, so I wonder if having other people teaching lessons and stuff would dilute that effect, but it would also take a big burden off of me if I only had to teach three or four courses a year instead of six."

Kim Bultsma: A Cup of Content

Membership Details:

Name: A Cup of Content

Topic: Content Marketing

Launched: November 2016

Website: acupofcontent.com

Interview Date: April 2018

Kim Bultsma is an SEO and content strategist from A Cup of Content and Content a la mode.

Content A La Mode is Kim's content marketing agency, through which she delivers content creation, SEO and social media services for other businesses.

The idea for her membership came about after repeated requests from people to 'meet for coffee' so they could borrow her expertise - for free.

"... some of these people I met with were really small business owners. Like solo entrepreneur types, and they didn't have a budget to hire someone like me.

But they really have the drive and the ambition to want to do it for themselves. I'd meet with these people and they'd literally want to pick my brain. Essentially, teach them how to do what I did over a cup of coffee I ended up buying for myself. And, they're walking out the door, and I don't have a client, and I'm like, 'I really need to capitalise on this.' I have a teaching background. I taught high school and

university level for over 10 years and I was like, 'I can do this. I can teach people
how to do this.' That's how A Cup of Content came to fruition."

Kim's background as a teacher comes in handy when it comes to creating content for the membership site, but her initial journey from teacher to self employment was out of necessity rather than choice.

"My daughter was born in end stage kidney failure. I knew when I was pregnant
that there was something wrong with her. We just didn't know what exactly was
wrong until she was born. My husband is mandatory staff at the hospital here in
town...I was a teacher, and when you're a teacher you work 70 or 80 hours a week
and it was really hard to have a child with medical conditions. All of a sudden, she
would get sick...

That was kind of the thing that really got me and my husband talking about, let's be
realistic here as a family. We've shelled out over $100,000 of our own money in
medical expenses. That included daycare, because you have to have specialty daycare
in order to take care of a child that is an end stage kidney failure and is catheter
dependent.

...But all of those things kind of built together and I just all of a sudden was like, "I
can't do this anymore." And my husband was like, "Don't. Just quit. Be done at the
end of the year contract and let's find something else." And I did. I started selling
cameras at the local camera store, because I had a photography background.

A couple of months into it, I was like, "You guys need a marketing person." And
they were like, "Okay, you want to do it?" So, I got a job as a marketing director at
the local camera store and was eventually hired away by an agency... It turned into

the hours of teaching again, where I was working a tonne... And I was like, "I can do this on my own and I can be there for my daughter." That's really was the whole thing that really made me, kind of pushed me in that direction of, I need to be my own boss and that's best for our, family for our marriage. It's been the best thing for me. I'm such a happier person now."

A Cup of Content was launched on Cyber Monday of 2016, teaching small business owners how to do their own blogging, social media, SEO, Facebook ads and other online marketing.

Member Sprints

Kim's intention was to release new content to her members every month, but they were struggling to find time to implement it.

"I have these on demand courses people can take. But in addition to that, I've got something that I release every month. So, I had new content I would release.

And the teacher in me was putting together this giant lesson plan that would take them two months to do, and it was too much stuff. I was listening to my feedback that I was getting from the members and I'm like, 'Maybe I need to narrow this down.'"

Now, instead of expecting her members to work steadily through the month's content, Kim runs 5-day sprint challenges.

"It allows me to schedule five days out of the month. Each day, we go through the pieces of that five-day challenge, and it has exploded in there. The engagement increased, they got excited, they're taking pictures. Little sneak peek pictures of what they're working on. They're sharing it with their friends."

Complementary Services

Kim's future focus is on growing A Cup Of Content, but dividing her time is a challenge, because Content A La Mode, her done-for-you content marketing business, currently provides more revenue and demands more of her time. *"My biggest challenge is juggling time between Content a La Mode and A Cup of Content. The reason for that is because Content a la mode pulls in a bigger recurring revenue for me each month, and it's deadlines and it's a lot of work...*

...I definitely want to shift it toward my membership. I enjoy it so much more, and it brings out my passion for teaching and interacting and building relationships with people. Not that Content a la mode doesn't do that, but I've actually had to... I hired a social media manager for that business because this is my focus. I want someone else to start managing more of that, and I can put more of my focus here."

A surprising side-effect of having the membership, is that it has been a source of clients for Content A La Mode - a good reason to keep both sides of the business running.

And she keeps the membership in mind when deciding which clients to work with:

"I just want to make sure that I'm only saying yes to the things that I'm really passionate about, and only if it's going to help me better my craft, and be able to help my members."

Learning to Say No

Coming from a teaching background, with no prior business experience, Kim was primed to say 'yes', eager to help as many people as possible. She quickly realised that being able to say 'no' was an important skill too.

"I had to change my mindset in not saying 'yes' to everybody, but saying 'yes' to the right people and how to say 'no'. As a business owner, in general, I think that's a huge thing. That it's almost like the crux of your business is being able to articulate a no that you feel comfortable with, but also to choose the right yeses."

Sharing Wins

Hearing member wins provides motivation for Kim, but also allows other members to see what's possible for them to achieve, if they engage with the training and content.

"I'm that teacher at heart, and I think my favourite part is when people tell me their successes from what they've learned in the membership. They shout it from the mountaintops and I love it...

...That's the stuff that I really get excited about. Because I was just like, 'Look, I did that. I helped her to feel that way.' That really is what makes me happy about this, helping small businesses do things that they didn't think that they could do."

No Obligation Trials

When it comes to marketing the membership site Kim has found that a completely free trial without any commitment has been most effective for helping her to attract members.

"I know that when I put myself out there and I get in front of people, that they can see the value of what I can offer. That's usually a great way to just say, 'Hey, go try the trial. It's free. You get 100% free access to the membership.' That trial has really been super beneficial for me. I did try a dollar trial for seven days in my demographic, I got like one person that signed up for it and she did actually join. But it was like crickets.

And so I brainstormed around that and changed it to a completely free no credit card required 14-day access. They get full access.

Am I scared that they're going to download stuff from the membership? Yeah, but really what can I do about that? Who's to say that they can't just pay their $30 a month and go in there and download a bunch of stuff and then cancel their subscription?

I feel that the value that they get not just from the courses and things like that, but the value of the community is totally worth the price of admission. If I can get them into that community, that's the clincher...

...That's just something I've learned with marketing: The least resistant point of entry - that's what people want."

Building Relationships

Kim uses social media, particularly Facebook groups and LinkedIn to build relationships with potential members, then continues this nurture process after they've joined A Cup Of Content.

"The one thing that I have been doing lately that's really proven to be good in terms of getting myself out there is spending one hour a day just going out and engaging and interacting with people, regardless of whether or not they are in my target demographic. The reason for that is because if I expect people to engage with my content, I need to go out there and engage with theirs…

… I'm getting involved in different forums and getting involved in Facebook groups, LinkedIn groups. I'm not just getting out there and saying, 'Hey, I got this great membership you should try.' But giving my true honest ideas and suggestions, and that has been huge."

During live calls and office hours sessions, Kim uses personal mentions to help members feel seen and recognized, using names when answering questions, or highlighting interactions in the Facebook community.

"Even if you got 7000 people or if you've got 70 people, they somehow have to feel connected. Creating content that really makes them feel like they're connected helps you to retain them longer…"

What's Next For A Cup of Content

Aside from continuing to grow her membership base, Kim is starting to add a one-to-one coaching component to the membership site as well to provide additional support.

Looking to the future, Kim would also like to run an in-person retreat for more focused help.

"I really wouldn't mind creating some sort of a weekend retreat and get people to come here where we laser focus in on what's a good content strategy for their particular business, and how can we get that more intimate one to one help? That would be something I want them to implement."

Scott Baptie: Food For Fitness

Membership Details:

Name: Food for Fitness Inner Circle

Topic: Nutrition & Fitness

Launched: January 2018

Website: foodforfitness.co.uk

Interview Date: May 2018

Scott Baptie's membership site, Food For Fitness Inner Circle, helps busy people lose weight without punishing fitness regimes or extreme diets.

Before creating the membership, Scott had run a separate programme, the 30-Day Fat Loss Challenge. He was able to piggy-back onto the interest in this by telling his audience the next round of the program would look different, and rolling it into the membership, along with additional content.

"Launch went really well. I've done a standard Jeff Walker style pre-launch content hype and build up and all that for various online programmes that we've run, so had the framework already there. It was just a case of, again, building anticipation, getting people going, because what worked quite well was we used to have a monthly programme, which was called the 30-Day Fat Loss Challenge. And that would run each month.

So a lot of people at the end of last year were saying, "When is this coming in January?" And we're like, "Well..." We kind of teased them, saying, "It is but not as you know it." Then they had to join the membership in order to get access to it, so everything, we offered a second individual programme, or a 1-on-1 coaching, or individualised meal plans and all that, all just wrapped up into the membership. It was like, "Wow, I get all this?" And we're like, "Yep, that's the plan." It worked quite well for us, doing it that way."

Scott's business, Food For Fitness, had been running for six years, with an audience of around 150,000 across social media platforms, and a large email list by the time he launched the membership.

Switching from selling individual products that required constant launching, to enjoying recurring revenue through a membership made sense. It also provided the opportunity to deliver the long-term support needed when creating a lifestyle change - something that short-term programs can struggle to deliver.

"I wanted to get away from the general launches every month, which I just found exhausting. And again, I wanted to have a more predictable income…"

While Scott could have carried on offering his existing programmes and products as well, it made more sense to go all in on the membership and reduce the number of things he was selling. Now he just sells books and the membership.

"…if you're just selling fewer products, you can focus on them more, you can again really get your messaging on point rather than saying, 'Okay, do I want to try to sell this to this person? Or this to this person?' You can think, 'Well, this is what we're selling, so let's niche it in a little bit.'"

Making The Membership Sticky

Realising the key to retention is to keep members coming back to the site over and over, Scott is making some adjustments to how his members can use the content.

"So a lot of our meal plans and stuff that are in it, people could essentially come in, download it all as PDFs, and leave. We're tweaking it slightly to make it rather than PDF downloads, they're gonna be more embedded within the site, so actual pages... And rather than it being a spreadsheet you download to track your progress that we get people to do weight measurements and measure their waists and hips and so on, that's going to be again within a dashboard and they have to log in and they'll be able to update it there. And again, just give people more incentive to keep coming back, really."

When it comes to content, then while Scott adds new content every month in order to keep things fresh, it's not where the real value in the membership lies.

"It's trying to find that balance of giving the people the content so they think, 'Okay this is really great, good value for money,' but the value isn't necessarily the content but the community and the support from us. Because if you ask us a question, we'll answer it. And you know who's gonna answer it, and you know it's gonna be evidence based and hopefully we've got the trust of people for them to realise that it's correct, to the best of our ability..."

Private Coaching

Recognising that a new fitness regime can be a difficult lifestyle change for people to stick to, Scott has integrated a number of different features into his membership to keep his members on track, including a private coaching area within the forum.

"Why did I do the private coaching? Because that's what I saw quite likely as the future, and again, because of the nature of what we're offering with weight loss. And so the data or information that people were sharing was quite sensitive, and they might not want to post in a forum and being like, "Oh hey, guys. How do I lose X amount of stone?" Especially if it's a beginner and they might not have succeeded in the past.

The private coaching is a bit where they can share experiences or if they'd fallen off the bandwagon and again, don't want to feel like a failure…It just, again, gives them a bit more of a private space to chat about things."

The private coaching feature also gave something for Scott to benchmark the membership price against in the sales page copy:

"We use an example of, if you're getting individual, personal training with a trainer, you'd be paying at least £50 a week. So 200, 250 a month, versus £25 a month [for the membership]. And also, again, the advantage of having built that quite large social media following, it was quite a good offer for people thinking that they'd get direct support. Because I pitched it as, "I will personally coach you inside the community." And I think that's a feature that people like, because I go on it every day, and I'm helped out by some of my team, as well. But I'm still answering all the posts."

A features comparison chart on the sales page also benchmarks the membership against the benefits and price of two other leading weight loss subscriptions, providing even more price anchoring.

Sampling the Goods

Insta-story ads have worked well for Scott, converting cold traffic into email subscribers, using a simple video pitch:

"We've always done quite well on Facebook advertising stuff. We do run Facebook ads, but Insta-story ads, and it's the kind of ones where it's like me right in the camera being, 'Sorry to interrupt, but if you'd like me to send you a free whatever, free meal plan or recipe book and so on, just swipe up to get it.' And that converts stupidly well. That's the main one, is give people little tasty bits of the content that they'll get, and so if they sign up and they get a seven-day meal plan as a lead magnet, and saying, 'Okay, if you'd like another, the rest of the days then, you need to join the membership.'"

Scott uses lead magnets and free content to give a taster of what's available in the membership, then adds a gentle pitch to let the user know they can get more when they join the Food For Fitness Inner Circle.

And anyone who visits the sales page, but doesn't sign-up, gets an irresistible offer:

"we've popped in that little pop-up of, 'Wait, wait up, don't go. How about you try it for a pound?' And then it just takes you on to the trial sales page, and it's working pretty well."

Connection Through Regular Contact

When a new member joins, Scott sends them a personalised welcome video via the app, Bonjoro. They then start receiving an automated sequence of onboarding emails, and they get a weekly round-up email of what's been going on in the membership.

Alongside the private coaching option in the forum, members can also join an accountability group to help stay on track, something that is essential to their weight-loss success.

"We've got a thing called Accountability Group, so it's a section of the forum where we pair up people of like-minded goals and if they're beginners and they're just starting out, we'll say, "Okay, you're the three, let's be all together." And we try and encourage them to post every day inside their Accountability Group, even if it's just saying, "Oh hey, great day, stuck to the plan." Or, "Oh no, disaster. lunch, totally went off track." And again, just trying to encourage them to use that every day, even if it's just to say "All good." That's working quite well, too.

And the whole thing with weight loss is accountability, and that's what we're trying to sell, so if you've got three or more people in your social support group, you've got 176% greater chance of succeeding, which is an amazing statistic…That's why, for the accountability thing, it's really important to try and get people making use of that."

Crowd-Sourcing Marketing Content

Scott uses both a blog and a podcast to bring in traffic and grow his audience. He's kept content-creation from becoming too time consuming by inviting guests and a team of 20 regular contributors to create 70% of the material, and using audience questions to inspire topic ideas.

"… you'll see the same questions come up over and over again, to which I'll just email the writers, 'Guys, who wants to do an article about whether you should do cardio on an empty stomach or not?'… So that when people do ask that question

again, or simply just email us, we're like, 'Here's the article. Or here's the podcast interview that covers that.'"

Team Support

Scott has switched his team members' focus from their in-person services, to helping him manage the membership so he can focus his time and energy on engaging with the members and creating new content for them.

"I've got a really good team that's helping out, I've got really good developers, I've got really good people who do the maintenance side of things, as well... I try and avoid getting bogged down with that, because I think there's so many more people that are way better at doing this kind of thing than I am...so I can focus on turning up and supporting people and helping them out."

What's Next For Food for Fitness

Scott intends to keep growing the membership and reducing churn by keeping up their existing strategy, but also by running group challenges and implementing on site tools.

"It's just giving more value, again we want to try and create more challenges inside it and give people a reason to stick around. We want to try and do some meet-ups as well, which we'll probably do up here in Scotland and Aberdeen. Or maybe we'll do a couple down south, as well, because I think that'll be a really good for community.

And yeah, just add to what's already there and like I said, that tracking tool, to get people using it more often rather than just downloading things. Possibly doing live events."

He'd also like to try some print-on-demand branded merchandise to bring people together and give them a sense of community.

"And also another thing that I was hearing about on Russell Brunson's podcast, was talking about creating swag and merch to really unite a community and people have asked us, do we do T- shirts and hoodies and so on, and I was like, 'I can't create more stuff to sell to people', but then I found I can print and post on demand and not have anything to do with it. So we're getting some T-shirts... to again try and unite people and just make them really feel like they're part of a group, because like I said earlier, for this nature of weight loss, the group is key. The more people that know that you're doing it and have got your back, there's a lot less chance of you falling off the bandwagon."

Tim Topham: Inner Circle

Membership Details:

Name: Inner Circle

Topic: Piano Teachers

Launched: January 2018

Website: timtopham.com

Interview Date: May 2018

Tim Topham is a piano teacher turned membership site owner. His Inner Circle membership helps piano teachers to improve both their creative skills and their teaching businesses.

In 2010, Tim was a regular piano teacher at a school. Other teachers would ask him for help, particularly with teaching how to play pop music, so Tim started a blog, and then later a podcast, and a course.

Tim recognized a gap in the market for helping other teachers, rather than end-users, so focused his efforts there.

"I didn't want to go down the route of teaching students how to play, because...there are millions of YouTube channels devoted to that, and videos, and already a lot of memberships...My skill has always been in speaking at conferences and talking to teachers, so it made sense that I differentiate myself that way anyway."

After releasing a course, Tim found himself investing a lot of time and energy responding to student emails.

"I'd be getting this back and forth emails directly to people, answering questions, and just thinking, 'This is insane. All this, I've got to scale this more and be able to spread this to a larger number of people.' And so it was a combination of that, providing more close support, and allowing people to get together as a group, that formed my thinking around creating the membership."

For Tim, his membership has enabled him to scale up his impact as a music teacher and ultimately help many more students and teachers.

"I did a lot of accompanying at my old school job. This is where the pianist would play for a solo instrument student going for an exam. And I was up to my 12th rehearsal with a little 8-year-old kid playing their first year of violin and scratching away. And I was kind of thumping around on the piano, and I was just thinking, 'Why am I doing this? This is not what I should be doing with myself.'

And so for me, another aspect of this whole membership going full time and building it enough to sustain me means that I can have a much wider impact than I would have had if I was just teaching my 30 students.

I can now teach a thousand teachers who all teach 30 students."

Build An Audience First

Tim attributes building an audience as an important pre-cursor to launching a membership site.

"I would encourage people who are considering memberships to preferably have some kind of audience already, some group who you know want what it is you're

offering, because it's so sad when people put all this effort into launching something and there's crickets.

Having that was a big part of me being able to start, but like everyone, my membership started with a beta launch. I gave an initial crew a month's free access and then the best discount of all time, which they're still locked into. And most of them are still there. And we built from there. Started with about, I don't know, 30, 40 people. And it's grown since then."

Selling to a Challenging Market

Tim has found it challenging to get the price point and sales strategy right. Although he runs a business-to-business membership, he recognises that many of his target audience don't see themselves as business owners, and find it hard to financially invest in a subscription that will help them grow their business.

"In my industry, a lot of teachers unfortunately don't charge enough for their own services, and 9 out of 10 of them aren't business trained, and probably half of them don't really think naturally like business people. So pricing a membership like mine is quite challenging... a lot of these businesses that I'm selling to are so small and nascent and aren't sort of rolling around in cash.

So I have to take a different approach to a lot of other memberships that clearly go enterprisal, business-to-business in a big way."

Tim has struck on a marketing strategy that works - combining monthly webinars with a discount offer on the membership price (usually $39 per month).

"I have live and automated webinars. So these live ones we do one a month towards the end of the month normally. And we tend to get about a thousand registered people for those. And I use Facebook advertising to drive traffic to our registration page as well, so that helps build up our numbers.

And then we also have a number of - I think there's probably six or thereabouts - automated webinars that people can join anytime and they have all been previously live webinars. So I've just converted them from live to the automated system. And some are linked up to email, auto-responding sequenced and all that kind of juicy stuff as well."

Speaking to Raise Awareness

Tim speaks at national conferences for music teachers in America, Australia and the UK which is great for raising his profile and creating more brand awareness. However, it doesn't tend to result in immediate membership sales.

"Speaking at those big conferences, it's a great thing for branding and awareness and connecting with people. And I'm a great networker. I love doing that. It's not such a driver of immediate memberships though….

… But what it will do is give you connections. It'll allow people to see you and you've got one more touch point in their process of deciding whether they go with you or not. "

Adding Personal Touches

Tim likes to provide a more personal touch to his members so that they know he appreciates them and that they're not just another number, however the way this is done has evolved since the membership first launched.

*"In the earlier days, we tested sending all our new members handwritten welcome cards, and all our monthly members would get little chocolate gifts at key points in their membership. And that was really successful. **We got great feedback from it, and it certainly positively affected our churn rates when we first introduced that.***

But what we found was that it gets really expensive as well. So I've more recently, just on the starting new members off, started doing Bonjoro, which is the personalised videos...And that's been getting some great responses as well.

And I can also, with that, which I couldn't do with the gifts, direct people to take action. And for me, that's introducing themselves in the forums..."

Increasing Engagement

Engagement is something Tim takes seriously and is continually working to improve, from his onboarding sequence to running regular member challenges and gamification.

"At the moment, I'm working on the onboarding sequence...we've been using Intercom for quite awhile, and we're only now just setting up the customer attributes and event tracking so that the member onboarding is related to events that people are taking rather than just a time-based sequence. So I think that's going to have an effect as well.

Obviously, general emails are important. And also for us, challenges. So we run four week challenges, three or four times a year... We give them about four sections, so teaching ideas, business ideas, personal, health, and they set their goals. They journal each week, and we award a winner, in inverted commas. So I think those things are really good.

But also for us, just getting the technology right so that things like progress tracking can be more effective. So people can see where they are in our roadmap or in a course. And they can get a certificate at the end..."

Tim is even having an app created to make his onsite forum community easier for members to use, and more like the familiar Facebook experience.

"We've got forums in our membership with BB Press and Buddy Press. But they're really clunky on mobile. And I don't want to use them on mobile, so why would my members? So we're working really hard at an app which will present our forums more like Facebook, which is what everyone's used to and what seems to work so well. So that's another one for the future."

Introducing Gamification

After an initial unsuccessful attempt at gamifying his membership using Badge OS, Tim is looking to introduce a more thought-out points system that rewards course completion, posting in the forum and attending live webinars and coaching.

"What we're going to be doing now is a much more planned, earning points system with rewards that the teachers want, things like private coaching, lessons with expert teachers, discounts on sheet music, things like that...

...it's not going to suit every member. I know that. But by encouraging some of those members to make an effort to join some of those live events, they're going to learn more, they're going to get more engaged, they're going to meet more members, they're going to hopefully make more change, which has more success, and also they get these points which they can then convert to some coaching, or whatever it is."

Getting Content Right

Members get access to all the content when they join, and a new course is released each month.

"We also each month do quite a few quick win videos, or I might have an expert interview that's not available elsewhere. And we also do a live coaching each month, so I'll invite on a special guest, we'll have a particular topic, so it might be teaching group improvisation, or teaching preschoolers, which is coming up this month for us. And then we'll have a live coaching call with everyone in a Zoom room on screen, all having a chat about whatever it is and the members will ask questions of that expert...

...in surveys that I've given teachers, I ask them once, 'What do you think about the amount of content we're putting out? Too little, too much, just right?' And most of them say 'just right'. So I'm going to stick to what we're doing. It seems to be working."

Team Work

Delegating tasks to his team of freelancers helps free Tim up to focus on adding the most value to his membership, without the long-term commitment or inflexibility of hiring staff.

"I think we've got about 12 at the moment in various freelance roles around the world. Isn't it amazing how we can use people wherever they are in the world? I think it's phenomenal...

...I started with just me doing everything, and my advice I guess would be to just find one or two of those jobs that you do regularly which is incredibly repetitive and that if you just recorded a screencast, if you could find someone, they could follow those instructions and do it.

*...And what I'm learning is that **I've got skills in certain areas, and I should be using my skills in those areas and not wasting time trying to code my website, or design a logo, or upload things, or whatever it is**, if I can find other people to do that so that I can focus on the next level stuff, the high level things."*

Bringing in Experts

As the nature of the membership has evolved, Tim has needed to bring in different experts, who have happily contributed (without a fee), as they appreciated the opportunity to get in front of Tim's audience.

"I've built the Inner Circle membership community primarily as a way to help teachers get more creative in their lessons...starting with the pop music, or teaching kids how to jam and play the blues and things like that.

But over time, as more members have come in, it's morphed a little bit into that, plus business strategy and support. And while I've run my own studio from home, I haven't run big studios. And so that sort of thing I needed other people to help me with, because I'm not the best person to teach that...

...definitely reach out to people and get help because it's all about the collective genius. I stole that term from somebody else, but the collective power of the group is what is most important in a membership. It's not just all about me."

A Meaningful Business

While Tim enjoyed teaching, he had always had other businesses and wanted something more. The membership appears to be what he was looking for.

"I'm more happy now than I've ever been in my working life.

As much as I enjoyed teaching piano, for me, there was always something more. I was always an entrepreneurial kind of kid. I ran a lot of businesses through my life, and none of them stuck and had shown success like this one has.

*So I'm doing what I want. It's 100% my passion, which I'm very lucky...**And to be able to have such an impact on people, but at the same time, be master of my own destiny is great**. Not having to ask people for permission to do this or that, and be able to make my own decisions, and drive my own vehicle I guess. I think that's really meaningful. And for someone that wants to do that kind of thing, I can only say just go for it. Get yourself set up right. You don't want to take a complete leap into the dark. But when you're ready, even if ... No, when you're* *not ready, but you think you might be, give it a shot. Because you never know quite what will come of it. "*

What's Next For Tim Topham's Inner Circle

As well as completing his new community app and putting the finishing touches on his gamification, Tim's main goal is to continue increasing the membership so that he can impact as many piano teachers as possible. He also plans to start running live events.

"I would love in the next 12 months to run or be very close to running my first live event. Probably here in Australia to start with, and then perhaps in the United States if I could work out how to do it right. So doing some live stuff would be great. And I guess getting the membership, the technology all at the point where I don't have to think about it anymore and it just works, so that all I'm really concentrating on is getting more great people in to help create great information and support for teachers...

... And it comes back to what I was saying before about having an impact. I mean, it's already having a significant impact on the lives of many, many teachers and students. And if I can continue to expand that, then that's a great thing. But it's already doing what it was designed to do, which is have an impact around the world."

Anissa Holmes: Delivering Wow

Membership Details:

Name: Delivering Wow

Topic: Dental Businesses

Launched: February 2017

Website: deliveringwow.com

Interview Date: June 2018

Anissa Holmes runs a dental practice in Jamaica, while also delivering high end coaching programmes, and running Delivering WOW, a membership and training programme for dentists.

The site started out as an online community for dentists, but is now repositioning as a year-long programme giving owners of dental practises everything they need to help their small business be successful.

When Anissa moved to Jamaica with her young family, she set up her own practise and needed to get patients quickly:

"I figured out how to build an amazing team. We became the number one practice, known for delivering amazing wow experiences. Our testimonials are crazy. Right now, we have over 55,000 people following my practice's Facebook page."

After achieving such huge success with her own practice, Anissa's business coach suggested she become a business coach herself, and Anissa agreed. She chose to specialise in helping businesses in the dental industry because she'd seen for herself that no-one was doing that.

To kick start her new business venture, Anissa started a podcast, and from the very beginning she aimed high.

"My first podcast guest, was John Lee Dumas. I joined his podcast community... I reached out to him and asked him if he would personally coach me with building that podcast. And he respectfully declined, but at least it started that relationship."

From there Anissa invited him to her podcast and gave him an opportunity to pitch his Freedom Journal to her audience of thousands of dentists.

"... the first piece of advice that he gave me was that you want to build out a recurring revenue model. That was it. He's like, 'You might want to help people, and coach people, but the one-to-many approach is going to be huge....for you to get your time back, but also to be able to help people, not only in your local area, but all over the world.'

He was so right. What we did was we started a Facebook group. Then we started building content for our membership site. I started it, actually, by having a bootcamp, which was eight doctors. I charged them $3,000 for eight sessions and we recorded live training. Then, from there, I was like, 'What else do you want? What else do you want? What are your pain points? Tell me everything.' Then I told them, I said, 'I'm going to be building out this site for dentists. Anything you need, just tell me what you want.' And that's how I found out what courses to build. I actually created, by that time, maybe 15 little extra courses, in addition to our live training. I didn't sell that live training. That was just for them, but I built up all these accessory trainings and that was, actually, the very beginning of my membership site."

Before she launched, Anissa invited beta testers from her free Facebook group, which at the time had around 500 people, to join for a lifetime access fee of $397.

"By the time we launched, we had 35, or so, courses and we had testimonials... I had all of this social proof... we had a huge launch, actually. Very interesting, because we probably did about $25,000, or so, that week of the launch and we launched it at $79 [per month] or $797 a year, just for that one week. Then we bumped it up to $97 and $997."

Giving back has been integral to Anissa's business model from the start.

"We donated $20,000 of it to World Teacher Aid. That was really cool. That's part of our culture and messaging, is that we're also changing lives. And I made it very vocal that we actually took the first profits we made and we gave it away. That goes into our brand story and messaging, that we want to make an impact."

Now the membership acts as an entry level product to introduce clients to Anissa's higher-end coaching programs.

"It's also a great opportunity to actually have people to come in at a lower level, build that trust, and get value and then they buy our higher level programmes, which, right now, our bootcamp is now $5K... We've increased the price. And we have a $24,000 inner circle mastermind. It all starts off with people beginning in this lower level and getting value, and then ascending up."

Repackaging The Membership

Delivering Wow is now being marketed as a year-long program for dentists and their whole practice team, as opposed to a traditional membership site.

"We're going to teach you consistent systems to get 10, or 20, new patients. We're going to teach you how to grow and scale by using your team. We're going to teach you how to hold your team accountable, so that they can help you grow.

It's a programme. It's the same thing. It's the same content. Our content is not changing.

We're just changing how we're marketing it."

To benchmark the annual fee against something her audience can relate to, Anissa is planning a webinar that compares the program to in-person training conferences.

"In our industry, in our space, you can certainly take your team to a conference, that's going to cost you thousands of dollars by the time you fly and get a hotel. When they leave, they forget everything."

Instead, Anissa's program offers the opportunity for the whole team to learn online together, and there's even accountability checklists and actionable activities built in to the end of each training.

"That's how we're changing it.... Instead of it being the online community for dentists, where I'm just preaching to dentists about how they need to grow their business, we're actually, now, having the courses and it's not just for you, it's for you and your team. Some people, some doctors, don't want to do anything. They just want their team to do it. Great, put your team in there, we'll train them. We'll train them and you'll get profits."

The program will also include resources needed to run Facebook ads for popular products like dental implants and Invisalign.

In her marketing Anissa compares the cost of the program to the potential revenue it will help them generate by scaling their team and increasing their sales.

"'Are you willing to invest $2,000 a year to make an extra $30,000 a month?' It becomes a no brainer. That's how we're going to be selling our membership site and, again, positioning it, not just for dentists, but dentist and teams. I believe this is going to change everything."

Getting Members Results

Initially Anissa priced her membership site at a low rate to make it easily accessible, but she later realised that low pricing actually reduced commitment, and in order to help her members get results she needed to charge a higher amount.

*"I had the false belief that if I just give people a low price, they'd want it. But what I found is, people signed up and then they send an email and they're like, 'Can you cancel, because I've just been so busy, haven't even had a chance to login?' I want people to login, because there's so much gold in there. It can change their life. So, for me, it is my responsibility. It is my duty. **I serve people by charging people higher amounts, because then they feel it. They don't want to waste their money. They'll go in and they'll do the work..."***

For Anissa what she charges isn't the important thing, she just wants to ensure that her members benefit and take action as she sees this as her legacy.

*"I've had a shift in my mindset, in terms of how I sell my membership site, because all I really care about is getting people results. **I am actually good with money now. I'm debt free. My practice is doing well. This is my gift. This is my legacy. If I have a programme that people are not benefiting from, and they're not doing it, I'm not really fulfilling my purpose.** That's what it's all about."*

Being committed to a product after paying more for it is something Anissa has experienced for herself:

"I'm a member of a few membership sites and I never login. But I've also paid $36,000 for a membership site, as well... It's a year-long programme, but it's a membership site and I'm paying a lot of money to be there. But guess what? I'm doing the work."

Although Anissa has raised her rate and plans to do so again with the newly repackaged programme, existing members are grandfathered in at their existing rate.

"I believe a lot in being appreciative for people who helped you to get where you are. People who believe in you from the very beginning, I think they should be rewarded. Those are the people that wind up being your biggest fans. They've been loyal with you. They'll give you testimonials...I think you can win from those members without charging them more."

Product Ascension

For Anissa, Delivering Wow is hopefully just the first step many members will take with her and her team.

"We've been able to ascend these people up to our next level programmes. Honestly, to me, that's my ultimate goal. I don't want people to stay here, watching videos, I want to work with them. I want to feel them. I want them to come to our live workshops, where we can really dive deep and help them at a higher level.

The membership has been, really, the stepping stone to get people into our online bootcamps, and our inner circle programme, and, again, that's where we can serve people at a higher level.

That's where everything changes. My inner circle, this week, it's the beginning of a month, and I asked all of them to share their wins for the month. I had at least, half of them say, 'This was the best month ever.' We always get that, 'We made an extra $30,000 this month.'...

That's when it gets really cool, because you know you're making huge, huge impact. Again, the membership site, for me, has been part of my total ascension plan. I think that's been the key for me, as well."

Attracting Members

Anissa's free Facebook group, which has reached almost 14,000 people, is a great source of new members, especially as some members of Delivering Wow remain inside the free group, and talk about the benefits they get from it.

Throughout the year Anissa delivers free trainings and lead magnets to give prospects a taste of what's inside the membership. She also uses Facebook ads that speak of the pain points associated with running a dental practise.

She also occasionally runs an offer to buy lifetime access to the membership for a one-off fee.

"We offered a lifetime access for three days. At the time, it's $997. We put it out to our Facebook group, which has 14,000 people...we actually had 175 people sign up. So that was $175,000 that we made in three days, which is nice."

And, she uses a genius method to get video testimonials to use on sales pages and social media:

"We're doing Zoom calls, where we can actually interview them with specific questions, in a specific order, and a specific way where we can get their testimonial...where it's speaker view, so we can just get their image and we're just chopping up those videos."

Venturing into Live Events

When Anissa wanted to extend her sphere of influence recently, she felt a live event was probably the way to go, but didn't know how to get started as she had never run one before. Russell Brunson (her business coach) suggested that as she was in Jamaica she should have a big party and invite all the top influencers in her market to speak.

She contacted friends and people who she'd interviewed for podcasts, and on each call she listed who had already agreed to attend.

"I actually built what Russell calls a 'stack'...and actually just talked to every influencer and said that other person is in, this person is in, this person is in. In one hour, I actually had all the top leaders and influencers in my space to speak at my event.

We hosted an event and it was amazing. It was in Jamaica. I hired an amazing photography team, video team. We had drones build all of these amazing images. We really over delivered in every single way.

We actually sold out 75% of next year's event, at that event, which was huge. Now, we have our movement. So, people know who we are. They know what we do. Now, the next level is actually using our speakers, who were there, as affiliates for our Delivering WOW U programme."

The Right Team

Anissa balances running her membership with delivering high-end coaching and running her own dental practice as well as enjoying time with her family. Getting the right team in place, she says, was crucial to being able to achieve this.

*"**You can't do it alone. Hire the right people. Hire the best team you can find. Outsource things that you don't need to be doing...Every time we got a little money, I started to think, 'What can somebody else do that I don't have to do?'***

Now, there's a lot of things being done, but sometimes I'm like, 'I don't have anything to do,' but I'm the strategist and I'm the visionary. I say, 'This is what I want,' and I hire amazing people and let them do their jobs.

*That's how it happens, but it doesn't happen right away, but that's how I did it. A little money, hire somebody to help you, who is better than you...**Be honest with yourself and do what you are most passionate about, and put your focus and effort into what no one else can do.***"

Financial Freedom

Even though the membership site is less than 18 months old, it's already had a huge impact on Anissa's life and is a 7 figure business.

"For me, personally, I have now financial freedom. In a really short time, which was really interesting. It's that one-to-many, so you're able to earn more than you ever thought possible. We're debt free. We pay cash for everything. We were on holiday, last year, in Europe, for a month. We just purchased a boat, actually, which is crazy. Why? Because I work too much, and I know that… So I needed to have that time with my family, where it was just us to be able to connect.

…It's not about the money that I make and, actually, I'll just say this, money is actually good. You know why? The more money you make, the bigger impact you can make, because, now, we're earning and our membership site and everything else that we're doing. I'm able to keep reinvesting in the programme to make it even better. I'm able to hire the best people, so I'm able to help people get results. To me, that's what it's all about. It's just impacting more people, changing more lives, and it's awesome."

What's Next For Delivering Wow

Once the restructure to a year long programme is completed Anissa plans to start selling the membership via a Facebook Ad to webinar funnel, live at first and then automated once the process is converting well.

"We're actually going to do them live, until we get them right. You know, you're a podcaster like me. My first podcast, the one with John, I mean, it sucked. It was really bad. It was okay, but it was bad. Now, when I get on a podcast, like we're on a podcast now, nothing is scripted out. I don't need any questions to think about

ahead of time. I'm super comfortable with it. I'm confident. I wasn't competent, at first. Even with webinars, you have to do it over, and over, again until you realise like, "When I say this word, this is the response that I get," or when I position it this way, or when I give the offer this way, more people buy.

I think it's going to be a process and once I get it right, and we have a lot of conversions, then I'll just put it on auto. That's my plan."

Mark Warner: Teaching Packs

Membership Details:

Name: Teaching Packs

Topic: Teaching Resources

Launched: 2012

Website: teachingpacks.com

Interview Date: June 2018

Mark Warner runs Teaching Packs, a membership providing resources for teachers and that has already helped more than 15,000 teachers in 5 years.

Mark started publishing teaching resources online in 1998, on his first website, Teaching Ideas, while he was training to be a teacher at university. The site was a way of sharing teaching ideas and resources that he'd made. That website is now 20 years old, and receives millions of people visiting every year, making it a great source of new members.

By 2012, Mark was struggling to balance his full-time teaching job with managing the website and his young family. At the time Teaching Ideas was funded by adverts, but that didn't generate enough money alone to support Mark and his family if he left his teaching job, so he started to think of other ways to monetise his large audience.

"I was a little bit reluctant to charge them, but that seemed to be the way that other sites were going. It seemed to be a good way of me increasing my income slightly, so that I could dedicate more time to the website."

As a result Mark launched Teaching Packs, providing done for you teaching resources for a low annual fee (currently £20 per year).

"It really took off, and fortunately I was able to give up my teaching job. Which I do really, really miss, but running the membership site is equally as rewarding...we're supporting thousands of teachers, and those teachers are working with children in classrooms all around the world. It's wonderful to know that the things I create in my mini office, here down in Kent, are being used in classrooms with children of all ages, in completely different parts of the world that I'll never, ever get to visit."

Filling Content Gaps

Mark has an continuous challenge on his hands trying to ensure he has the right content on the site, given that curriculums frequently change, not to mention catering for different countries needs as well.

"Content is always my biggest challenge, because there are gaps in the site that I don't have content for at the moment. If a teacher is teaching something about mountains, and there's nothing on my website, then for them, at that point in time, the membership isn't useful for them.

I always want to fill those gaps, to make sure there's as much useful content for them as possible...

...And the curriculum's always changing. The government is always meddling in things. They're always moving the goalposts, adding things to the curriculum, taking things out. Again, that's happening all around the world. So I have to cater for that content in many different situations."

Growing a Team

Initially Mark was doing everything in the membership himself but as the site has grown he's begun to grow his team so that he can focus his time more.

"I started by doing everything myself. Over time, gradually, I've got extra help.

My wife only works part-time, so she's able to help. She does lots of research for content, and she's started to make teaching resources. She's also a really good illustrator, so on some of our packs you might see some of her pictures.

Over the past few years, I've been getting extra help from other people. I found a fantastic teacher on a site called PeoplePerHour, completely by chance. Over the past few years, she's been doing lots of research and content creation for me.

I've also been outsourcing a bit more over the past six months. By getting graphic designers to help with the illustration, developers to help with some of the interactive teaching tools that we're adding now.

A couple of months ago we also added a new VA to our team, so I've got somebody doing admin stuff for a few hours every week.

Which really takes the load off, but the bulk of the content creation is mainly me."

While Mark's team is still small, he does wish that he had started bringing other people onboard earlier:

"I've kind of spent the first 15 years doing everything on my own, thinking nobody else could do it. Then over the past five years, as I mentioned, all those people that I've been getting help from, it's really enabled me to create more content, to help more people, more quickly. Taking much more off my plate, so I can plan the business now. I'm not just working on a pack, getting it out the door as quickly as possible. I'm actually planning packs that might not be published for a couple of months yet...So I think getting extra help earlier on would probably have helped me to serve my audience better at that time."

Member Review System

For Mark, the testimonials are proof that his hard work is paying off, and they are often a source of additional sales.

"The feedback is just incredible. We get amazing comments, amazing emails every day.

We have a review system on the sites, where teachers can post reviews of our packs, and we've got over a thousand five star reviews, which is just amazing.

Feedback from teachers, saying, 'We use this with our children. It had such a great impact, the children loved it.' That feedback is just incredible. It's just amazing to get those emails every day. We also have a gallery where teachers can take photos of their classroom displays. So if they put some of our resources up on their wall, then they can take a photo and send it to us, and we'll share it in our gallery...seeing something that I've made on screen actually printed up on the wall, in a classroom, is just delightful."

Mark's site uses a Wordpress plug-in that makes the reviews and star ratings visible on search results displayed on Google, which is great for enhancing his SEO and marketing efforts.

"So if somebody searches for a topic on Google, then they'll see a little star rating next to the Teaching Packs link. Then that's an instant eye-catcher, and it brings people into the site."

Expiring Memberships

Despite competitors charging up to four times as much as Mark, he's reluctant to increase the price, or tie members into a subscription, because they're often paying out of pocket, and he knows their circumstances may change year on year.

Instead he focuses on creating great content to keep them coming back to the site, and choosing to renew year after year.

"The site has renewal reminders. A week before and a couple of days before the expiration date, they get some emails. Then if they want to log in and renew then, they can. If they want to wait a few months, or even a few years, then they can log in at any time and come back, and their renewal rate is slightly lower as well. So there's a bit more of an incentive. I've also got automation sequences in Active Campaign, that encourage people to pop back in. If they don't come back for a while, then there's an even bigger renewal discount. To try and tempt them back in, if they'd like to join."

3 Million+ Facebook Fans

Mark has amassed a hugely impressive 3 million Facebook fans but it wasn't done quickly or easily.

"I've worked 20 years to build this up. It hasn't come overnight, it's been a huge amount of work...Social media reach is a constant worry, because Facebook is always pushing us to pay to share posts online. At the moment, things are still working well for me with Facebook. I'm trying different avenues as well. I'm trying Pinterest and Twitter and Instagram, but Facebook is the big audience for me."

Mark's Facebook growth is all organic. He's total lifetime Facebook ad spend amounts to around £100 spent experimenting with boosted posts.

"I've been trying to find and share lots of useful resources that I think my audience would like. Not just my own stuff, lots of content from other sites. Lots of things I've discovered on Pinterest, or other teaching blogs. That really resonated with the audience, and has really helped me to grow that audience, which has been very beneficial for me with the membership.

Teaching Ideas was one of the first educational resource sites on the internet. There weren't many people doing it back then, so it certainly got its foot in the door very early. It grew, with lots of teachers sharing their own resources with me. I was able to post those online, and then even use some of those in my own classroom when I was teaching. So it was a really fantastic, two-way thing. The audience it's got now is incredible."

Giving Sample Content

Mark's huge Facebook following and large audience for the Teaching Ideas website is his main source of new members.

Mark also gives away frequent samples of his paid resources so that people know exactly what to expect if they become a member.

*"At the bottom of every page on Teaching Ideas there's a link to Teaching Packs. We also include lots of free samples. **I post a selection of the content from Teaching Packs on Teaching Ideas, so teachers can see what is in each pack.** They can download it for free on Teaching Ideas. Then if they like it, they can go to Teaching Packs and download the full pack.*

*Facebook has just been amazing for me as well. I've been very fortunate, we've got three million people who like us on Facebook. So we've automatically got a very big reach there. Organic reach is always declining on Facebook. **We're very lucky that if I post something on our Facebook account, it does go to tens of thousands, sometimes hundreds of thousands of people. That brings a lot of people to the site as well."***

Teachers also help other teachers discover the site:

"There's lots of staffroom conversations about what resources are working well. There are lots of educational resource groups on social media…teachers put their posters up in their classroom, and in the corner of each poster there's my little logo."

Community Isn't a Priority

Despite creating both a community forum and Facebook group, Mark finds that his members aren't there to socialise.

"Unfortunately, the site's community isn't really very busy, because teachers tend to pop onto my site during their break times, before school, after school, evenings and weekends even, so it's not the place they want to hang around, unfortunately... The community isn't a big part of my site, so I keep pushing out content, that is my main way of bringing people back and getting them to renew."

Despite the community element of the site being quiet, Mark does spend time talking to his audience to ensure he knows what they need and want from the membership.

"I get so much wonderful feedback from my audience via Facebook, via Teaching Ideas, via email and reviews. Knowing exactly what they need, what they want, when they want it, has really helped me to direct the memberships to meet their needs. They're giving me a little bit of money out of their own pockets every year, so I want to make sure they get the best value possible. Following that feedback is the direction that I need to go every time."

Transitioning from Teaching

While Mark loved teaching, transitioning to a membership has allowed him to have a much greater impact, helping both teachers and children on a wider scale, while also giving him more control of his own time.

"It's a very different environment. Teaching is incredibly social. You're always spending time with your colleagues, you're always in front of this group of 30

young, amazing people. I love that environment, it's fantastic, but it is completely exhausting.

I'm very lucky now, with the job, that I can spend so much time at home...

It's completely transformed my life.

Before I started it [the membership], I was struggling a little bit managing everything. I remember sitting down with my wife at Christmas, before we set up the site, and thinking what could I possibly do to juggle all these things I've got going on?

The membership site grew, very fortunately, and I'm very lucky to be in the situation I'm in now. I'm master of my own time. I do have to support people, but I don't have a boss. I'm the boss. I can control when I work, when I want to work, and I do love doing it. I love getting the feedback from teachers. I love knowing that the stuff I create is being helpful to them, and to their children around the world. That's an amazing feeling."

What's Next For Teaching Packs

As well as continuing on with his content creation and quest to fill all the content gaps he can, Mark is also starting to add interactive teaching tools into the membership as well, an extra bonus for members.

"... content, content, content. I need to keep pushing as much as I can out the door, to fill those gaps that teachers need.

We've also started, over the past few months, to add some interactive teaching tools. So things that teachers can use on an interactive whiteboard, like a classroom countdown timer, a stopwatch. We had a random pupil picker tool added to the site a couple of weeks back. We're working on a classroom jukebox as well, which plays background music while children are working. So I want to develop that range of tools, because we've had some great feedback about that lately."

Mark is also facing the unenvious task of having to change membership plugins, a significant endeavour for a membership with over 15,000 members and thousands of resources!

"I'm possibly thinking about changing membership plugins as well, which is a big challenge that I've been reluctant to try. I think it's possibly best for the future, because our membership plugin isn't really in active development anymore. So it might be better to switch to something that's a bit better supported...So that's going to be an immense job, which is what I'm putting off, but it needs to be done at some point I think."

Terra Dawn: Uncork Your Dork

Membership Details:

Name: Wham! Bam! Business Plan!

Topic: Subscription Products

Launched: January 2017

Website: uncorkyourdork.com

Interview Date: June 2018

Terra Dawn from Uncork Your Dork runs Wham! Bam! Business Plan! A membership site that helps people create various types of subscription products.

The idea came from her own experience of going too quickly from idea to launch, and not making the revenue she needed.

"...you have this amazing idea, you don't quite think it through, you don't quite polish...When you launch you get a little bit depressed 'cause it makes 200 bucks and you're like 'that's all'. That's like one trip to the grocery store. That is not going to do anything for me.

... I could launch something and have $6,000 but then the next month I either wouldn't launch anything and I'd make $200 or I'd launch something and I'd launch it incorrectly or a button wouldn't work or something like that and I'd make $200.

So it was totally inconsistent. And so I got into memberships to help with that consistency."

To launch her membership quickly, Terra took four online challenges she had already created and moved them to Teachable, offered it to her free Facebook group for $20 per month, and had 150 people join. From there she was hooked on creating new courses for her members.

"I was very, very excited and I was already coming up with different courses and different things that I wanted to put in there. And then I realised really, really quickly that I wanted to do so much more."

Changing Platforms

While Teachable worked for getting the membership up and running quickly, Terra quickly found that it wasn't the right platform for her membership and community needs and so moved to WordPress instead.

"Teachable is a wonderful platform but it's got one purpose, to hold your content and to take payment for content. And it does that really, really well but there was no room for me to create that community. There was no room, when you got into Teachable, it didn't feel like a community, it felt like a course. And I didn't want that feeling…

…So yeah, I went from Teachable straight over to WordPress with MemberPress and the Memberoni theme which I absolutely adore."

Unfortunately, when Terra switched her membership from Teachable to her own Wordpress site, she lost 50% of her members.

"I think it was a re-sign up thing. Teachable is very comfortable for a lot of people. And I think the reason people joined is because they're familiar with the Teachable platform. They were familiar with me. They'd taken these challenges, they wanted

these full challenges. They were interested in those challenges. So when I said, "I'm moving these challenges and adding a bunch of great new content." They were like, "Yeah but we just want the challenges and that would involve me going and signing up." Plus a lot of people may not have seen the email when it came through. It was just a bunch of different reason why we probably lost that many."

Switching Communities

As well as changing membership platform, Terra has also changed community platform from an onsite forum to Mighty Networks. This turned out to be a great decision and helped to increase engagement amongst her members.

"...I knew that I wanted to build a community around the membership and not just have it being like a little side project which is kind of what it was at the time 'cause like I said, my mind wasn't in it either.

...It's [mighty networks] a phone application so if I'm out hanging out with friends or if I'm out running errands or if I'm at lunch just chilling and someone in the forum posts, I immediately get a little ding on my phone and I can go in and respond really quickly. Or if I have it up, I try to always have it up on my computer and so when anyone posts in there I get a little ding. Or if someone joins I get a little ding and it's great 'cause I can go in, I can welcome them. I can be the first one there.

Yeah, it's fun. It's a very welcoming community. And all the members also have the app on their cellphones so whenever someone comments they can either have it set to only subscribe to certain people, subscribe when anyone posts, subscribe when the host posts."

A Ready Made Audience

For Terra, having a membership means having a ready-made audience, eager to use her courses.

"With a membership, what I love about it is, I can get an idea, run it by the community. My community says yay or nay or crickets. One of the two, one of the three. And then I can go on ahead and create it that week... and I don't have to try to go out and find a new audience for it. I already have an audience who's excited to get that content. So it's fun....

... You know what the worst feeling is? It's when you create something that you absolutely love and then no one buys it. The worst part is not the fact that you're not getting income in, it's the fact that no one is seeing this amazing thing that you've created... I absolutely love being able to launch to a ready made, already paying, already excited audience. That's been literally one of the best things ever. "

A Culture of Sharing

Beside the sense of accomplishment from seeing her newly created content being put to use, Terra also gets a lot of enjoyment from her growing community. Something she particularly encourages is sharing useful resources into the community, creating a community packed with useful links from both herself and members.

"One of the things that I've always been a fan of is sharing out ideas, outside work. We don't just keep it to the articles that I post on my blog. We post everything from you guys. We post things from people who are doing stuff on YouTube...I post anything that I think will help them regardless of where it comes from.

And so that's been really, really fun because the community's starting to do the same thing. If they find an article, if they get something in their inbox they're like, oh that's a great read.

And it's great because we're starting to get articles from small names, big names, medium names and we're starting to... I just feel like we're growing the community outside of the membership as well. It's been really, really fun."

Alumni Community Access

In an unusual move, when someone pauses or cancels the membership, Terra sends them an email inviting them to stay in the community portion of the site. This has been helpful in both encouraging members to rejoin and increasing resumes from pauses.

"Whenever I post any new courses, whenever we have any summits, whenever we have any events, I make sure everyone in that community are the first people to know.

Now if it's an event happening inside the membership obviously, or it's a course, they can't get that unless they're part of the membership. But they see it. They're more aware than just an email passing through their inbox that they may or may not see. And most people are not quitting because they hate the content. Actually no one as far as I know has quit 'cause they hate the content. They're quitting 'cause they're having either financial issues or they don't have time or something like that. **So keeping them as a part of the community has been huge for keeping them interested in becoming a member again.** *And keeping them as a member of the Uncork Your Dork family.*

…The second we started doing that we starting seeing memberships unpaused at a higher rate. I think we've had five members unpause in the last two weeks which has been great. I think that has to do with I've been making a lot of announcements… And so I think people have been unpausing because they've been seeing that inside of the community and they're like, oh yep, I want that. So they've been unpausing…"

Virtual Summits

Terra is a fan of running online summits for both increasing her audience and promoting the membership and runs two per year.

Previously, all the content from a summit was made available to purchase for $97 on a standalone website, but with her next summit the content will be housed within the membership instead.

To add a sense of urgency, people must join the membership by a particular date to access the summit content immediately.

"So you get it immediately if you join before the clock ticks down but once that clock hits zero, any new members will have to wait two months. They have to be a member for two months. Which means they're paying twice what they are paying to get in for the summit this year.

Anyways it's all kind of an experiment at this stage. We've never done this before. But we've already seen an increase in sign ups so that's fun. And people are loving the summit content."

Free Challenges

Terra currently uses live challenge events hosted inside her free Facebook group to encourage people to join the membership, a strategy she's planning to supplement with an automated webinar.

"I launched a challenge three months ago and it was a tools challenge. I went over, it was like five days of tools basically. And it got really great reviews and we saw a really great, a really large number of people join the summit around that time. I think we had, it was a five day event and I think we had 30 something people sign at that point. It was like 36 or 37 people sign up at that point. So which is good. That's really good for us. Really, really good for us."

...I think the huge thing that I'm learning about marketing is you can't just set it and forget it...there's a certain amount of automation to marketing but you have to be present. You have to be talking in the group, in the limelight, in front of people. And so that's why I think challenges work so well....

... I'm going to do a couple of live webinars, see which one really resonates and then try to get that one automated and up and see if we can at least get a little bit of automation going in the system. 'Cause right now it's very hands on."

Changing Focuses

Now that the membership is established, the kind of content that Terra is creating has changed, along with where her day to day focus lies.

"So at this point I focus on releasing videos. I focus on events like the summits. I focus on creating smaller content not the large courses. 'Cause I think we've got seven large courses in there right now that walk people through everything. And then we've got a whole bunch of smaller stuff. So right now, I'm kind of focusing on the smaller stuff. I'm focusing on really being a part of that community and making sure people are being held accountable for what's going on in their business."

Initially, Terra simply uploaded all of her courses and let members pick and choose what they wanted to work through, but this wasn't the most helpful approach for her members.

Now, Terra has created a pathway through her content to make it easy for members to consume and stay engaged.

"When I launched the membership initially, I launched it in Teachable and then I had to move everything over and then I started slowly pivoting and growing my content and I realised really quickly that it was messy. It was organised because you can log in and you can see all of the courses...but there was no clear direction on where you should turn. Where you should go.

So that's why we've started putting everything in the success path. So when you log in you know exactly where to go and where to start next, and where it's going to not necessarily end, but where the end goal is kind of a thing."

Terra also adds to the membership content regularly, ensuring that there is always something new for members each month. One of her favourite things about the membership is running a live monthly goal setting call.

"I put out a lot of content. Not an insane amount. I usually put out about two to three pieces of content a month. But there's always something new. There's always something fun to explore.

We do something called Goal Diggers. So every single first of the month, we go in, we plan out our month. We plan out our marketing. We plan out our launches. And we do that live together as a group. So that's really fun. That's actually one of my favourite things I think."

Mindset Shifts

Now that the business generates recurring income, Terra has experienced a mindset shift - she no longer feels like she HAS to do the work, she WANTS to do it.

"I do it because I want to do it. And I think that that is a huge part of being a membership owner is you're doing it for your community now. You're not just doing it for whoever might hopefully want to buy it. So it's a wonderful mindset shift thing. So yeah, I'm starting to enjoy myself as a membership site owner actually. So it's fun."

Tunnel Vision

Before launching the membership, Terra admits running her business was a struggle, but now she's found her focus.

"It's kind of like tunnel vision now. I've been able to narrow my focus down to my membership. How do I market my membership? How do I make my members happy? Not my customers from 10 different products. How do I make my members happy? I've been able to singularly focus down on everything.

My boyfriend knows what I do for a living now which is great. My family knows what I do for a living now. My message has become very, very focused and very, very singular because I'm talking to one audience. I'm not talking to people who want to learn email and then also people who want to learn Facebook. It's one audience. So it's fantastic."

Pricing Too High

When making the move from Teachable to WordPress, Terra also increased the price of her membership, something she wishes she hadn't done immediately.

"I should have started at the lower end of the pricing scale. I should have started initially on that WordPress launch at $20. And that would've given me room to grow and expand and get people excited in at a lower tier and get the talk going.

Or even give people a little bit of a timer saying, 'It's $20 now but it's going to be $30 next week.' There was no ladder for me to climb at time.

I knew $39 was about, that was my perfect price point…But when you start at the perfect price point, there's like I said, there's no ladder to climb. There's no way for you to offer urgency. There's no way for you to tell people the price is going up.

Kind of bit myself in the butt on that one. Wish I had started lower and launched bigger is what I wish had happened. But you live and you learn."

What's Next For Wham! Bam!

After running her next online summit Terra will experiment with closing the doors to her membership for a while and only letting members in during short launch periods.

"Right now it's an evergreen membership. Right now everything is open but we're always in the mood to guinea pig so I think what we're going to try to do is by the time the next summit comes around, this is a version, it's going to be more about the summit or the membership is closing its doors for a little bit. 'Cause I do want to focus on that organisation inside of the membership a little bit more. Focus on the members. And yeah, I want to see how it all works. It's going to be an experiment. We'll see what happens."

Nigel Moore: The Tech Tribe

Membership Details:

Name: The Tech Tribe

Topic: Managed Service Providers

Launched: February 2017

Website: thetechtribe.com

Interview Date: June 2018

Nigel Moore is founder The Tech Tribe, a membership site for Managed Service Providers and IT business owners.

Nigel ran his own business-to-business IT support operation for around 10 years, which he sold in 2016. During this time he often coached other IT businesses owners, which gave him the idea of starting a membership to teach, coach, train, and mentor other Managed Service Providers (MSPs). This became The Tech Tribe.

"This is actually version two. I started a site similar to this back when I owned my IT company, back in about 2013 with a friend of mine. And we built it up. So a kind of tiny little site, but it was fun. And it was because back then when I owned my company, I found that I was coaching and teaching other people in the industry a little bit on the side and enjoying that a whole lot more than I was enjoying owning my own IT business. And that put the writing on the wall to go out and figure out how I could go out and do that for a living.

So we had that little one on the wall, running for probably a couple of years. And it was working pretty well for a little side gig for us. And that was probably the impetus back then. And then when I was selling my business, that process took about a year, but going through that process I always knew that this would be what I would be jumping into afterwards in a more full-time capacity. And we turned it into the business version two, and relaunched."

While the membership site is now the main business, Nigel also runs a private investment business, Teeth Capital, to buy and invest in small businesses that show scope for improvement.

When Nigel first opened the Tech Tribe, he ran launches for the first four months, however now the doors are open all the time and he gets 1-2 new members every day. I

"We originally ran on a launch cycle for the first three intakes. And that probably went over a four month period. And that was while we were getting the balls rolling and trying to figure out how things work, and we just didn't want people coming in will nilly during that process. After that, we opened it up and it's been open ever since. However, we're now starting to get to the point where we've got enough members that things are starting to stretch in certain areas and whatnot. So we'll probably, in the next three to six months, we'll probably close it again and just expand our capacity inside for a little bit, and then go to some kind of relaunch thing just as we go. Or some kind of intake thing as we go from there. But at the moment it is wide open. People could join, and we get a couple of people joining each day. Or at least one every day coming in and joining us, which is cool."

Free Coaching Calls

Nigel loves to make his new members feel welcome and getting to know them and so offers all new members a free coaching call.

This approach doesn't scale well however - in a normal month this may be 30 calls, but when running a promotion and getting 5-10 members a day it becomes more difficult.

"When people join us, I go a little bit overboard because I love talking to our new guys. And so every person that joins I give them a free coaching call. So right now we are not doing any marketing, but we are still getting a person to join us every single day. So we're getting 30 members a month, which means 30 coaching calls a month...."

...when we have campaigns running, we could sometimes get between 5 and 10 new members a day. And when you're offering a free coaching call as a bonus for everybody that joins after that, it kind of doesn't scale very well."

Despite the one-to-one coaching calls creating a bottleneck in the member onboarding, Nigel appreciates the opportunity to connect with new members, get them off to the best start, and get them engaged early on with the membership. As a result retention rates tend to be better with people who have had that initial coaching call.

He also offers a private coaching area in the forum, an idea borrowed from James Schramko, but again he is finding there may be a scaling issue.

"We get some really great momentum and conversations happening in that private section as well to help people out. But of course because it's me in there that's coaching people, that kind of has a capacity limit."

Facebook Ad Funnels

When not using Facebook ads, most of the new members find Tech Tribe because Nigel gets tagged into posts and questions in Facebook groups.

But he's not dependent on these organic referrals alone. After much trial and error, he's been able to create a marketing funnel that generates new members when the Facebook ads are turned on.

"...we only have one Facebook funnel that we use and that works incredibly well.

It took us about four months to get it working well, and many, many, many thousands of dollars to learn the marketing process, and figure out what works and what doesn't. But that marketing funnel, when we do turn it on, works great. And we get some really solid metrics out of that. But right now we just don't need it. We're working on too many other things and just trying to fine-tune a couple of things. And once we're ready for a little bit more scalability and growth, we'll go back and turn that marketing engine back on."

The funnel that has been so successful is actually surprisingly simple:

"So the funnel is a Facebook ad to a lead magnet that goes into a basic, a very, very, very basic email funnel. And we were closing ... people were joining within about two to three days. The majority of people were joining within about two to three days of downloading the lead magnet which was very relatable to stuff inside our Tribe."

Ad Hoc Content Delivery

Nigel doesn't have a pre-set monthly content schedule. Instead he tries to find a balance between what the members are asking for and what he has capacity to produce, while also avoiding flooding the members with too much material.

"We don't set a strict schedule of 'we're going to roll out one template, and one resource, and whatnot'. Kind of comes down to my capacity, how much stuff I could roll out. As well as what people are yearning for at the moment…You join some membership sites…and then they just blast you with new stuff every single week.

And we're the polar opposite, I'll only put stuff in there if it's really high quality. And that means that some months we might only put one or maybe two things in there. However they're typically pretty high quality… We do have a roadmap, but that changes pretty regularly because the industry changes, and peoples' needs change, and whatnot as well. So we kind of keep it fairly fluid."

With 20 years industry experience, Nigel has accumulated a wealth of knowledge he'd like to share with his members. Finding a structured manageable way to share that with them has been difficult.

"The biggest challenge is getting everything out of my head and into some sort of structure, or training, or framework.. Being in the industry for nearly 20 years, I have got a crazy amount of stuff I'm throwing around, and jumping around, and bouncing around up in there. ….

…And my biggest challenge is getting that out in a timely manner without overwhelming me, and without overwhelming other people that are around me as well."

When he first started it took a long time to get content created, taking hours to script and record each 10-minute lesson.

"Back then I was scripting out my slides, and reading them from a script instead of doing it ad-lib. And so that process was incredibly painful for me, for at least the first six to nine months in there. Now we're getting a whole lot better at it, and I'm getting a whole lot more comfortable in it, and I've got some really good frameworks that I've learnt that are helping me roll that stuff faster. But that, to me that was definitely my biggest challenge in there."

Nigel also got plenty of practice in front of the camera sending welcome videos to new members:

"I'll tell you what, I am extremely comfortable in front of a camera now after doing 250 welcome videos compared to what I was when I first started."

Creating a Mastermind

After spotting a need for greater accountability to help members implement what they are learning, Nigel created a high tier programme.

"We created this programme called Tribal Masters which is our next level up.

And it's a mixture of some accountability, some peer stuff in there, as well as coaching support from me underneath the whole thing. It's for those people that just want to dive in and go the extra level, and they need that external accountability, rather than just trying to rely on their own motivations…

...And that's more my zone of genius than creating training, because I love getting on those things and helping guys out in more of a one-to-one, or even a tiny group kind of basis."

Each new person gets a 90-minute one-to-one coaching session with Nigel, so instead of doing large group intakes, he's focused on onboarding a few new people at a time.

A Happy Folder

Nigel stores every note of feedback and thanks in a single online folder, making it easy for him to see at-a-glance the impact his business is having for his members.

"And that to me is the most amazing, fulfilling thing for the whole thing. Seeing that whatever I've created, whatever it is, is out there and getting results for people. And especially in the industry that I came from. I come from IT support. Now IT support is a pretty thankless industry. People are ringing saying, 'Hey, my stuff's broken, fix it.' They're angry, they're cranky. So coming into a business like this where I'm getting thank yous at least a couple times every single week, out of the blue... That to me is an enormous highlight. It kind of lights me up and I've got this, I call it my Happy Folder, whenever I'm having a struggle day which we all do, I would jump in there and I'll have a look. And I'll go, 'Man, this is why I do it.' I love seeing those things, which is great."

The 'Happy Folder' also helps him cope with the ups and downs of running a membership.

"I guarantee you every person that dives into this business model, it's still going to be a roller coaster. But once you learn to enjoy the ride, and notice the dips, and

have tools in place to be able to help get through those dips, like your Happy Folder, it just makes the process so much easier."

Removing Community Distractions

Although getting traction for the community on a forum rather than in a Facebook group was initially hard work, for Nigel, the productivity and focus benefits of being away from social media have been worth the effort.

"You can come in, you can do some work on your business, you can get some advice. You're not going to be distracted by all of this red button, red numbers that are sitting at the top. And you're going to be able to get back and work on your business.

...we focus very heavily on making it like a pizza shop. They come in, they get what they need, they don't get distracted by anything else, and then they can get back out. There's no advertisements in there from vendors. There's non of this red dots up in the corner trying to take their eye away from things. You come in, you get your work done, you figure out what pain points you've got, you learn a little bit about what's been said on the last couple of months, or couple of days, or couple of weeks, or however long it's been since you chimed in. Then you jump back out and you back into working on your business.

...Engagement is nowhere as good as a Facebook group...However, the quality of conversations is far better...And so those, while there is engagement issues between having an off-Facebook kind of group and having an on-Facebook kind of group, you've also got to take the bigger picture into view as to what kind of quality conversations those things are."

The old adage 'people come for the content and stay for the community' has proved true in Nigel's case.

"As most people say in a membership program people come for the content and they stay for the community. And that's pretty relevant in ours. You see a lot of people as you follow their journey when they join, they're always going into the library and downloading documents, and templates, and whatnot. But then we've got a pretty big push in getting them engaged in our private coaching section, and getting them engaged in the community. And getting them engaged and getting some help from me in different things as well as our monthly Tribal Gatherings. And that's typically what keeps the majority of people around is just giving them a vision for the future of what's coming. Making sure they've got the support around them."

The community didn't start to feel active and engaged until Tech Tribe hit 75-100 members, but now, with 250 members, there are multiple conversations happening each day.

"There's not too much, there's not too little. It's just right. The term I like to use is we're 'right-whelming' our people. We're not overwhelming them, we're not underwhelming them."

Membership Pausing

Tech Tribe members are able to pause their membership for up to 6 months, without losing entitlement to any lower price they were grandfathered in at.

"I want to say 8 to 10 people that have paused, they have come back within the 6 month period. Which, if we didn't have a pausing option, they probably would not have come back."

Nigel collects feedback on why a member wants to pause and then after six months, members are invited to unpause (if they haven't already) or cancel their membership.

To keep paused members engaged, they still receive a weekly round-up of what's gone on inside the membership.

"The paused members still get the weekly digest. But at the top of it, we've got a little bit of conditional logic that says if the member is paused, put a little note saying, 'Hey, we know you're paused. We're just going to keep sending you this just so that you can see what's happening inside the Tribe...feel free to log back in and press the resume button, and you'll be able to jump back into it.' And that means that they're still keeping weekly tabs on what's popping up, and what training we're doing and whatnot. And a couple that I have spoken to personally after they've un-paused, they've said... that's what got them back in."

Location & Time Freedom

Nigel has a small team of two helping with development and admin, plus his wife Nancy does all the accounting and bookkeeping, enabling Nigel to focus on creating content and interacting with his members.

He spends around an hour a day in the forums replying to coaching threads, and blocks out Tuesdays and Thursdays for calls with new members. The rest of the time, he's working on resources for the membership, or focusing on his investment business, or surfing.

"My plan is to grow this and to deliver excess value.... So I would say the minimum I need to put in to keep things going really well and to get the stuff rolled out is probably at least a half a day every day, so five days a week."

Nigel enjoys travelling with his family, so having the flexibility to do that is a huge motivator. As is the scaled-up impact he's been able to have for his members.

"The biggest thing for me is that location and time-independence. That is the biggest impact for me. Well two things. The location and time-independence, as well as getting into a business where I can see that my results and my output matter. And where I can see that I'm out there and there is a tribe of people out there in the world, that I've created something that's helping them do better, that's helping them have a better day, or wake up better, or do something better for their clients. Or go to sleep at night with a little less stress on their shoulders. To me, they're the two biggest things. Location and time-independence, and impact with my Tribe. And they absolutely, both of them drive me to do what I do every day."

What's Next For The Tech Tribe

Nigel's main focus is continued growth of the membership, although when it comes to member numbers he's wary of growing too big and diluting the membership benefits.

"I'd love to see it at somewhere between 500 and 750 members. I've got this vision in my head of all the content, and training, and whatever that I want in there. And a certain number of people inside the Tribal Masters, the high level programme. But my vision is it's a thriving, engaging community of people helping each other out at that point in time.

We're at 250 now, so I'm a third of the way where I see it getting to.

I don't want to go too much bigger than that. I've been in membership programmes where there's thousands of members and they just dilute, and it becomes crazy. So I see, my vision is that we get to that, maybe 750, maybe a little bit more if we could handle it."

Nigel would also like to connect with his members in-person more while he is travelling.

"Whenever I'm travelling I put on a dinner for people in that certain area. In 12 months time, once we've got 750 people, there's going to be a lot more people in local areas as I'm travelling around."

Kim Jimenez: The Business Lounge

Membership Details:

Name: The Business Lounge

Topic: Online Business

Launched: January 2017

Website: kimberleyannjimenez.com

Interview Date: July 2018

Kim Jimenez is the founder of The Business Lounge, a membership site for online business owners.

The Business Lounge helps online entrepreneurs take their idea and scale it online. It's designed for authors, and coaches, consultants, course creators, and others who deliver their products, programmes, or services on the Internet, and want to grow or scale.

"At the beginning, we kind of launched it as an experiment because, truth be told, I didn't know if a membership would work for my audience and my business."

Kim recognized there was already a lot of membership sites in this niche, and when she asked her audience, their response was not encouraging - they preferred webinars and courses over a membership option.

"Initially, I launched my one-off courses. The first launch was horrible. I mean, we barely made any sales. It was an epic failure. The kind where you lock yourself in the bathroom and cry the ugly cry, and mascara is streaming down your face…

The second and third launch did better, but it wasn't there, like the revenue wasn't enough for me to say, okay, I feel like I have a solid way of transitioning from a service based business to the online space and teaching and training. It was a lot of hard work to figure that out. I was confused and trying to figure out what I wanted to do."

It was Kim's dad who planted the idea of having a membership site, even though he's got an academic, rather than business, background.

"He was like: 'No, listen. You need recurring revenue. I think that this something that you should look into.'

Then, my husband was talking to me about the same thing. He was like: 'You know what? I think a membership site would be really good for you. You're already coaching all these people. They're asking so much of your time and energy. Why don't you just transition into a membership site?'"

Kim wasn't warm to the idea because she hadn't enjoyed the memberships she'd been a part of, and felt that a monthly payment model would diminish the value of the courses she'd created, which were selling for around $500.

Then one day, on Pinterest, Kim discovered The Membership Guys and 4 weeks later she had launched her membership site:

"I found one of your guides, so I downloaded it. And I thought, oh my gosh. These guys, all they teach is membership, so let me read a little bit more about it. I started reading the blog, listening to the podcast, and then it just kind of hit me, like, okay, there's something here. Like, I need to look at this a little bit more. I prayed about it

a lot. I'm Christian and so my faith was really important. I thought, okay, all signs are pointing in this direction. I need to at least pursue it…

…But I was also really tired of launching courses, nonstop. I felt like I was on promo-mode 24/7, or my business wasn't going to succeed. That was just not a place that I wanted to be in for the rest of the year…From the time, I think from the time I joined the membership, it took four weeks, and we launched The Business Lounge. It was like pretty fast

… I needed to figure out my revenue strategy, and I needed to make it happen, or I needed to go back to launching online courses. I was so scared of having to do that. It was like, we have 30 days, and we're going get it out whether it's perfect or not. And so, we launched with three courses, and the rest is history."

Now the membership forms the core of Kim's business. Lower tiered, standalone courses feed into the membership, and higher level courses are available once a year, but the main focus is definitely the membership.

Handling Cancellations

One of the most challenging aspects of running a membership site for Kim was accepting that people would cancel.

"I think one of the biggest challenges I had initially was getting kind of like over the whole idea that members were going to leave every month, and that it wasn't personal, and it wasn't a big deal, just people are in different places in their business. Some solutions work and some don't.

For me, it was really, really hard the first couple of months. I think the first six months, oh, my gosh. **Every time I saw a cancellation, I was like, I'm a failure** *in life…What am I doing wrong? 90% of the time, it had nothing to do with the membership, and everything to do with what was going on in their lives and in their businesses…it was very, very hard at first to get over that hurdle and not feel like a terrible person because I thought, I'm not a good marketer, I don't know what I'm doing.*

 But I think with time, you just start realising that, A, you can't control other people's decisions, and you cannot control their commitment level; B, you have to do a better job at bringing in people that actually are committed and are ready to take on a programme that's intensive…It was kind of like that transition to, 'okay, I need to let go and not freak out because I can't control what other people do.' Then, also bring in more people that are committed and are in the right mind-frame or the right mindset to join a membership site."

Being Present 24/7

Kim also initially struggled to switch off and find the balance with her working hours until her husband reminded her that she should lead by example:

"I felt guilty not being there 24/7….my husband was talking to me about this, he was like…'You're teaching other people to have online businesses and run them profitably and sustainably. So you have to lead by example…your members are looking at you and thinking, I have to be on all the time. I have to be on. I have to deliver tons of value, nonstop. If I take the weekend off, or if I shutdown at night, I'm being selfish. And so that's not a good example. You're not leading by example. They don't expect you to be on at 2:00 A.M. in the morning.'

…Of course, at least for me, understanding that balance came as a result of, wow, I'm actually doing a disservice to my members by just being on constantly. I think it also drains you and doesn't allow you to show up as the best version of yourself and truly deliver the value that they need."

A Deeper Understanding

The membership has also been valuable in the other areas of Kim's business, allowing her to understand the needs and challenges of her audience more, as well as providing a testing ground.

"Everything that we create is based on our members, and their needs, and their questions, and their challenges, and the things that we see every single day. It's great because I get to create content for the YouTube Channel, and podcasts, and the blog that's based off of problems that people are having right now. I think it makes you that much more relevant, whereas, if you have only one-off courses, or only maybe services, you're not in the trenches as much, with as many people, and so you don't get to see those trends and those challenges as much…I think that that's just amazing to be able to tap into that direct line of feedback and understand where people are at, what their challenges are, and even test and experiment inside the membership before you release them publicly, it has been invaluable to the business as a whole."

Webinar & Course Funnels

Kim uses two funnels for bringing in new members: one using webinars, the other offering low-cost courses.

In the first funnel, Facebook ads are used to bring in new cold traffic via a value-giving video. Video viewers are re-targeted with an ad offering a webinar. Then from the webinar, viewers are directed to the membership.

The other sales funnel offers an introductory level course, which then upsells to the membership, at the point of purchase, and again as part of the follow-up sequence.

"We have three courses right now that are just introductory courses, kind of like those little wins that we can give people that are going to attract them no matter what stage they are in business.

They're around social media, building an email list and creating content. Those courses are $9.00. They're very, very inexpensive. Then, we upsell them into either the membership as a full paid member, or they get a 7 to 10 day trial to test it out...just giving people a little bit of a taste of what they're going to get inside, and getting them in the website, engaging in the community, has really worked for us."

Audience Building Using Social Media

Right now Kim is active on multiple platforms, but her advice for those just starting out is to stick to one of two social media accounts.

"You don't need to be everywhere because then you're just going to be nowhere really. You're not going to be consistent. You're going to create subpar content and you're not going to build a following that actually cares about what you have to say.

In the beginning it was, for me, Facebook and YouTube. Those were the main hubs for us. I had already built a decent following on YouTube and a decent following on

Facebook, not crazy numbers, but enough to where I knew that I had a decent relationship with our followers. YouTube has always been the main social hub for us, even though it's not really social. It's more of a search engine. We love it and we get tons of members from there, Facebook, as well.

Now, we're expanding a little bit more. That's why you're seeing more of me on Instagram. We're expanding on to Instagram. We've always used Pinterest, as well, for traffic. Those are the main ones. We do Twitter, as well, but it's not as much of a focus. Now, I'm like, okay, it's Facebook, YouTube, and Instagram. But, we're not expanding more than that for now because we really want to be able to monetize the audience in an authentic way, and know that what we're doing on the platform is working, rather than just putting up content and seeing what happens."

Throughout her YouTube videos, including as ads and as part of the closing sequence, Kim makes sure The Business Lounge is promoted.

"I feel like that's one of the biggest mistakes I made the first year, was like, I wasn't telling anyone. We just kind of had it on the website, and then we were putting out all this content and never letting people know, hey, we're adding a new course, we have this awesome stuff here. It was just like a tab on the website. Now, we're trying to be more vocal about it, just telling people, hey, we have this awesome thing that's going to get you results faster, and if you'd like to check it out, here's the link."

Adding a Roadmap

To help members jump into the content and stay on-track, Kim developed a roadmap:

"One of the big things that we added last year that was totally inspired by Membership Academy, 100% giving you guys credit, is the roadmap. Just having a very, very consistent system of, how do you start, how do you launch, how do you grow it, how do you get to the place where you're able to replace your salary or your income from a different stream, and then we scale it. We have a full blown success path that really keeps people engaged."

From the moment they join, members are encouraged to join in with the community. Access to some materials is even restricted until certain milestones are met, to stop members becoming overwhelmed.

*"**The first thing that they do when they join the membership is we really bribe them to get connected and plugged into the community**. I have, literally, a bribe. It's a challenge inside of the membership where they introduce themselves in the forum, they share their goals, they update their profile, and they dive into the success path…Then, we also have benchmarks to when they're allowed to move into the next stage. At the beginning, we didn't have that, and so a lot of the members were like, where do I start? I was having to go in and manually tell people, these are the courses that you're going to take, this is the order in which you're going to take them. Now, we have a full success path. That's been so helpful."*

Managing Two Communities

Kim's members have access to both an onsite community forum and a private members-only Facebook group, each with its own distinct role.

*"Initially, we only had the Facebook group… Three months in, we launched the forum. We had the Facebook group, which was fine, **but I needed a place where I could go deeper, give people more insight.***

There's only so much you can do on a Facebook group with the tools that you have right now. Having the forum, we got a tonne of pushback at the beginning. People did not want the forum. They wanted to be where they were at, hanging on the Facebook group... **Now, those people who were pushing back at the beginning, are avid forum users.**

Our forum is where they go to really go in depth with the feedback that they receive, ask questions. *And, a lot of the members don't want to be on Facebook groups, which was very surprising to me...*

Then, the Facebook group is there for quick conversations. *I do weekly check-ins with the members to see where they're at. They share their wins, some challenges. Sometimes they ask quick questions. Then, we go live. Sometimes, we go live more for our Q&A, so I'll just go live for a minute and share something with them. They appreciate that. It's kind of like that quick and fast touch point. Also, we get to post news and updates. A lot of our members were missing out on a lot of the new stuff because they weren't opening their email. Now, we get to connect with them via Facebook in the group and share what's new...*

It's kind of an interesting dynamic, but we do have both and they work very well together, which I thought at some point I needed to close the group because the forum would suffer, but it's actually been a really nice dichotomy."

A Business That Fits

Selling one-off courses wasn't something Kim enjoyed. She disliked the constant launch cycle, and wanted to provide more ongoing coaching and support than a standalone course allowed for. Moving to a membership model reduced stress, while improving her business' financial stability.

"In terms of grounding our business and growing it financially, it's been crazy positive, in that sense. Everything we do feeds off of the membership. **It's the core of our business. It changed the game for us. It helped us to multiple six figures. I would have never been able to do that without a membership that allowed me the mental head space to not be on promo-mode, 24/7...**

...It just feels really nice to not have to stress every single day *and think about where are my sales going to come from today, where are we going to make money today. That space was very negative for me because it was extremely stressful. I don't think that you can put out the best work when you're constantly bogged down by financial pressure. The membership came right on time for us, and it made a huge impact, not just psychologically for me, and being able to grow the business, but also in terms of putting out our best work and challenging ourselves to, every single day, provide value."*

Scaling Back Content

When launching her membership, Kim put herself under too much pressure to reach perfection and pushed herself hard to create plenty of courses, something she has since changed.

*"If I could go back, I would say to younger Kim: 'Don't do it. It's not worth it and it's not serving anyone'...***If you can put out higher quality stuff that really helps your members, you don't have to make it absolutely perfect, or put it out as frequently as you think you need to in order for them not to cancel.**

Making that switch was huge for me because I was terrified. I thought the minute I don't put out a new course, members are going to leave...and it was the opposite. We grew the membership because I had the mental space to put out higher quality content and focus on other areas that didn't necessarily involve creating more, and more, and more every day."

When Kim decided to scale back on the amount of content being produced, she expected some push-back from members, but didn't get any. Having their own roadmap to follow, they were focused on what needed to be done next, and didn't need new courses.

"They were already working on certain strategies and they either were not even paying attention to the new courses, or were okay with them being delayed because they'd be like, hey, that makes sense. You are the expert. We're deferring to you. You know what we need.

That was like such an incredible, validating moment for me because I was like, okay, **I've gained their trust enough to where they know that I'm not going to let them down,** *and I'm not trying to be lazy."*

What's Next For The Business Lounge

In the next 12 months, Kim would like to add a layer of gamification to her membership, to make the content more fun to implement.

"Giving members more perks, and more bribes to encourage them to implement and reach their milestones, their goals, should be really interesting to test out."

And she'll be creating more courses, but in a more strategic way:

"That's a really big focus for us this year, is just being more strategic about the courses that we come out with, and the format of the courses, so that they're easy to consume, and really help our members implement fast."

Kim will also be creating content specifically for the many niche's of business represented in the membership:

"We have our e-commerce group, and we also have our authors and writers, and we have our bloggers, and our course creators, and our service providers. We just started a new series last month where we're creating kind of like a 101 programme for those individual niches."

Jared Falk: Musora

Membership Details:

Name: Drumeo / Guitareo / Pianote / Recordeo
Topic: Music Education
Launched: 2012
Website: musora.com
Interview Date: July 2018

Jared Falk, founder of Musora, has three, soon-to-be four, membership sites, all in different music niches.

The first and most well established of these sites is Drumeo, the world's leading site for drum education.

"It's basically like Netflix for drummers. I always use that because right away people get exactly that it's a bunch of great content from drummers for people to learn the drums. And so we work with the greatest drummers in the world and we film lesson content with them and we publish that within our platform."

For the first few years it was just Jared creating the content, which became tiring and led him to look at other options and start bringing onboard other drummers.

"I started [teaching] around 2003. I had a baseball cap and my little practice space on the farm... So for the longest time it was just me and my business partner was the tech guy. So that went til around 2006, 2007, and we hired a few other guys to do packages, like DVD packages that we sold. But it was primarily me, which got

tiring. So that's what led us to say we need to figure other ways that we can produce more content because with the internet, the larger your content footprint is, the more success you're gonna have, especially if it's high quality content."

Jared initially provided DVD based training before moving to a membership model when he started looking at how he could provide a better service.

*"I think for us, it wasn't necessarily a model where we said, "Oh we need to create a membership so we can make more money." It was never financially driven. For us, it was always about how can we provide a better service. We found that when students bought a DVD package from us, that's where the sale ended. The book Automatic Customer refers it to as a one night stand compared to a marriage, right? And we really wanted to get married to our students, and **we really wanted to be there to help them on an ongoing basis so we could answer their questions and give them the feedback when they needed it and do stuff like that.** It had to be a membership because there's no way we could charge a one-time fee unless it was incredibly high and deliver on an ongoing basis. For us, we just think it's the best model for teaching drums on the internet and for a student who wants to learn drums."*

Daily Content

On average, Jared adds an hour of content each day to Drumeo, far more than is recommended for most membership site owners.

"I'm breaking the rules. In some ways, it's way too much and people have actually left because they said I can't keep up with it. They feel like they're paying this amount of money and they're not using it, so they just leave. But in reality, anyone who tries to watch every single video would be absolutely crazy. It would take you

over four months, if you did 24 hours a day, because I think there's over 4,000 hours of content in there now."

While it may cause overwhelm for some, Jared is keen to have content to help with whatever a members struggle may be, plus he has a wealth of content available to share.

"My original idea for Drumeo was for a student to be practising , and every student, when they're practising, they have struggles within those very moments. And every single student's struggle is different…So my original idea was to have live-streaming 24 hours a day, 7 days a week, and then work with instructors all around the world, so we could hit all the time zones. That still might come at some point, but for now, we've said let's just focus on producing really, really great quality content with these amazing artists.

… And the reason it's so much is because we had so much opportunity to bring in the artists that we're not gonna say 'no'…Drummers have a spirit of sharing. They're very communal and they like to give back, and Drumeo is a conduit for them to do that."

95% of the content produced is used inside the membership, then the marketing team pick videos that they think will work well as standalone content pieces released to the public.

Attracting Top Drummers

Drummers who come in to record video lessons are paid for their time, and also appreciate the exposure offered by Jared's large online audience.

"Drummers were very used to publishing a DVD or a book and they sell that and then they get a certain percentage per sale. That's the traditional model and we did

that in the past. But there's no real way that we can say we're gonna pay you based on views... We're not gonna pay people based on how big their network is or how famous they are. We basically pay them a fee and they come in for a set amount of time, and we do it that way.

*...we have a large YouTube channel. I think we have one of the most engaged Facebook pages. Our organic reach on Facebook is incredible. Also on Instagram, we have a heavily engaged network there. **So the artists love the way we cut up the content and promote it and always make sure we tag them. They get a lot of residual benefits from the stuff that they do, and I think they really appreciate that.***"

Expanding Into New Markets

Jared recognises that as an early entrant in the drumming market Drumeo had a head start. Now his newer memberships Guitareo and Pianote are competing in a much more crowded online space, he needs to use a different approach to penetrate each niche, whilst also recognising that the culture among different instrument players also varies.

"The piano market is completely different from the drum market. Piano players... There's a different social culture there...You can't talk in the same tone. You can't even teach in the same way. Piano is way more traditional...

The guitar market is also completely different than the drum market. Guitarists don't like to share everything about what they're doing.

...Pianote started two years ago and it's a completely different world out there. There's way more people trying to create membership sites and trying to sell info-products, right?

You have to do different things to cut through the noise.

...Guitar is a much bigger market. There's way more people doing it and we're again late to the party there, so we have to do things differently..."

World Domination

Jared's music empire already spans 10,000+ active members in Drumeo alone, and he has a support team of 35 people, with big plans to span multiple niches around the world.

"The goal is to have something for every musician and even go deeper into the arts, like teaching painting or teaching dance or teaching photography or anything like that. So the platform we're building will be able to power all those different communities as well as moving into other languages, right? So I wanna create Drumeo in China, which is going to be entirely its own platform that we can provide support on....

*... It's all about world domination. **Why not think big?** I know it's sometimes crazy or sounds ridiculous or silly because there's so many other great companies and great other people doing stuff in this space, but I finally got to the point where it's like why not me? Why not us? Why not you? Why should it have to be someone else? I think if you just have that mindset, then we're gonna at least try. I'm not gonna guarantee that I'm going to do it, but I'm going to try.*

...When I started, I just wanted to pay my mortgage. I just wanted to be able to drive a nicer car than a 1985 Nissan pickup truck. I think the goals, the short term and long term goals, changed over time and when you have some smaller or medium sized wins, those are things that are going to inspire you to then create those larger goals."

Keeping 10,000+ Members Engaged

Jared acknowledges it can be challenging to keep his audience on-track, when they're used to quick wins and instant rewards, via video games like Guitar Hero. The key for Jared is taking the focus off delivering instructional information, and instead inspiring action, and providing enough entertainment value, that even when members take a break from practising, they stick around to enjoy consuming the content.

"...the biggest challenge is keeping people engaged and inspired to really want to learn. I think everyone loves music. No one falls out of love with music, but sometimes people get excited about learning an instrument and then decide it's not for me and then they quit.

...The music business overall is changing, right? Guitar sales are down because more things are going electronic. Less people are starting to play guitar because the barrier to entry, to get actually good at guitar, is harder than people think. Whereas getting really good at video games is a lot easier. So more people are just playing video games...

...We have to somehow inspire them through this digital interaction to take a physical real world action. That's actually really challenging when you think about

it. Video games do it well. Even though it's sometimes just with people's thumbs,
but the Rock Band and Guitar Hero stuff is good. **So our goal for each lesson is**
for someone to watch it, have a deep understanding of the concept that they
could just go to their kit and play it. Or go to their guitar and just instantly
get results. If we've done that, then we've succeeded...

... we're working on more educational content that's wrapped in
entertainment...really cool videos that are super entertaining, but also have
that element of education...The goal is, even if a student stops practising, they
can still get a lot of value out of Drumeo just through the content."

Bundling Physical Products

Jared realises that his audience can have difficulty understanding the
cost/value of digital products like a membership, and has found that
combining the membership with a relevant physical product has been
effective for tackling that and increasing sales.

"A lot of times people still have trouble seeing the perception of value for digital
products or a membership which essentially lives in the cloud. Nothing they can
touch or feel. It's hard for them to wrap their heads around that, especially if it's a
$200 a year membership like ours.

So we've got the exclusive license on this practice pad, which is something
drummers use to practice on, and we bundle that with an annual membership, and
that moves the needle enough for students to try it...In guitar, we're doing strings,
so if you sign up for Guitareo, you'll get, I forget what it is, it's like a box of strings
and we work directly with D'Addario, which is the largest string manufacturer in
the world."

Offering a physical product alongside just the annual membership is also one way that Jared stacks the odds in favour of annual signups, although he does offer a monthly option despite disliking it.

"I don't like the monthly. I always tell my marketing team, get rid of the monthly. I don't want it. Just get rid of it. If someone doesn't want to commit for three plus months, then they're not gonna see a result. Like how are you going to sign up for a month to learn drums and get a decent result to where you're happy about your progress. It's very, very difficult."

Targeted Sales Pages

In order to really talk to certain segments of his audience and increase conversions, as well as increase traffic from search, Jared has created certain 'sub pages' that act as sales pages for particular topics and problems people may have.

"A lot of our best results come from search marketing. People are trying to solve a problem, so they search for a solution on Google or wherever, and we want them to find that exact page that they're looking for. So if they search 'beginner drum lessons', they land on a page that says the 'best beginner drum lessons from the best drummers in the world', it's really hard to say, 'oh this isn't what I was looking for'. This is pretty much what they're looking for, right?

*We do that with a few other styles too. If someone's searching jazz or if someone's searching rock…**we created these sub pages, which are essentially different iterations of the sales page that speak to whatever they're searching for.**"*

Learning to Lead

Jared has a sizeable team of 35 people, most of which work locally in his substantial office space. The office also contains the recording studios used for content production.

"I think it's like 6000 square feet, around that. And we're adding another 2000 or 3000 square feet. We don't have a board room because we have two studios, so all of our big rooms are used. We're gonna get a board room and a different office and more communal work rooms. We're putting in a gym so people can exercise because we just sit here all day. So everyone's here for the most part…We're fairly flexible with our schedule and stuff like that. It's a really cool team."

Having his team onsite means that a lot of Jared's time is spent in meetings with various team members, and it also means that they are able to discuss and implement ideas quickly.

"So a lot of what I do is the new ideas and when it comes to what products we're doing and that. Then I'll meet with each individual department. So the marketing meetings. I have development meetings. I have production meetings. And then I have any sort of administrative, financial, or customer support meetings.

So my day is mostly spent up creating new products and services, or scoping out new ideas. Doing new research. And then meeting with all the different departments to make sure everyone's on track, and that happens weekly."

With the size of the business and team, Jared has also had to step into the role of a leader, something that he's found is a constant, but enjoyable, process.

"I know it was a deficiency that I needed to work on, and so it's something that I really enjoy getting better at something like that. But it's always a process. You're never done learning about becoming a better leader. It's like drumming. The more you know, the more you don't know. That's what I found with leadership. You think you're good and then you listen to a podcast or you read a book and you realise how much you suck at it or how many things you're screwing up on. But yeah I really enjoy that process of becoming a leader and seeing the strategies and tactics that I deploy actually have some sort of positive effect."

It's Not a Lifestyle Business

While many people start a membership site in order to work less and create a lifestyle business, this is not Jared's goal.

"Naturally I just really want to work hard and I'm not looking for a lifestyle business. I'm looking to create something big. For me, it all comes down to my personal goals. I like working every day. I like doing something every day. I grew up on a farm and I collected eggs every day since I was five or six years old...That's just the way I'm wired. I'm 36 and I planning on working another 20 or 30 years. I like hanging out with cool people every day...I still work hard. If anything I work harder than I would. I think I'd be a terrible employee. I'd probably be lazy, especially if I don't believe in what we're selling.

So the fact that I get to do this, I'm extremely grateful. I think anyone who runs a website like this, whether you do it because you want to create something big, or whether you've just created the perfect lifestyle for yourself, it can offer both of those things, right? And that's what's so cool about the internet and that's what's so cool about the membership model. I think everyone needs to just be very, very grateful.

I watch other marketing videos selling membership model and they're saying it's the perfect lifestyle. You don't have to do anything. They make it seem like you don't have to do anything and just sit around on your ass all day, right? It's not like that. You gotta work hard. You have to try and be smart. You have to be constantly learning. One of our mottos is you keep pushing. You never stop. Regardless of how bad or how good it is. Never take your foot off the gas and just keep working hard."

What's Next For Musora

Jared has invested heavily in building a custom platform that will allow him to run his entire business from one hub, better enabling him to scale as they venture into even more markets, including international partnerships.

"We're building that platform so we can scale and we'll basically be able to run everything from customer support, processing transactions, user management system, all the social features. Everything from one hub under Musora, and we'll be able to publish new content from there. It's a full blown CMS as well. So the idea there is to then take Drumeo to China. I have a meeting coming up with a guy who's coming to Vancouver from China to talk specifically about that. That market is absolutely massive and they love the Drumeo content. So language is our big thing…we need to make sure that we partner with someone who can actually provide the service. So when a drummer has a question, they can talk to them in their language… So I don't know if it's like a franchise or a brand licencing thing. I'm just figuring it out as I go."

Creating an app for a better mobile experiences is also high on the priority list.

"Another thing is we don't have an app right now. Everything's mobile friendly and really easy to use on iPads or iPhones, but not as good as it could be, so we want to create native experiences on IOS and Android and then all tablets. So that's the next thing. But the reason we built the platform is so we can create one framework for an app and then deploy it over all markets. So those are the two biggest things is new markets like home recording and different languages, and then becoming more omnipresent with how we're actually publishing and where we're publishing our content."

Mike Collins: The Green Room

Membership Details:

Name: The Green Room

Topic: Irish Heritage

Launched: February 2014

Website: youririshheritage.com

Interview Date: May 2019

Mike Collins from Your Irish Heritage, runs The Green Room, a membership site dedicated to Irish ancestry, alongside his wife Carina.

Mike and Carina are based in Ireland, and their membership site is targeted at the 80 million people of Irish ancestry around the world, helping them create a deeper connection with their Irish heritage.

The business started with a weekly newsletter sent out every Sunday, focused on different surnames, which eventually became a book.

Mike started to see the potential to make money when his newsletter audience reached 1,000-2,000 many of whom were replying to Mike with stories of their own ancestry.

"...So we started to do things like selling t-shirts.... which didn't quite work out.

I think it was around about that time Michael Hyatt started his first membership. I remember looking at that thinking, 'Well that's interesting, and that's kind of well laid out, and that looks good...how do we do that ourselves?'"

Mike launched with around 100 members, offering training, and research into family trees in a similar style to the popular BBC TV program, Who Do You Think You Are.

"...it's kind of hard to figure out exactly how we got started, but the attraction certainly was recurring revenue, plus looking at models elsewhere of how it could be done."

Mike likens the membership site to entertainment rather than genealogy research, although they do now have two genealogists on the team, his focus is on bringing stories to life.

"At this stage we have about 26,000 photographs, we have about 1,500 videos. You know so we have a lot of material, and we're essentially I would say a media company... we take advantage of that in actually looking up people's ancestry"

One of the most popular elements of his membership site has been a member spotlight feature, when Mike and Corina research the family of one of the members, visiting places relevant to their family tree.

"We realised from an early time that, if we want to offer people something above and beyond what they get in a place like Ancestry.com in terms of records and so on, we have to bring the whole thing to life.

... So we started early on to literally go knocking on doors, driving into farms, you know, taking down a bit of stone and shipping it back to Australia. So doing all kinds of weird things like that."

Mike and Carina have spent the last couple of years travelling around the world, creating content for their membership site, and to put out as free content.

"And I suppose about two years ago then, we figured out, you know what? We have about four-and-a-half, five million people in Ireland, but there's roundabout 80 million people of Irish ancestry around the world.

So with that, we started to actually travel to the places that folks migrated to as well. So we did a tour of Canada, we did a tour of the North-East U.S. we did a tour of Australia last year, UK, and so on, so forth.

...people want to see the pictures, they want to see moving pictures with people and real life people, they want to hear the accents. So we kind of need to go to all of the places where those things happen.

...our strapline early on was, 'Bring your Irish ancestry to life'...that was kind of the piece I guess the people were feeling they were missing as I said with joining Ancestry and so on."

Lifetime Memberships

Mike focuses on quarterly ($47) and annual ($147) memberships, although he does offer a higher priced monthly ($20) membership option too. Something he's found works well for his audience though is occasionally running lifetime membership offers.

"We also offer 20 per month if people still want that, but you know, that's kind of a high price, just to discourage some people really, or transfer them upwards."

A surprising source of income has been from people buying lifetime memberships not because they want to use the site, but because they want to support the production of Mike's high-quality publicly available content.

"We have an unusual situation when it comes to lifetime because what we do is not really that practical to a lot of people, it's not like a utility they need, kind of get from A to B, or to get kind of a job done.

So early on, we essentially figured out, we published a book, we publish a weekly letter, and we turned it into a business. But you know, people just like digesting books and letters, and not kind of thinking about, "Well, how useful is this to me?" So what we noticed earlier on was that we actually had to offer people, if you like, membership of the Green Room, but some of them let's say bought a lifetime membership and never logged on. We said, 'Well what's going on?' to them. And they said, 'Well I just want to support you.' "

At the same time, Mike recognises there is a large proportion of his audience that are only there for the free content and don't seem likely to ever buy.

His email list is currently at around 30,000 people, and the membership currently has around 2,000 active members.

"...it's a constant challenge for us to figure out ways not to run ourselves into the ground offering lots and lots of free stuff...I realise that we'll only ever convert maybe five or six percent of our list into being members. Well, what are we going to do with the other 95%, you know? We're still trying to get our heads around that, five or six years later."

Organisational Challenges

For Mike, the biggest challenge has been organising the materials and hiring in help so he can take a step back and have the membership work well without him.

"...the biggest challenge has been making it more self service for people, so it's just not relying on us...I mean, I haven't had what you would call a holiday in about six years, however, I've built all the travelling and holidays into our work, if that makes sense. So the biggest challenge certainly has been kind of downtime, turning off."

When it comes to hiring Mike's discovered through experience, someone can be great at the interview but not work out in the community forum, and other people can perform less well in person, but be engaging and personable online.

"I would personally say that two or three of the people we've had, you wouldn't necessarily say, if you met them in person, that they will be so good online, and so good, and so personable, and so expert, and so competent. But so you know, just uncovering those diamonds has been a learning process as well."

Meaningful Work

Running the membership offers Mike the opportunity to do work he loves, that has meaning to other people, while enjoying time and travel flexibility and the stability of recurring income.

"... we're doing something very meaningful for a lot of people. Surprisingly meaningful, and they let you know.

... it has that level of meaning for more people than I ever realised. And I don't mean it in a kind of, yeah, as soon as we remove it, their lives are going to be empty kind of way. But what I do mean is it just touches on something, which I think is surprising to a lot of us. You know, where people's identity comes to the fore, as opposed to just their skills and so on, but this is who I am, and this is what makes me who I am."

Self employment isn't new to Mike, but the membership model and recurring revenue has meant he's been able to move away from the time for money trap. If he didn't find it meaningful though he doesn't think he would have stuck with it this long.

"I've been self employed for about 25 years now, and a lot of that has been the sort of work where you kind of reset your time every morning and you go out and you hunt the buffalo so to speak and bring back the carcass.

So you know, this recurring revenue, and the ability to build a community, and to be doing something that's so meaningful to a lot of people has been kind of probably the best combination for us.

...if we weren't doing something that was interesting to us and meaningful to other people, I don't think I'd be able to, I wouldn't have lasted this long quite frankly."

Offers & Bonuses

Mike's weekly newsletter, A Letter From Ireland, attracts between 25 and 50 new people every day. Offering bonuses to this audience has been converting well recently, and is something that Mike is keen to continue doing more of, rather than discounting.

"...our membership tends towards... age 45 and up, and they tend to be quite careful with their money...so we do have to make offers, and we do have to include bonuses three to five times a year, and that really shakes people out the trees. We sell into the list then at that point.

...The real game changer for us recently has been bonuses, and making it something that people really want...[at] one level, we'll feature you in a letter, that's the weekly one. The other one then is we do a surname report. So you know, give us one of your ancestors and give us a name, and we'll give you a private report on that, which we can share on our free site, but also inside of the Green Room as well.

... I really, really do believe bonuses are the way forward, and we have to think up a few more bonuses that don't affect us so much, that people still want.

In future Mike would like to build more automation into his sales funnel as well as fine tune his sales pitch in order to get a steady stream of new members.

"...we're woefully behind on automating, on getting our sales pitch so it really hits people with a sense of, 'I want this, and I want this now.'... there's an awful lot of tuning up to be done around the place, which I'm very conscious of every day...we are doing some things right, but we would like to kind of get that more continual drip, if you like, into The Green Room, rather than just kind of dealing with 100 people coming to the door at once."

Encouraging Engagement

Mike's niche lends itself to good retention because people are used to working on their family trees over multiple years, so churn is at just 3-5%.

"But what we kind of notice then is that, and honestly, we try to kind of run with the things that are really running, and the members that are really running, and really kind of crank them up. When people are kind of falling by the wayside, well we don't get too upset by that quite frankly, we kind of say, "Well you know what? You can encourage people some of the way, and they have to meet you halfway as well."

Mike keeps people engaged with weekly updates telling them what's new, through short-term challenge events, in-person meet-ups, and a bi-monhtly magazine.
A huge part of the membership is the community and the connections created there:

"... we had to stand back quite a bit, just let people connect with each other.

So the community basically has become probably the biggest part of what we do... it's amazing to see the friendships that have built up over the years where people in Australia are visiting people in the U.S."

A fairly unique feature of The Green Room is that it offers tiered levels in the community, based on engagement. This includes a final 'hidden level' that the members don't know about until they achieve it, something that works well for retention.

"Inside we actually have different membership levels that people actually go up as they actually answer people more and so on.

They eventually get into this level they didn't know exists, which gets them into an inner circle, which gets them all really excited and interested...think of an apprenticeship. If you went and you did apprentice to be a poet, or a mechanic, or whatever, there's seven or eight different levels, so people actually advance up through that, you know?"

Mike has introduced an innovative feature to encourage new members to engage with the community, while also making it more useful in the long term.

"When you put your introduction in, we use a tagging system, so we tag your surnames. As soon as you introduce yourself and mention what surnames are in your family tree, you can hit on a tag and see all the posts from all the other people who also share those surnames...

...And then as you go around, inside the community, you can actually see somebody's ancestry tree, by clicking on it and you can also see the surnames in their family....

...and it's a navigation system then through the content too...if you click on either a place, a county or a surname, you can pull up all this relevant material and spend time going through it."

Re-purposing Content

Mike and Carina recently began publishing a bi-monthly magazine online, utilising content they're already creating for their members. While it's designed for members, it also acts a marketing tool and members are encouraged to share it freely.

"Just last December we started a bi-monthly magazine. That's been an eye opener... we're very visual in what we do, we've a lot of photographs, we have a big community, people want to see who is in the community.

*We have a lot of features that can go into magazine kind of format, because they're already made. **So we tend to use it as an actual way of focusing on what we have already, rather than actually coming up with new features**...I'd love to actually have a print magazine in time... at the moment, so it's built in Canva, it's downloaded as PDF, and it's roughly about 30 pages long. And people love it, you know. **It's available free as well, so we encourage people to spread it to other people. But if you click on the various links at the bottom, it brings you into the Green Room, if you're a member, or indeed, it brings you to the sales page, if you're not a member.***

So that's worked very well. We're quite happy with that."

Events With A Difference

Mike does enjoy connecting with his members in-person, but he's not a fan of sitting still, so instead of a member conference he and Carina arrange a multi-day experience.

"We bring about 38 people from all around the world to a place in Ireland...it's a moving story basically, because it typically starts off somewhere, and ends up somewhere else three days later.

So the last one, we started off in the middle of a stone circle in the middle of rural Ireland, with a druid facilitating a ceremony. We went through all the few hundred years from prehistoric times to the mid 1800s. Then we went to a place called The Queenstown Cove and we emigrated on a boat. So that was over about four or five days.

*... but the thing we didn't anticipate was how good it was meeting people in person and for other people to meet other people in person. **The bonding, and the electricity that came out of that and into the forum was actually quite phenomenal**, it really was.*

So I suppose as a result of that we decided to travel around the various countries and actually hold the conference every year- or-two as well. Yeah, so our next one is next month."

Mike encourages any membership site owner to start running some kind of events to allow members to connect with each other, and you, more deeply.

".I would encourage anybody if you've an opportunity at all, go have a conference, give people an excuse to come and meet all the members. It's not all about yourself, but what you can facilitate is actually magical, you know? Because people really will bring it back in spades, back into your forum again afterwards. You know, that connection, that sense of excitement. And suddenly realise we're all three dimensional beings, we're not just these kind of two dimensional online avatars."

Building A Team to Facilitate Growth

A small core of experts help run the membership, including a genealogist based in Belfast, who runs a section of the forum called Ask The Genealogist, a genealogist in the U.S. and a community moderator.

Mike can see the potential to grow the business, but first needs to figure out how to make the business less dependent on him.

"I think we've room to expand to double our size at the moment, double turnover, double whatever you want to call it. At that stage then I want to kind of move sideways into a few other bits. I need to start to replace myself an awful lot more...

...the decision we made strategically, was that we'd start doing an awful lot more lecture tours around the world. So up to now it's been book a flight, go somewhere, meet our members, have a meet up in a local pub. But now... let's arrange to be part of a conference or a special lecture in Boston for example, where people have to buy a ticket and there's a hundred people, because there's an awful lot more value put into that, and extra people tend to come along, they start to spread the word and the same person will pick up books, etc.

So to free myself up to do that, we need to kind of backfill I suppose an awful lot more, but that's a kind of a hard one, **because I think we've made a mistake, like many mistakes, of building the membership site depending upon our very peculiar skills***...*

... we've just kind of crafted everything just to suit ourselves. ...And it's no wonder another person has a problem...or we're having trouble let's say trusting another person to kind of do it just like that."

Survival

Mike's key advice to new membership site owners is to have patience, persist and keep going. And realise it will probably take more time and help to succeed than you think.

"I heard something just recently, which I thought was really, really good. It was, you need to be able to survive long enough to make all your early mistakes. You know, I think survival is very underrated actually, and it's the flip side of persistence, and realising - this stuff takes longer than you think. You're going to need the help of more people than you think. It's going to take way, way more time on a daily basis than you ever, ever, ever could imagine.

So therefore, make sure you're choosing something that you have an affinity with, and perhaps the change you want to see in the world."

Mike also encourages new businesses to start selling as soon as possible.

"In the early days we were part of a startup accelerator. The most noticeable thing in that accelerator with the other 15 companies was nobody was selling except us. It was interesting, because everybody's paying attention to the big stories about how the millions are going to be made eventually by the companies who weren't selling, and we were kind of the poor mice, if you like, because we were selling, and because the income was actually, what's the word, so small at the time, it was kind of being kind of looked down on a little bit.

But really, what was happening was we were truly experimenting because we were selling and truly learning because we were selling. So it's not about bringing the money in, it's about actually learning because you're selling as opposed to anything else.

So I would say, you know, sell early, not to get the money in, although that's good, but to actually learn what works and what doesn't. As soon as you make an offer to people, see how they respond. If they don't respond, well you know you need to change it, you know?"

What's Next For The Green Room

As well as doubling the size of the business, Mike is looking to expand and move from The Green Room being everything they do to just a portion of it, although he's not quite sure what that will look like yet.

"…I think over the next two years, we're going to have to make a few decisions and I suppose make the Green Room a portion of what we do, as opposed to everything we do. We're not quite sure how we get it there, but I'd like to think it's probably going to be about a third, thereabouts, of what we do, because you know, we've hit upon this kind of baby boomer kind of thing if you like where they're the folks we're going after. They know what we're up to and how we're up to, and there's a lot of people out there trying to reach that same audience.

We've decided not to do any advertising, not to engage with that, but to do everything to suit our actual membership and our direct audience. So we still have to figure out how to make that work as we go forward. So I think we're kind of an early startup. I think I'd like to double the business in size. That'll happen over the next 18 months-or-so. As I said, I'd like to see the Green Room become probably kind of one leg in a three legged stool after that."

Louise Brogan: Social Bee NI

Membership Details:

Name: Social Bee Academy

Topic: Social Media & Online Marketing

Launched: January 2018

Website: socialbeeacademy.com

Interview Date: May 2019

Louise Brogan from Social Bee NI runs the Social Bee Academy a membership for people who want to raise their visibility online through social media and online marketing.

Louise started her membership site because she wanted flexibility around her working hours and to continue to have an income even in the school holidays when she was unable to do in-person workshops.

"I have three kids, so they are 13, 11 and nine, and I created this business so that I could work around them being at school. I thought that having the membership just seems like such a good option for somebody who wants to have more flexible working, but also to have a recurring revenue stream in the school holidays and Easter holidays and Christmas, unless I'm paying somebody to look after my kids...I do workshops all over Northern Ireland, in person workshops, so I can't necessarily do those as much during those school holiday periods, and neither do I want to. Having my business online really works for me, and having the membership...the membership is just a really good business model I think for someone who's in my situation."

Louise was originally running online courses, then moved that content into her membership. After starting out using open-closed launch cycles, she switched to an evergreen model, which better suited her and her audience.

"I started out in the sell a course space and moved into the membership space.

The first course I created was called Facebook for Business, and that entire course is now inside my membership...there's literally an entire course on Facebook in there, and that's just one example of the kind of content that's in there...

...I tried it with the open and close cart initially, and you try and test all these different things and see what works, don't you? When I did open and close cart, it was almost like it was such a massive thing to try and launch it, and I was like, 'Where am I finding the time in my life to do this launch?'...

...I realised that by having a closed membership, you're really blocking yourself a little bit there. People come to you at different times through the year...if someone comes and meets me, or comes to a webinar I'm running... it just seems to work better for me that way [doors open] than closing a couple of times a year."

The Academy is available at two tiers, with the standard tier priced at £30, and the VIP level at £99 per month.

"I have people who want to work with me a little bit more one-to-one but don't necessarily want to book a one off strategy session. So, the VIP, I actually call it VIBs, it's £99, and they get access to all of the membership and the coaching and the expert webinars and everything, but they also get a one-to-one call with me every month for half an hour.

I really like that because you can see your progress with people when you're talking to them every single month and their business as well."

The Academy includes members from all over the world, although around ⅓ are from Northern Ireland (as is Louise), possibly due to the public speaking she has done through her connection with Facebook's She Means Business program.

"It's not supposed to be local at all…but I think the fact that people here know me more, on my email, I have over 2,000 people on my email list, and I would say a good third of them are from Northern Ireland, so it's just numbers."

Balancing Act

Louise has found it a challenge to balance her membership alongside her other revenue streams and she feels that with more time and energy focused on the membership, it has the potential to grow significantly.

"I have too many revenue streams in my business. I recognise that. I really see the potential in the membership, and I want to give it my focus for the second half of 2019 because when I look at retention rates, people stay. They get really good value out of it and they stay, so I don't have a lot of people who leave it, but it's not maybe growing as much as I can see it has potential to.

One of the things I've been trying recently is running webinars. I want to properly spend some time developing out that funnel, if you like, because when people sign up to my webinars, they really see that I know what I'm talking about, and then they join the membership as a result.

But because I'm doing local training, local workshops, talking at local networking

events, it's hard to find a consistent time for putting that webinar into my diary."

Positive Impact

For Louise, the best thing about running a membership is knowing she's made a positive impact on her members.

"I'm hosting a conference here in Northern Ireland at the end of May, and there's a lady coming on stage called Barbara, she is an estate agent in Northern Ireland. After joining my membership...she started making these really fabulous little videos and stuff for Facebook. She got shortlisted for the marketer of the year in the estate agents awards of Northern Ireland, and she said it was completely down to the help I'd given her.

Things like that, you just think, 'that's just everything this is meant to be.' You know? I love, love, the live calls and connecting with the members and being in the community. It's just I really, really enjoy helping people with their business.

I think a lot of my audience as well, people come to me and say, 'I just don't know how to use this social media.' There's a real fear of going and putting yourself out there a little bit, a bit of your personality out on social media. I like to think that what I help people with also is getting over the fear of doing that as well."

One to One Conversions

Louise has successfully recruited a number of new members through in-person events or online one-to-one interactions.

"I went out and did 13 local networking events, and at each of those I spoke to people about my membership, and I pretty much got members signing up from every event...Maybe one or two from each event..."

...I don't send out cold messages about my membership, but if somebody sends me a message or a query... so, I might get a message through Facebook messenger asking me, "When are you holding your next workshop?" Or whatever. I'll say, "It's not until da, da, da, but did you know that I have this membership to try out?" That kind of idea as well, and LinkedIn messenger works as well. Not so sure about Instagram messenger actually converting into any sales for me in any part of my business. But yeah, I think LinkedIn messenger and Facebook messenger, connecting those ways with people works well."

For Louise, once people connect with her one to one, whether at an event or online via messenger, they're far more likely to join the membership, so discovery calls are something she may test in the future.

"Connecting with people one to one, meeting people in person they realise they you know what you're talking about...meeting at events, meeting at network events or I'm talking at something and someone comes up and talks to me afterwards, but also through messenger. Interestingly, I haven't really done the discovery calls for the membership, so that might be something to explore as well. I don't know. I suppose part of me thinks where do I find the time for that. But if it was a strategy... you have to try and test everything out, don't you? Different strategies, if they work then you do them more."

Online Summits

Louise also runs free online summits to drive people towards her membership site, making the summit content only available in the membership after the summit is over.

"Another strategy that I have is I run two online summits. I've had quite big names in those summits, so people like Carol Cox and Kate Ericson have both been on my summits and given really amazing value. I've dripped that content into my membership. The quality of the training in there from other people as well as my own I think is high."

High Touch

Louise makes herself very available to her members in her Facebook group, which serves as a social media news hub, and she also provides them with high-quality content through recorded tutorials.

"I'm very clear with my members that they can ask me whatever they want whenever they want. We have our communities and a Facebook group, which works for me and it works for my members. They pop questions in there all the time. In fact, interestingly, **sometimes they send me a private message about the question and I say, 'Do you mind putting that in the group so everyone can benefit from that?'** *So, the Facebook group is active, and people ask questions in there."*

Louise's collaboration with Facebook means she is often among the first to know about new developments on the platform, which she feeds back to her members via the Facebook group, giving them the 'inside scoop'.

*"I'm in a Facebook business group that Facebook invited me into. They share stuff with us there like brand new things and trainings that I can then share into my group as well. Also, if there's breaking news on one of the social media platforms, I will share that into my group as well. **It's a source of what's happening right now and what's the latest news and what do we all think about this?** For someone who teaches social media, that does not mean that I am Facebook's biggest fan either. You know? I'm quite happy to be... critical is not the right word, but to be honest about what I think about some of the things that go on within the social media industry as well."*

Finally, Louise keeps tabs on her members via their social media activity, and interacts with their content to let them know she's there for them (even the ones who don't tend to engage with the membership community).

"There are some people who are in the membership, and I'm sure it's the same with the Membership Academy, who never, never come to a live call and never comment in the group. Sometimes you forget they're there....

...I try and follow my members on their social media, so if I see they're posting, I will comment on them...I keep tabs on what they're all up to."

Content Planning

Louise creates regular fresh content for her members, but tends to be guided by what they need, and the latest industry developments, rather than planning too far ahead.

"...people will raise questions about things, so I'm more inclined to create training for the next month... But then if something major happens, because you never really know with social media... then obviously that would need to be my focus."

Guest experts need to be planned further out, but Louise's level of expertise makes creating the new monthly content relatively straightforward.

"I have to be organised... I have my guest experts lined up for the next five months and they're booked in the calendar, so those are set in stone.

Creating the content itself doesn't take me a huge amount of time...I know my content and my topic so well...it's just being organised and making sure I block out time in the calendar to give that focus to the membership."

Commitment & Passion

Commitment to the project, passion for the subject area, and a joy of interacting with others are all attributes Louise sees as essential in a membership site owner.

"I think it is quite a lot of work. It is quite a lot of work. You've got to be committed to producing every month.

*And I think you've got to like people as well, because **I think the reason why my retention rate is so good is because members know that I like them. I like connecting with them and communicating with them.***

*So, **if you're thinking about starting your own membership, you've got to understand that it does take time and effort. You have got to show up every month**. You can't just think, 'Well, I'm going to produce 50 webinars, stick them in a membership and charge people a fee and then not really do anything with them after that,' and having the community is really important.*

So, it's not for everybody. I don't think it is for everybody.

...find something that you know really well that you can help people with and be able to produce enough content to keep it going month after month."

What's Next For Social Bee Academy

Louise knows that she needs to dedicate more time to her membership site in order for it to reach its full potential in terms of growth, so this is something she now intends to focus on, with the aim of making the membership her main income stream.

"In 12 months time, I would like to at least have doubled my membership. To me, there's so much potential in it that I could see this being my main, if not solo revenue stream. It's just me making the time to give it the space it needs to grow.

Also reaching more people and helping more people as well...becoming, a much bigger audience that can help more people and have people just connecting with each other as well from all over the place. I love that concept for it."

Melissa West: Yoga with Melissa

Membership Details:

Name: Yoga with Melissa

Topic: Yoga

Launched: November 2011

Website: melissawest.com

Interview Date: May 2019

Dr. Melissa West started her yoga membership eight years ago, after being an early content creator on YouTube.

Melissa began teaching yoga in 2003, teaching 10 classes a week, alongside offering Thai massage, and yoga therapy during the day.

"I would get up at 6:00 in the morning, practise my yoga. I would teach a morning class or two, then I would come home and I would see Thai massage clients, and yoga therapy clients, and then I would go out again at night and teach more yoga, and I'd get home at 10:00 at night, and do the whole thing again.

So, it doesn't take long for that to become a recipe for burnout, which happened to me. I got a migraine. It didn't go away. So, I had to give the whole thing up and come up with another idea."

Melissa had started filming and uploading her classes to YouTube, and inspired by the Freedom Ocean podcast by Tim Reid and James Schramko, she settled on the membership community business model.

"In 2009, we had started filming my classes for YouTube because people loved my classes. They were themed. So, if they missed them, they felt like they really missed out, but I'm pretty creative, so I was always coming up with new ideas for my classes.

So, we started filming them, putting them on YouTube. We realised that we needed a business model behind it because we weren't making any money on YouTube...I was like, "Okay. I need to figure out how to make some money doing this."

*The membership community made the most sense to me. **It was something that I felt like I wanted to continually contribute, and build and connect with a community of people that were connecting with me on YouTube.** So, I felt like that was something that I could do. So, in November of 2011, we opened our community."*

The membership model gave Melissa and her husband Tim the flexibility to move from Toronto to Vancouver Island, and a couple of years later Tim started working full-time in the business. While Tim handles customer service Melissa is freed up to focus on her community.

Letting Go of Difficult Members

In the earlier stages of her membership, Melissa found herself spending too much time and energy on just a few members. When she learned to shift her focus on members making the most positive impact on the community, her membership flourished.

"One of the things that I found would be a big challenge for me for a long time in the community was that the people that weren't contributing to my community in a positive way were taking up a lot of my time.

So, people that were complaining, are having problems, they were just a big time suck. I wanted to be spending my time with our A-team members, the ones that were contributing and giving a lot to our community...

....now, I recognise when those things come up in our community, it's like, 'Okay. Hold on a second. Is this a person that's contributing in a really positive way in my community? Are they one of my A-team? Are they making a big difference in our community or is this just somebody that's draining my time?' I can usually very quickly see if I need to put a lot of time into the situation. That's been a huge learning curve for me....

...As soon as I did that, our community, it flourished because you can spend a lot of time with people that aren't really making a difference in your community...

I'll be the first person to tell you that the most important thing to me in our membership community is community. It's the people. Also, the most important thing that I learned is to let go of people."

Creating Success On Sub-Optimal Tech

For the first few years, Melissa's membership and community was run on vBulletin, a forum solution neither she nor her members were fond of.

"We're a yoga community, but that site, that option, was put together by techy nerds. Our people hated it. They hated it with passion for all the years we used it. So, it was desperately in need of revamping. So, when we found you [Membership Academy], when we saw what you guys were running, we're like, 'Okay. We want that.' We just completely copied what you were using because it looked good and it ran like social media sites."

It's a testament to the community that she built that even with the tech being less than optimal and not what she, or her members, wanted she was able to build a successful membership that stood the test of time anyway.

"I think that speaks to the philosophy behind our whole membership, which is that we're about community. I'm always asking myself, 'What can we do together?' So, even though we had this total garbage platform that everybody hated, we are always doing things together. So, in our community, we have something called the Daily Yoga Connection. We have monthly themes…

So, everybody is practicing the same class everyday. They're talking about how it for them. Our guardian of the community makes sure that everybody gets a response and acknowledgement, 'Woohoo! You practised today. That's awesome.' That's one of the ways that we're doing things together everyday. That's a very community-oriented thing."

After 7 years, the membership site has amassed a huge amount of content which can appear quite overwhelming. Providing a monthly theme and daily recommended class for members helps to avoid this, and provides much needed guidance to members while also bringing the community together.

"It takes away from, also, the overwhelm of, you go to the video library, and it's like, 'Oh, my God! There's 500 [videos] here. I'm so overwhelmed. I'm going to spend my whole yoga practice time choosing a video.'

...We've just taken all that choice overwhelm away for you and today, you're going to practice this. If you don't like that practice, then Tuesday's practice... Just take one for the week, whichever is good for you, right?"

Volunteer Members

To help run her membership, Melissa relies on a team of volunteers, who are also members. They have defined roles to contribute towards the community, and in return they enjoy closer support and coaching from Melissa.

"We do have actually quite a big team. It's a volunteer team, and all come from the community. Right now, there's around 11 people on the team because that team grows, and is growing and shrinking all the time, too, because it's volunteer...

That team is integral to the community... That took a long time to grow as well, and it's something that I'm super proud of. I mean, every part of running a community is a learning curve. That was something that I had to really learn and grow into was creating a team of leaders as well.

There's the Carriers of the Teachings. So, a big part of that team runs the DYC, the Daily Yoga Connection, where they rotate through who presents. We also have somebody who runs a Moon Phases section. She goes through the waxing and the waning of the moon, which is really cool. I have somebody who runs a book club, some recipes, somebody who does a more spiritually focused section. So, every month we meet, and I meet with them and they get a more close mentorship with me...So, they help me a lot, too, because part of that holding all the balls in the air and being the only one making the decisions, it's hard. So, yeah, they really help me see clearly around some things...

...It's just really great to have that team around you to support you with that. So, yeah, the volunteer teams have been amazing, and they have special names, and they're recognised in the community."

Limiting Access to Advanced Courses

When Melissa launched live dharma talks and meditations on Mondays they were initially popular, and then attendance began to drop.

Melissa was holding classes twice a day to hit all the time zones, and started to feel frustrated that her hard work wasn't proving valuable for her members.

"I came up with the idea of courses instead. I put some prerequisites on them. I was asking people to apply. I was turning people away. I called them advanced courses, too. So, I wasn't taking brand new people to the community..."

Because the courses involved deep spiritual work that could bring up a lot of emotions, Melissa restricted access to those she felt were ready, asking people to complete applications, although there is no additional cost involved.

Now the classes are always full, the students are engaged in the work, and members find the courses more attractive.

"It was also with applications. Also, me going into the community... tapping some people on the shoulder and saying, 'Really, you should be applying for this course because you are more than qualified.'

So, that took my engagement in those classes. To me, they were always full. I like my class sizes to be around 12. So, they always had 12 in them. Also, it meant that they were engaged. So, I always give them homework now, too. So, it meant they were doing things between classes, they were more engaged, and they were more committed. So, to me, that made retention really good. It also brought in new members, too."

Success on YouTube

Melissa has two YouTube channels, one with short 5-10 minute videos, and the other with longer content. Between them they have around 80,000 subscribers and are the main sources of new members.

"Our tried and true is the freemium model with the YouTube funnel. We have a YouTube channel. We put out yoga class every week. We funnel that into our membership. The best way we find is to get people on our mailing list. So, we have different opt-ins. We have a whole bunch of different opt-ins. Tim keeps track of all of this, but he usually finds that people that have become members are in one of those email opt-ins. That's the usual way. But I do have to say that every time we change something...that's when members come in.

I like things to be steady and calm, but honestly, it's the change that makes people, the constant newness that ... It just must pull different people in, *right? You speak to different people in different ways."*

Look After Your Weaknesses

Melissa has found that she resonates best with her audience, and gets the best results, when she tries something 'out there' or new or different, rather than what other people recommend.

"You definitely have to find what works for you, and not do what other people are doing. That takes, I think, a lot of courage, and it takes putting on the blinders, and staying in your own lane or if you're into yoga, just keeping your eyes on your own yoga mat and figuring out what works for you, for everything. Because honestly, that's what's going to resonate with your own audience the most.

*I think about some of the things that we've done that's most popular. It does well, but **anytime I come up with something that I think that I'm excited about, but I think, "I don't think this is going to fly because it just seems too out there," our audience always goes nuts for it.** I think you have to go for it. The more I do that, the better it goes."*

An important lesson though is to actually know what works for you, what you need and what will be fun for you, and not worry about what others are doing. For Melissa this means taking a lot of breaks, rather than having a 'hustle' mentality.

*"I tend to tire quickly, so this is something that I've learned, it's taking me a long time to learn, is that I need a lot of breaks. So, I take a lot of breaks. I use an adapted Pomodoro. I set a timer for 25 minutes when I'm working especially on screens. I stick to that. I work for 25 minutes, and then I break, but I break away for more than five minutes. I need it, and I take that...**I think that each one of us has to figure out what is fun for us, and just really go for it and don't worry about what everybody else thinks, and play to your strengths and look after your***

weaknesses...I can't believe what some other people can do, but it doesn't matter what everybody else can do. I just have to look after me, and have fun the way that I can have fun, and then everybody else, my members are going to be better for that."

A Giving Mentality

For Melissa, the best thing about running a membership is the time freedom it gives her, enabling her to spend time helping the members that need her the most.

"My most favourite thing is helping people...

.... Just this week, there was a woman, a longtime member in our community, who was diagnosed with Parkinson's. So, over the last few days, I spent a lot of time with her, and talking to her about what her doctors have been telling her she can and can't do, and then we've been talking about how to make lifestyle changes, and what yoga is going to be appropriate, and just recommending certain books, and yeah, all of that, and just being able to be there for her, and letting her know that I've got her back.

I really love being able to know that I can put in that time with individual people.

...Knowing that what I'm doing and having this platform is able to have that massive difference on people's lives and to be able to have that personal impact, I'd do that all day long. That's amazing.

The freedom to be able to spend your time the way you want to spend your time, I think that's an amazing part of being self-employed and to take it and to be able to do what you want. Yeah. That's the best part about having a membership, and being self-employed. Just saying that I get to choose what makes me happy about this, and my version of success is going to be unique to anybody else's. For me, that one- on-one and small groups and spending a lot of time with people, that really lights me up. So, I love doing that."

What's Next For Yoga with Melissa

After completing a big site revamp and moving the membership to a new platform earlier this year, the membership is stronger than ever and Melissa would now like to start running in-person retreats for both members and non-members.

"My biggest goal is to run in-person retreats.

In the next year, we have a couple of things left to do with the membership redesign on our main site and stuff. Once that is done, then our next goal is to run in-person retreats. First, here on the island, and then we have some key locations that we're looking at in Australia and Europe.

They're going to be open for everybody, but basically, members are going to get a discount."

Chris Marr: Content Marketing Academy

Membership Details:

Name: Content Marketing Academy

Topic: Content Marketing

Launched: 2015

Website: thecontentmarketingacademy.co.uk

Interview Date: May 2019

Chris Marr runs the Content Marketing Academy, a membership site teaching content marketing to entrepreneurs, business owners and in-house marketers.

Although Chris had been considering a membership business model way back when he was still at university, the Content Marketing Academy membership came about as an extension of an in-person training series on content marketing.

"The membership started as a move from a six monthly in-person event that we used to run in two different locations. Then once that wrapped up we moved it into an online coaching programme. That was the end of 2015.

I was running six month masterclasses... I had one in one location, one in another and then as they started to wrap up I was like, well what are we going to do? How are we going to provide an ongoing service for this group of people? There were about 20 or 25 people at the time, so what we decided to do was just pull it into an online forum. That morphed from a Facebook group into a more private community where I was providing content and teaching. It was very, very organic."

Means Based Pricing

For established businesses, membership costs £49 per month, but businesses making less than £10,000 per year can join for just £4.99 each month, and still access all the same content and features. The rate is available for one year only. Members who do the work are expected to be in a position to pay the full rate within a year.

"We realised that there was a big part of the marketplace we were working with in our [free] workshops that may not have the cash flow or the budget to actually join CMA. As much as they wanted to learn and develop their business, they just couldn't make it work, so we introduced our starting price as well, which is actually £4.99 a month or £49 a year for the first 12 months.

That allows people don't have the budget or they haven't fully established their business yet or haven't even got their first customer yet, they can actually join us still and learn about content marketing. *We've got those two prices....*

... We didn't really know that it was going to work until we did it, and then it's worked. Loads of people are taking advantage of it now, which is great for any membership, to have new blood coming in and new members coming in and a new audience to teach and all the rest of it. It's been great."

Despite newcomers enjoying a 90% reduction on their monthly fee, Chris didn't receive any push-back from his current members.

"[we]...explained to the members why we were doing it and why we felt it was important. Most of the people that commented were saying we totally get it, we understand why you would do this. A couple of years ago if you had done this for me then I would have absolutely taken advantage of it."

For Chris, making this pricing available for just the first year gives responsibility to both him and the member for making sure they get the results needed to pay full price for the following year.

"...there's a little bit of responsibility on us as teachers that we're saying basically if you're not going to get up to that point where revenue is going to be at the point where we feel that you can afford the normal pricing tier, then perhaps you haven't got the value from CMA and we're saying it's our responsibility too, to help you to get to that level. After 12 months they would go on to the normal pricing tier."

Consistent Marketing

One of the biggest challenges for Chris has been finding a marketing strategy that can consistently generate new customers, and avoiding distractions along the way.

*"The membership site is, in my mind, no different from any other business in the world. **It's about finding the thing that works...there's just so many tactics and strategies and gurus and blueprints and all of that stuff, to help you do this, it's so distracting trying to find something.***

For me, the single biggest challenge is being able to take a strategy, build that strategy, implement that strategy, stick to that strategy, have the patience to see if it

works or not and then being able to change that when it doesn't, and not be
distracted with all the other things in the meantime."

For Chris, consistently practising what he teaches about content marketing, is the key to growing his membership base.

*"We don't do any advertising for our membership, no paid ads. It's all through content marketing and essentially what we teach…**the one thing that truly has changed for us in terms of how we get customers is having just ultimate consistency in our marketing**. I've seen the days where we've been inconsistent, I've seen the days where we're consistent and making sure not just that we're turning up consistently at the same time, but also that our brand is consistent across all platforms as well. That's been absolutely key to getting new customers, essentially the way that we're showing up on all social platforms with our content and our brand. That whole consistency has been a game changer."*

Free Local Workshops

Besides online content, Chris also markets his membership by delivering free in-person workshops in his local area.

"One of the challenges that we have, with what we do, is that people just don't know what it is. When we say 'content marketing' it could mean many things to many people. What we were hoping to do there was attract people to our workshop. They would come for free and even if they didn't join CMA, they would at least walk away knowing what it is that we do and why we do it."

Chris aims to convert around 30% of these workshop attendees into CMA members.

*"It looks as though we're going to be hitting our targets, hitting our goals. **The free workshop obviously costs us money but if you think about it, it's just the same as putting money into any marketing or advertising activity**. Let's say it costs £500 for me to run the workshop, that's £500 for 30 leads and it's up to us to convert those leads into sales....*

...I think that when people come to our workshop, they join us, it's a really strong qualified customer. They've seen me, they've met me, they've learned from me and they understand exactly what we're doing. I feel like it's a big part of that trust that's needed, it's just dealt with in that two or three hours at that workshop."

New Member Experience

Chris drew on Joey Coleman's book Never Lose A Customer Again, and his course, First 100 Days, to create the best possible experience for new members.

*"Essentially what he says is you don't have a customer until they've been with you for 100 days... **When someone joins we send them a membership pack in the mail with a notebook and a pen and a bookmark and a badge and a sticker and our manifesto and a welcome letter from us. Everyone gets that, whether they pay £5 or £50 or £500.***

*Then we've got video, we've got a Start Here track, we've got the whole onboarding thing. I would say we've got the onboarding part pretty much nailed, especially in the first 14 days. **They have a one to one call with me when they join. We have calls at six months and a year, we're doing weekly Q&As, weekly calls, monthly calls, live training, course content.** We're engaging them in all* *the different ways, audio, video, written. We've got our forums, so we're really active, we're on it. Private coaching as well, loads of stuff. We're doing everything that we can to keep our members engaged...we're essentially trying to touch all the platforms and do it in a planned way as well....*

*... **nobody should ever feel like they never saw me this week.** There's always a reason or an excuse or a way that they can join me on a video call this week. It's up to them obviously if they want to join. Not everybody does, but we're turning up and I think that's the main thing."*

Using Slack For Community

Chris started the community side of his membership in a Facebook group but quickly started looking for an alternate option. As Chris wasn't a forum fan himself, he settled on using Slack.

*"We did have a Facebook group but honestly it wasn't working. There was zero engagement and there were some assumptions around why that might have been but I think it was a case of, let's try something different. **We moved over to Slack and all of a sudden everyone was engaging**, so I don't know why. You can make some assumptions about that, but it worked from the very start."*

Whilst some members have struggled to adapt to Slack, Chris accepts there was no perfect solution, and less tech-agile members would likely have struggled no matter what platform he went with.

"...looking at the struggles they're having, I think they would struggle with any digital platform they were going into. Slack is so easy to use, it's just like using a messenger app. I do feel that the challenges that people have coming into Slack

*would probably be no different if they were coming into any digital platform. The reason that they're struggling is not because it's Slack, it's because it's new and it's a new platform for them…**how much is your responsibility as a membership site owner to make it easy?** We make it as easy as we possibly can, we've got all the tutorial videos, all the onboarding stuff is there and we help them as much as we can. But if you're not willing to try it then you can only do so much to motivate people, can't you?"*

Lifestyle First

Chris enjoys having a global impact, while keeping his work local - something that increased in importance when he became a father.

"Being able to work with people all over the world is something that I'd say is a highlight.

Because it's a membership site you really have got the global reach, instead of if I was still a marketing consultant and that's all that I did, then my clients would probably all be in my local area, typically. I think that's been one of the major highlights…

…I've moved from being a business owner with no attachments, living on my own, in my own two bedroom flat and I had an office and all the rest of it, to very quickly having a boy. He's three years old now, Spencer, and separating from my wife. Finding my new partner and having another baby and living as a stepdad, so we've got four kids now. Even moving city as well.

In the space of starting the membership and today, it's been this huge shift. There's never been a more important point in my life to have a business that I have as much control as you could possibly get from your business. You can't control everything but I feel like with the membership site, the lifestyle choices that you make are much more within your control than they would be otherwise....

...Every Wednesday I take the day off for daddy day. I don't work the weekends, my laptop gets shut on a Friday, it doesn't open until Monday."

For Chris, putting his lifestyle first is the key to running a successful business, and a membership model makes this possible, especially when combined with a support team.

"There's three team members in CMA and Cara [Chris's partner]is part-time. And then, like everybody, we've got our own external suppliers as well that we use for branding and website design and video marketing and all that kind of stuff too. Again, it's pieced together over the years. I started with just me, for a long time it was just me, but over the years I've again, just back to this lifestyle choice, need to have the right people around me in order to make this an actual business and to have an actual life as well."

It's Not Easy

The evolution of the Content Marketing Academy has been an organic process over the last three or four years, something Chris thinks he may have sped up had he understood from the start the work involved and made it his sole focus.

*"I think the amount of work that's involved in a membership site is not talked about enough. **If anything, I would like to have gone in with my eyes a bit more open, in terms of how much work it was going to take to really focus on the membership.** Not knowing that, meant that I did a lot of other things, like we did more live events, we did more consulting, I was doing more speaking. Ultimately, I think that slowed my progress with the membership. Knowing what I know now, I think I would like to have said no to a lot of things back then and instead focused on building the membership... it's just far more demanding than you think it's going to be."*

What's Next For Content Marketing Academy

While Chris already has a high quality member experience, it's something he wants to continue honing further, for both existing members and new.

"One of the big things we've been working on at the moment is trying to build a customer experience around CMA that goes beyond just an online product. We're just looking at everything, to make that experience for our members, regardless of how long they've been around, a special experience."

Chris doesn't want to compromise his family-friendly lifestyle by travelling to multiple in-person events each year, so he's exploring other ways to create a community culture.

"... we've got gifts that we send, birthday cards, branded water bottles, the welcome packs, T-shirts, stuff like that just to make them feel part of our culture. We designed a manifesto.

Just the other day actually, someone shared a picture with me, in the background it's all of our manifesto and our posters are on the wall behind them, they've got their stuff on their desk and things like that.

So I'd say that's the biggest thing that we're working on is making CMA a bigger part of people's lives at their work or in their business. I think going forward, that's the one thing that we're really going to be focusing on.

We want to be around for the next 10 years. That's always in my mind is what does this look like in 10 years time? If we want to have a real business and want people to enjoy that experience then it's going to have to go beyond just a few courses and a forum. It has to be something that they believe in and they want to be part of."

Jodie Clarke: The Empowered Educator

Membership Details:

Name: The Empowered Educator Member Hub

Topic: Early Childhood Educators

Launched: June 2018

Website: theempowerededucatoronline.com

Interview Date: May 2019

Jodie Clarke runs The Empowered Educator Online, a membership site for early childhood educators (those working with children aged 0-5 years).

Before launching her membership, Jodie's main website, The Empowered Educator, already had a large audience of early childhood educators, so she knew there was an interest in the topic.

Initially Jodie's blog was focused on reaching parents, then she narrowed down to childcare providers, realising these professionals felt unsupported in their roles. As she grew her audience, Jodie started creating resources for those working at management level too.

"I started to realise I was reaching larger childcare centres as well...the educational leaders and the directors and the managers are also not getting the support they need and it's coming right down from the top. If they're not in a good place it's not feeding down to these educators down the line, so now I've sort of broadened it and the Member Hub has become something that's got a little bit for your day to day educator just as individuals, and then also the family daycares because they're running their own business from home as well, it's not just that they're a teacher."

Jodie was creating free content, plus standalone resources available to buy separately, until she decided to launch a membership to make it easier for customers to use what she'd created, and to smooth out her monthly income.

"I noticed more and more saying, can I get this all in one place? I'd pay a monthly fee for that…

…I think the final tipping point for me was the constant launching, and also just not having any recurring income. I was starting to do quite well monthly, but you never knew… If I had a launch that month or I did a promotion to my subscribers it might be a really good month, but it was that uncertainty… I wanted to try and see if I could get even just a small amount of recurring income so I could have some sort of baseline to say, yep, we're going to have that this month to pay the bills."

A VIP Waitlist

When launching Jodie invited members of her email list and free Facebook group (13,000 members) to join a VIP waitlist if they were interested in joining the membership. Then she nurtured this audience with additional training, a webinar, and by providing early access to the membership, before it went on sale to the public.

"I had what I called my VIP Wait List. In my free Facebook group and through my newsletters and ads I did a lot of hype, I try to drum up a lot of hype before I do a launch. I started that a fair way out, it'll be probably about two months out…I find with my audience I need a really good lead in and they need to see a few things…I would get them onto the list by saying, 'you can get onto the wait list now and

you'll receive some samples and some freebies from Member Hub, and some training.'

And then what I had set up was an automation… It was things that were out of Member Hub that were also from my resource shop. It was just like a little teaser and they'd just be once a week, so it sort of became like a regular, like you'd send out a newsletter, but I gave them that feeling of connection.

In my [Facebook] group… I called them the VIPs, VIP Eds. That became a little like club and they knew that they were the only ones getting that email. I had special pages set up where they could go and view videos and things like that, and then they actually got a 24 window where when I launched, the emails leading up to it I said, you will have first access, I'm only going to be giving it to VIPs, I'm only taking 100 members for this intake.

… I did stick to that even though we went over, I think it was 150, but that was because they just came too quick. The VIPs, I emailed them out and they had a full 24 hours. They had a special link and they got to go in a special page…that worked really, really well."

From Launch Cycles to Evergreen

Jodie ran three launch cycles in the first year of her membership and hit her target of 600 members far earlier than she thought she would.

She's since switched to an evergreen model, using a pre-recorded webinar, and advertising to cold and warm traffic. This funnel now brings in between 5 and 10 people per day.

"The one this year, I actually did a live webinar and I got about 150 people signing up on that night just from the webinar, but they were going to a bonus page that was only available for that night, we sort of ended at midnight.

That was a lot more popular than I thought and a lot, lot more exhausting than I thought it was going to be. Because as well as launching the Member Hub I also have a lot of products and things that I do, and other courses that I do launches throughout the year. I got to the point where I was thinking, I can't do this for another year....

Now I've gone to an evergreen model so I'm open all the time. Basically the main way I'm feeding in new members, grabbing new members, is by doing that same webinar. I've taken it and I did it again but made it into a recording that I'm using through Easy Webinar...it's a lot less stressful, just that gradual drip. I feel like I can onboard people better."

Coping with Cancels

Even with a low churn rate, having such large membership numbers early on means Jodie was facing large numbers of cancellations after her launches, which knocked her confidence. She's dealt with that by tightening up the sales page, so only the right people are joining, and redirecting cancellation notices to a separate email.

"Even though it's not that many, it seems like when you've had those big launches and you've got people joining in all at that one time because it was an open and closed hub. There's this big bulk couple of days and then suddenly you lose people because they've been charged again.

...you think, oh no, you know all that work, I did all this work up front for you and now you're pulling out. So yeah, that's probably what I struggle with most at the moment. I've set up another email inbox and those notifications I get from MemberMouse to say someone has changed their account or cancelled, they go straight into another email address now."

Jodie also found she had to make the fact it was a recurring payment very clear.

"I've found I needed to...on my check out page and in a few other places...make it really clear that if they're doing a monthly payment it is a monthly recurring payment. I've had a lot of people say, 'I just thought I'd pay the $39 and have access', and I was like, 'well, what, forever?'
...I've been a lot clearer that it's a recurring payment, I've even likened it to Netflix and something like that... I'd rather do that and perhaps lose a few at the checkout because they see that and go, 'I'm not doing this every month.' I also make it very clear that they can, with one click of a button, cancel."

Demanding Customer Support

One of the most surprising things for Jodie when she first started the membership site was how much customer support would be involved.

"I didn't realise that was going to be such a time consuming task... A lot of my audience... aren't very digital savvy, they're not very computer savvy... and you need to walk them through the buying online process and how to download and do all that sort of stuff."

Jodie's started to set up training videos to help members get the most from their subscription and this has cut down on some enquiries, but customer support is still a time-consuming part of running the membership.

"I always feel like I'm on, I'm always switched on like, they might be messaging me or they're in the group or they're emailing me, and **I sort of feel like, oh, all these people are paying me money, I need to answer them and keep them happy***, and yeah, so that's been a big struggle."*

Customer messages aren't always demanding though, something that Jodie is grateful for.

"I was just complaining about the customer service emails, but on the other hand, I also get a lot of lovely emails or private messages saying, 'I was about to give up my job and go into another field altogether and you've just reignited my passion in childcare...'

I think for me that aspect, just to know that these people who weren't getting the support and were right down to that level, which is a lot of the people in Member Hub, I've just taken them back to basics, given them some simple tools and some explanations that they weren't getting.... The children are the ones that are benefiting from that because there's a lot of passionate educators out there but because of all the paperwork and regulations and all that sort of thing, much the same as any industry, they're thinking about leaving, which is really sad."

Retiring Her Partner

One of the biggest impacts the membership site has had for Jodie is that she's been able to retire her partner from his job, something that has not only improved family life, but increased her productivity as well.

"I've actually been able to retire my own partner so that he can spend more time at home with our kids and I don't feel as torn now. He had a really awful job, long hours, going at 4:00 in the morning and be back late in the afternoon.... Since he got home he's back to the guy I knew before this job, because it just was sucking the life out of him, which wasn't good for any of us either. It's actually then in turn made me more productive because now I know I can just go to work in the morning and he's there...to see the man out there vacuuming past while I'm on the computer, instead of me doing it, on a Monday morning is just a rare thrill."

Providing Direction

With a lot of resources on the site, Jodie is aware of the need to provide increased direction to her members and does so in a number of different ways.

On her website Jodie uses Intercom to help new members find what they need. She also uses onboarding emails, and fortnightly round-up emails to keep members coming back to the site.

And she's creating a range of pathways to guide members through the content they need depending on the demands of their current role.

"I've just started setting up, I call them simple pathways, and I've pulled out roles like, 'I'm a new educator', or 'I'm a leader', or 'I work in family daycare and I want

to fill my vacancies', and then I've put drop downs under all of those on a separate page where they can go, different resources, different training, a webinar, wherever. I've linked them up so they can just follow down that path...small steps, but they're working quite well too."

Free vs Member Engagement

Creating a members-only community has been a struggle due to the popularity and success of Jodie's free Facebook group.

"We have a [members] Facebook group. That's probably been the biggest struggle engagement-wise and I think that's mainly because a lot of those members that are in there have come from my free group, which is a really big engaged group. There's a lot of discussions and a lot of things, they're used to that level. When you've got 13,000 members and it's an engaged group, as you know it's a lot easier to get people talking...

...what I've noticed is, when they're posting, a lot of the time members are posting in my free Facebook group and they think they're in the Member Hub group. I think because it's all meshing in they aren't always able to make the distinction between that private content and the other two, but that's Facebook, it keeps changing."

Starting to Outsource

Jodie has one VA (virtual assistant) helping her at the moment but is looking to start outsourcing more tasks, although it's difficult to let go of her perfectionism.

"I've now got a VA who is a fellow blogging friend, but she's also a teacher so she knows this world and how we speak and what my resources are. We started on about 15 hours a month and now we're up to about 25. Her main role is just helping me out with scheduling social media and she pops into the groups and helps me with answering and keeping those connections going.

The biggest help - and this is what I would recommend anyone even if you've only got a little bit of money, this is the best thing I ever did - she does the majority of the support emails now...all that sort of stuff that I was spending hours on every day... so that's been really helpful. I'm hoping, my goal for this year is to start outsourcing all of it. I've just got to loosen the reins on the perfectionism and do some videos so I can show others what to do."

Jodie is also supported by her business coach, Melanie Miller, who encourages her to keep an eye on the stats and facts, so she can make informed decisions about her business.

"...if I didn't meet her four years ago I think I was ready to give up. We've come a long way. She helps me do the figures side of thing... I don't like stats... but I see now after keeping those figures and those records why it's important, especially with doing a membership site, that you need to know the money coming in, money going out, members coming in, members going back out."

Avoiding Perfectionism

Jodie wishes she'd spent less time getting the website perfect for launching, and more time designing a content production plan to use month on month.

"I knew what content I wanted to be in there and I'd done my pages and the fancy categories and worried about all of that stuff, and uploading and all of that great stuff that takes ages, and that I perfectionized myself over every minute. Then I realised after that first influx of members and people started saying, 'have you got next month's plans', 'where are next months plans'?

...I think I would've done better content planning and how I was going to organise that, and yeah, just thinking more into the future....

Suddenly you've got all the customer support and the new members and the payment processes and all of those great things as well, and you think, but when am I going to do my content? I think that's what I would've liked to have had in place, a content plan."

Imposter Syndrome

At times Jodie has felt that choosing not to do public speaking has undermined her credibility, but travelling to in-person events doesn't fit the lifestyle she wants to create for herself and her family.

Instead, she's enjoying using her blog, social media presence and membership to reach more people, from around the world, while she remains comfortably at home.

"I've struggled a lot with that whole imposter syndrome because I don't talk, I don't do the speaking circuit. I've done talks and things over the years but it's not what I want to do now...

...I can reach more people and make more money by sitting here at home in my pyjama pants doing a webinar and helping out 100s of people, especially in rural areas that can't get access to that sort of training.

I want to be able to do more of that and help people in regional areas that aren't getting access to that support."

What's Next For The Empowered Educator Member Hub

While Jodie hit her target of 600 members soon than she thought, she's not stopping there and is now looking to get to the 1000 members milestone. She's also looking to start having guest experts create some of her monthly content.

"My goal is to have more guest presenters to help me with doing those monthly webinars.

I want to grow to at least 1,000 members...It's not so much about just building those numbers but knowing that I'm making that difference."

Varvara Lyalyagina: Start Blog Up

Membership Details:

Name: Start Blog Up Studio

Topic: Russian Entrepreneurs

Launched: June 2018

Website: startblogup.com

Interview Date: May 2019

Varvara Lyalyagina from Start Blog Up, is the founder of The Studio, a membership focused solely on helping Russian-speaking entrepreneurs build a personal brand and grow their business.

When Varvara started looking for a mentor or coach herself, she struggled to find a package that matched her budget, until she came across a membership site.

"Those people whom I wanted to be coached by, they didn't offer the coaching or mentoring programme or the price was so high that at that point of time I couldn't afford it....

...And then I joined April Bowles Olin's membership site, Sunday Society. And I was blown away how great it is.

And I'm like I need to do the same for my clients. I just, I really think that this kind of thing is missing on the Russian-speaking market, because I was amazed that you pay really small amount of money, but you still have access to the expert. You have all your questions answered, you have trainings, you have the community, you have it all and this is just less than the coaching session, and it's like peanuts compared to the price of the coaching with this kind of leader.

I was like okay, I need to do this."

It took Varvara more than a year to develop her membership site, and open it to beta testers. Now, the membership forms the core of her business.

"Membership is now in the centre of my business. I would say that, in terms of income, it's about 70%. 30% would be, or maybe like 25% would be coaching. I still do one-on-one coaching with clients. Most of them, basically they transferred to the new membership, and this is basically how the idea of the membership appeared because those people with whom I work they asked for the longer support.

I also have some small products, like I have the bloggers diary to write to track the content…I have some few webinars info products that I also sell. Basically, they are all in my membership. I was thinking about closing it and leave it only in membership, but currently there's a few online products that still exist and they bring me some money too, on an ongoing basis, but I do not do anything for that."

Pricing Locally

While Varvara's membership site is entirely in Russian, her members are based around the world. While she does have an international audience, she charges in Russian Rubles to keep things more affordable.

"I have lots of people who emigrated. Russian speaking people who are located in Europe, in the States, in Latin America, and they buy my services. And for them, with European, American, Australian prices, the price that I can offer is much

cheaper. Is much better than they can get locally, but they have a very quality product...And I provide the Western approach, but with the Russian specifics, you know? I think this is a very good and unique product for my people."

Moving To A Closed Door Model

When Varvara first launched she used an open door model where people could join the membership any time, but she has recently closed the doors, and is now planning to use multiple launch cycles throughout the year to generate new members.

"I started the membership with an open model and I transferred to the closed model just recently...

...One of the biggest struggles for me is to find the balance between the internal and external content. To create quality internal content for the members. And at the same time, to talk about this all the time and to create blog posts, Facebook lives, and all this kind of stuff."

Alongside this difficulty, Varvara had also noticed that many people would be thinking about joining but were stuck in in-decision.

"...there were so many good people and I knew them and I knew that it would help them, but they really needed this incentive to join. They needed this push. I don't like to be pushy, but I know that they needed this. After closing the doors now I have people who thanked me for closing the doors and for making this decision for them basically. So I'm experimenting, I will see how it goes to the end of this year, but so far I'm glad how it is going."

Success With Online Parties

As the Russian market isn't as familiar with membership sites as many others, Varvara has used some creative ways to bring new members onboard.

Noticing that Facebook Live tours of memberships often convinced her to buy, Varavara started doing the same for her audience. She also showcases her members-only workbooks.

"I usually do very beautiful workbooks that come along with the courses. I can show the make-up of this workbook in Facebook for example. People love this because they are beautiful and people ask me can I buy it separately, and I say like no. So I started to use this showing more of the workbooks because it catches people."

Varvara also started throwing online parties to celebrate certain occasions, such as her launch, and opens these to both members and non members.

"I have online parties in Facebook, in the format of Facebook Live.

I adapted this idea from Chris Ducker...I did an online party opening the membership and I did it in a really funny way. I was with the balloons, I was dancing happy dances because this is what I do in my membership - I dance happy dances for members at the beginning of every video call."

Varvara invites her current members to join the party, so they have an opportunity to talk to people who are thinking of joining.

"I can talk brilliantly about what's in my membership, but what works the best is when it's not me talking about membership, but somebody else like my members are talking about my membership."

And to sweeten the pot further Varvara also runs a giveaway, open to those who join the membership during the live session.

"I usually at these parties, there are guests, there are some fun things and I keep talking about the membership within the breaks, and I do a giveaway. Those who join the membership during this live session will be in the giveaway. The giveaway is like some nice things - it's my calendar, my things that I produced, and it's also some nice stuff like tripods or some colourful keyboard covers, something like this which I do have and which I love."

The first time Varvara ran one of these giveaways she was scared no-one would join the membership while the party was happening, which proved not to be the case.

"[I thought] Should I change the rules right now and say it will be the giveaway within those who buy to the end of the week maybe? And then I was like okay, no I will stick to the plan and even if nobody buys, I will be embarrassed but I will stick to the plan.

And can you imagine? People buy while I'm live! It blows my mind even now. And it happened over and over again.

People really like this somehow. They join live and they have this giveaway at the end of the one and a half hour session and send them the gift then, they post it online...So yeah, these online parties are like my jam."

Getting To Know Members

Varvara accepts that not everyone is there for community engagement. Some people prefer to grab the content they need without much (or any) interaction.

"... I totally respect this, but if they reveal themselves on the video calls, on the Facebook group, in the community, then I really try to get to know them as much as I can.

I use this Crowdcast service for video calls...close to the name there is a user pic of the person.... when people join the membership, I really encourage them to go and to make this user pic, not just a picture that is by default there, but to make it their photo.

This is such a tiny thing, but it helps really to know people in the chat, they know each other better, they see the faces, I know them better....

...From time to time I do not just answer the message in the Facebook group, but when the question from the member is really deep or I want to go deep into answering them, I do the recording in the video format...it could be five minutes plus... You never know when you'll get this answer from me, this video answer. So it's a bit of a surprise when you get it...

... I also like small personalised gifts. For example, for the one year anniversary we send a small package for everybody who stayed with us a year, for a year or longer."

Emotional Challenges

Varvara has been surprised at the emotional challenges running a membership has involved.

"For me it was extremely emotional for a long time when people were leaving. It still is. Now I'm much better at this, but when I see the email when somebody cancels the membership, at the very beginning I took it really very personal. I didn't transfer it to the member, but myself like that day was ruined.

And I was like 'oh my God, I do not understand, it's so wonderful here. The price is so low. There are so many amazing things and I'm working so hard...' It was really difficult because I worked before the trainings, the group trainings, I do this one on one consulting all the time, and it didn't feel this hard and this emotional for me.

It has also been difficult seeing competitors launch courses on similar topics, but at a much higher price point.

...The other thing was when I see some of my competitors are launching the courses on the same topic that I have in my membership and just the price of this training is twice as big you know, than the price of my membership... I want to run to people and say hey, don't buy. Look I sell here the same, it's great quality. Same topic, but you will have a ton more training of this kind and you will have this, this and that.

Yeah so to get into this membership mindset as you guys call it, it was very challenging for me to cope with all these emotions. Explaining to people what membership is, seeing people leave, seeing others are doing similar stuff and selling it for more. Yeah, so I think this was the biggest challenge for me."

Financial Stability

While running a membership presents many challenges, Varavara enjoys the financial stability the business model has provided her with.

"It's hard to make it work every day, basically, but I love that I do not need to worry every month now, will I have this money coming or not. I know that I will have this money and I can plan according to this. And I really love this feeling of being in the Russian speaking industry of this. I feel myself like I'm leading this, I really believe in the membership model. I think that more and more businesses will come to this community and this is what I see is really happening and I'm already there. I think it's good for me, it's I think also beneficial for my members to be with the leader. So it's nice and flattering."

The regular, predictable income from her membership enables Varvara to enjoy a more comfortable lifestyle.

"...if I want to go somewhere I can go somewhere. I can do this travelling. I can afford some nice more comfortable stuff for myself. For example, not thinking about using the public transportation, when I do not drive my car but to use the taxi...Just a more comfortable life, not thinking about every penny where I'm spending and being able to travel to meet my friends, to go to the good restaurants, again not to look at the menu what to chose there. In the grocery store, not to look only at the red price tags, but just to buy and to do whatever I feel that I want to do. This I because I have this constant income that I really can rely on."

What's Next For Start Blog Up

Varvara's main focus right now is seeing how the closed door model works for growing the membership, so that she can decide which approach to take long term.

"I really want to see how this opening, closing the doors really goes to make the final decision for me on this experiment."

In addition to this, Varvara is keen to start delegating more tasks so that she can free up some more time for herself.

"And to have all the content creation rolling, because looking at whatever I do now, I understand that lots of things that I'm doing could be done not by myself. The workbook creation for example, editing videos that I still do, and sometimes I am afraid to delegate, I do not have a person to whom I can delegate this, to whom I can really trust. I'm a little bit of a control freak. On the other hand, I sometimes do it such last minute, I film the video, I record the video and I need it to be done by the end of the day. So I cannot delegate this because nobody will be able to do it instantly right?

...this is what I'm working on, this is why I have this videographer, this is why recently I delegated more processes to my VA. So I'm coming to this but this is like internal stuff, this is where I want to be, more relaxing life for myself.

And some new features for the members as well. I really want to introduce the feature of finding their accountability partner for example, or online masterminding. So not only me talking, but they can talk in the online room, so I really want to introduce it too. But this will be possible when I free up some of my time. So it's kind of interlinked."

John Hatcher: Blues Guitar Institute

Membership Details:

Name: Blues Guitar Institute

Topic: Blues Guitar

Launched: August 2015

Website: bluesguitarinstitute.com

Interview Date: May 2019

John Hatcher runs the Blues Guitar Institute, a membership site teaching acoustic blues guitar.

John first started teaching online in 2011, while working full time as a CPA and tax accountant.

"I was teaching online without any real business model behind it. My background is in... I'm a CPA and a tax accountant. That was my former day job, and so I had a lot of this business training, but I think for the first couple of years that I had Blues Guitar Institute, I really kind of treated it like a hobby, which was fine and it was kind of getting that creativity out of me. Then when I tried to monetize it for the first time, I did a little cheap, standalone course, and it didn't sell well. Then I don't know exactly what put me on the membership model, but I knew it was out there. Other folks were doing it, so it was kind of the proof of concept was already tested."

One of the first things John did was start posting videos to YouTube. Initially these were quite sporadic, but by 2014 he was consistently posting a weekly lesson. While doing this he was also growing his email list.

"I started in 2011, late 2011. I think I put one video up on YouTube in December of that year, but then, a couple of years rolled by and I was just putting out a lesson here or there and nothing consistent at all.

Then in 2014, I started doing a weekly lesson on YouTube, and I was very consistent with that. I mean, every single Tuesday, I was putting out a free lesson and collecting email addresses. And so that helped me, especially the consistency of that, it really helped me to grow an email list.

Then I surveyed that list to find out if they would be game for a membership, and honestly, I got kind of mixed results back on that. Some people are like, 'No, I never sign up for anything recurring.'

But I felt like I had enough yeses that I was going to give it a go. Like I said, I was kind of thinking about how the membership model fit me a little bit better anyway, and fit my goals a little bit better, and I had enough of an audience to justify giving it a shot, and so I did. I don't remember what sizes the audience was or anything, but I definitely had some folks that were following me almost since the beginning that were on that email list. I had enough, I think, to justify putting this out and that it wouldn't be crickets."

After researching the market, John settled on a price of just $9 per month or $75 a year.

"Back when I started, I did some market research. I mean, there are obviously other folks out there doing online guitar memberships, and I definitely priced myself kind of on the lower end. I think that initially, the thought was, "Well, I've got to build up some content to really make this seem like a good value."

Surveying people on his email list showed that many of his audience had some past experience playing blues guitar. They hadn't played for a while, as family life and work ate into their time, and were returning to the guitar as they reached retirement age. So John targeted his membership content at beginner to intermediate skill level.

As a member of guitar teaching sites himself, John could see the potential in the model.

"'If you do this, you won't have to do taxes anymore.' That was a big motivator for me. I mean, that's probably the biggest reason that I really kind of doubled down on the membership model and really tried to grow this into a business that I could support my family with."

Three years after launching the membership site, John was able to quit his job and he has been working full-time on the membership ever since.

One Core Focus

In an effort to keep his working life as simple as possible, and knowing his own strengths, the membership is John's sole focus.

"Membership is the full-time business, and that's by design. I'm not one that can wear a lot of different hats successfully, and so I wanted to really just have one product that I knew how to structure and market. Not that I know all of that, I'm still learning, but it's nice for me to just be able to focus on this one type of model. I've toyed with having some outside standalone courses that people could just buy because maybe that would fit their purchasing habits a little better than the recurring membership, but I find it easier for me at least at this stage to just kind of

stay on the membership model and learn that because there's... I'm learning stuff every day when it comes to how to operate this thing."

Only having one product and focus is also beneficial for John's audience, making it very clear to them how he could help, as well as encouraging commitment.

"I didn't want to confuse people at all. I wanted this to be very upfront that it's recurring. I think with what I'm teaching, there's a great case for a recurring model. I want somebody to really invest and come back. You're not going to come to a blues guitar lesson and learn everything you need to know in one lesson, and not even in one course. That's one thing that kind of put me on the membership model in the first place, is it just didn't make sense to me to just have a one and done course because you're not going to go from A to Z and then all of a sudden be a blues master. It just doesn't work like that. I thought that the recurring nature of it, whether annually or even just monthly, will keep people coming back and hopefully encourage results."

From Crickets To Conversations

Although the community is now John's favourite aspect of running his membership, it hasn't always been a lively, thriving forum. In fact, initially, the community didn't exist at all. Once a community was added, it took some time for John to embrace it.

"I didn't start building it right away. I think I was probably... Gosh, I was two years into the membership before I really started building up my own community like on a forum on the site, and it took a while. For a while, that was me posting to crickets. No one was there, but lately, I'd say within the last year for sure, it's just

been very active, and it's a whole lot of fun. There are folks that are active posters that have been with me since almost the very, very beginning. It's just a great group of folks, and we get to get in there and talk about the music we love every day.

*It started out, I didn't have one at all, and then I added a forum. Then there was just no activity. I made very few posts on it. That was very much a mirror of my activity. I wasn't in there posting questions or drumming up conversation, **so I wasn't active and no one else was, which makes a lot of sense.***"

Once John started making the community a priority and taking time to encourage engagement, it flourished.

"But within the last year to 18 months or so, I've really started posting more in the forums. I encourage people to come and introduce themselves as they come into the membership as part of an onboarding....

....when the courses go out, I set up a topic that says, 'If you've got questions, post here.' I set up a little button that they can click to go directly to a course discussion....

.... and then I relaunched my site back in January, just with some different tech and everything, and that has a link to the forum on every single post. It's like, 'Want to continue the conversation? Click here. Need to get help? Click here.' That kind of stuff.

I feel like that's helped kind of passively generate some conversation."

John has also started direct support tickets to post in the community instead, re-training members on how to get their questions answered.

"Then one thing that I've done over the last little while is I'll get a lot of support tickets that really should be forum posts. I'm like, 'Hey, post this in the forum. People would love to get in on this conversation, or if you don't want to…' because some people are kind of privately-minded, 'If you don't want to, do you mind if I do?' That has been helpful as well. I think just coaching people even one-on-one to go post in the forum has been helpful."

Now that community engagement is high, John has started creating content focused on member activity as well, highlighting his most engaged members.

"Then lately, I've started to do a Member Show where we highlight some of the members in the community, what they're doing, because people have started posting videos of them playing through the course content and things like that. It's just been an amazing experience, and honestly, those videos are my favourite to make every month."

Although using a forum doesn't come naturally to John, by making it part of his role as a membership site owner his feelings have changed.

"I'm not a very active person on social media and my personal life and things like that, but I think having this community has kind of… I don't know. It's changed me in a little way. I enjoy it so much that I'm posting in there all the time and I absolutely love it. I never had the habit of posting in a forum before. I would lurk, I would read, but I certainly wasn't an active poster, and I think this just kind of excited me so much that I'm in there all the time just having a blast."

Experimenting On YouTube

John's weekly YouTube videos have provided a reliable way to build his audience, attract new members, try out membership content ideas, and improve his video-making skills.

"I've kept the weekly lesson on YouTube, and it has been just the best thing to get the word out. I feel like I provide full lessons in there, and so people get a sense of my teaching style. Then I try to either get them to subscribe to the YouTube channel just to grow that and make sure that they see more and more videos or give away some sort of free download or from time to time, there's a free little mini course, things like that. That has done pretty well. I think that that really is the thing that has helped me to transition full-time and grow it to the point that I needed.

Probably 99% of it is new content. There are some courses that will take a series of lessons from the free YouTube stuff and just take it to a whole another level. It's kind of interesting, it's kind of my little laboratory in a way, what I put out for free. When I get something which resonates with people, my members, or my YouTube audience are commenting and saying, 'Hey, we love this, we want more.' I'm like, 'Okay. Well, I'm going to put my head down, go to work, and develop this into a full-blown course.' Those are the courses that really tend to do well, be popular in the membership. Then I'll go back to YouTube and say, 'Like this? Come on in, I've got more.' It's just a great little testing ground for what's going to work."

The Content Treadmill

Now John is working full-time on his membership, he's been able to give his week more structure which helps him to stay on track.

"Each day has a job and a focus. I tend to work better that way rather than just being a firefighter and putting out all the random tasks. If I can just think about one section of the business on a given day, I'm better for it. Because a lot of what I do is creative and writing music for lessons and things. I've got a schedule for that, and that helps to just get me in that creative mode, and write what I need to write. I know I've got this time to do it, and it helps me to keep on track and to keep things coming out…"

He spends around 40 hours a week working, and the bulk of that time is spent creating videos and content.

"… the courses really take a lot. I'll spend a couple of weeks just getting the course plan written, filmed. Filming is just a whole another thing. That is a huge time suck really. I'm getting better and better at it, I've come a long way, I guess, in a sense, but it still takes me a long time to film, edit, and get a video up on the internet. That's definitely the largest portion of it for sure.

…It just takes practice and tying back to that Tuesday show that's the testing ground, it was my testing ground for all that stuff too. For editing, for lighting, for different cameras and all those things. It's kind of like that 1% better mentality where I just tried to get a little bit better than the last lesson. That was the only way that I could get it done on a weekly schedule."

A big goal for John is to streamline and start batching content, so that he has some breathing space if anything unexpected happens.

"I think now, my goal is to start batching content and have at least a month's content in the tank ahead of time so that if I get sick or something like that, there's

nothing really stopping the flow of content to my members. That's a huge goal for me..."

One downside of the time that content creation currently takes, is that it has affected John's ability to focus on retention activities.

"I spend so much time producing the content that I don't think I pay attention enough, just because of available time, to things in this category of how to just make the membership sticky and keep people coming back."

A Solo Business

John doesn't currently have a team and has always done everything for the membership site himself. This is something that he's looking to change now however.

"...I'm definitely at the point where I'm recognising some of my shortcomings and really want somebody to support me and play at the level that I think I play at, in my strong suit.

For me, that's first and foremost, marketing...because it's fascinating to me, but I find that I think I'm a little unsure of what I read and what I study, and so I don't implement good ideas.

I'm looking for somebody that can take good ideas, formulate a strategy... and then implement them. That's clearly where I need help, and that'll allow me to not worry about those things, certainly make sure everything's going well, but I'd rather spend my time pulling together lessons and just creating the best courses that I can."

What's Next For Blues Guitar Institure

John is focused on membership growth, however isn't quite sure what that looks like just yet and whether it will require growing a big team, or simply becoming more efficient.

"I certainly want to grow the site and want to bring more and more members into this cool thing that we've got going at BGI.

But I'm not sure - does that mean growing out a big team, or does that mean just getting super efficient and making it with one or two other key people?

I'm really not sure as far as how the next thing and the next chapter looks.

But I can tell you the number one goal is really growth. I've been able to sign up new members month over month and I want to do more. I want to bring this music, these lessons to more and more people."

Deborah Engelmajer: Tizzit

Membership Details:

Name: Tizzit HQ

Topic: Handmade Businesses

Launched: September 2018

Website: tizzit.co

Interview Date: May 2019

Deborah Engelmajer runs Tizzit HQ, a membership site offering business and marketing support for makers and handmade businesses.

"Tizzit HQ is a membership site for makers, handmade business owners, Etsy sellers, anyone really that's making something with their hands, and trying to sell it online. We do cover offline topics as well, like setting up markets or retail, but mostly I teach makers how to do business online."

After completing a Masters in Business and Marketing, Deborah briefly had a corporate job in Paris, before deciding to freelance. She offered website design, marketing strategy and SEO to small businesses, and her client base began to lean towards small handmade businesses.

"More and more people were coming to me from word of mouth, being handmade shops. So I just dove in and decided that I was going to focus exclusively on that.

I'm a maker myself. I make a lot of stuff. I just don't sell them because honestly they're not quite as good as that."

Although Deborah was keen to try out the membership model early on in building her business, she decided building her audience first would give her a more successful launch.

"I knew about membership sites when I was just getting started in the online business...I quickly realised that I didn't have enough of an audience to do that...

...Then somehow along the way, I sort of forgot about them a little bit. I think we hear so much about, build a signature course, and launch, and do your webinar, and all of these things, and I think I was sort of getting caught up in that."

For a while Deborah sold workshops, creating a new one each month. The workshops were free to attend live, then the replays were sold after that. As she was already creating this new content every month, Deborah realized she had the beginnings of a membership.

"I remembered about membership sites and thought, hey, how about we do this, and incorporate that Maker's Roadmap in the middle. So it all kind of made sense."

Even though Deborah had spent years building her audience and had already sold other products, it was a pleasant surprise when she launched the membership and attracted 250 founder members.

Low Key Launches

Deborah has been active on a number of social media platforms to build her audience and draw people onto her subscriber list, giving her a healthy audience to launch to.

"The most important part of my strategy has always been building my list to start with, and then selling to that list... Pinterest works really well for me, always has. Facebook group is a big one. Then YouTube as well. So I have a weekly video show, and that's working better and better, which I really am happy about, because I love doing those videos. It really helps in search as well. So people find me through my YouTube videos."

As a result of having a large audience, Deborah's launches have been fairly low-key, yet successful.

"I came in with that advantage of having an audience already, which is definitely something I would recommend people focus on doing first, and then build your membership site, because it makes it so much easier.

Because really my launches... when I was opening the cart the last few months, I was just sending an email to my list to announce it's open now, and then maybe three, four more emails over that week."

While her launches worked well, Deborah didn't like what happened after the doors closed, and has found a different mindset is needed for membership growth.

"It's scary then because you do close your doors. Then for two months, you just have people cancelling. You're not getting new people in. So there's definitely that mind game with the memberships where you're constantly looking at yeah your growth rate, but that's your churn rate as well. So it's definitely a new way of looking at business, and those retention numbers and all of that. So you can launch, but if you can't keep people in then it's definitely not going to stay for too long"

The membership has been through a few launch cycles since it first started, but now Deborah is leaving the doors open.

"I think I've always wanted to have evergreen, but I just didn't have the system, or even my website wasn't really optimised for that. It's barely mentioned on my website actually. So that's what I'm doing at the moment. I'm just redesigning the whole thing so that it's everywhere, and it makes sense...

But mostly it's because I am not a big fan of launches. It's a personal thing. I know they work really well for some people. They work well for me too, but it's not something that I necessarily enjoy doing. So, you know, that's kind of why you start your own business, to do things the way you like doing them... so I kind of wanted to move away from that launch model, and also just offering people the ability to join when they want to join, and when they need it most. I hate the idea of having people that need help with something right now, and having to say, 'Hey, we're closed for maybe 60 more days, so come back when you don't need us anymore.'"

Content Concerns

Although Tizzit HQ already has a huge library of content, Deborah still has a long list of resources she'd like to add.

"I launched with a lot of content already, but I have a list of things that I want to have in the membership that I don't yet. After that I probably will chill out a bit more, but I really want to push those out, because I know they're really important for my members.

I sort of wish now looking back that I had like three months content scheduled and planned and recorded like ahead of time, which I didn't.

...It's not like me. I'm this person that does everything in advance. So I kind of wish that I'd organised myself a bit better for that."

The content inside the membership includes courses, one-off guest workshops and shorter tech tutorials.

"Some courses I know I want in there because they're important building blocks for their businesses. But as soon as those core courses are in there, I'm more comfortable doing less, and just sort of like updating...I'd rather make sure...people get up-to-date information, rather than just constantly building new content."

Deborah launched with a monthly live Q&A call, but as most questions got answered in the forum, it's evolved into a hot seat style experience.

"... this has moved more into a critique, or a feedback, or a shop feedback kind of thing where I'll share my screen, and we go in depth into someone's website, or someone's Etsy shop, or someone's strategy. We're able to sort of look together at, hey, this is what you should change in terms of your SEO strategy, or your pictures, or your conversion, like how to optimise your site."

Reducing Stress & Increasing Predictability

Less stress, greater financial predictability and a clearer focus are the three main benefits Deborah enjoys as a membership owner.

"I don't really like launches. I've tried them. They've always done well... I just don't like it. It drains my energy. It stresses me out, and it just makes me anxious. It's just not good for me honestly.

So, I love that I don't have to do that. I love that I'm going evergreen. I love that I know I can predict my revenue. It feels so much less stressful than having those big peaks in cash flow, then having to deal with all that type of cash flow management.

...With a membership site...you can see trends happening... you can predict and react accordingly. I've really liked that. That has an effect on my personal life I guess as well. I just feel so much less stressed.

I love that I found what I'm doing. I feel like I have my core offering now. For a couple of years, I was selling different things, and I wasn't really sure what is it that I'm really focused on.

Right now it's so clear that I make decisions so much more easily because I'm like, 'Does this help my membership or not?'"

An Engaging Roadmap

The membership was actually inspired by a physical planner that Deborah created, the Maker's Roadmap, which now acts as the main pathway to help members navigate the content.

"It's really my system for starting and growing a successful handmade shop. So it's a productivity journal that you know… you would have your weekly spreads, monthly spreads, and every three months there's an assessment that you take to understand where you're at on your journey, what you should be focusing on, what you should definitely not be focusing on, to help people focus and fight that sort of overwhelm….

...that Maker's Roadmap is really the base of everything I do now. It's kind of like my core concept if you want. So you'll find it in the planner. And that helps you figure out when you need to do what. And then you'll find the exact same stages, inside of the membership. So that you start where you should start, and then slowly grow."

In the membership site, high quality content, organized around the Maker's Roadmap, keeps her members engaged and ontrack.

"The Roadmap is very big, that's the most important part of everything I teach.... that really helps them navigate the content inside of the membership.

I made the Roadmap pretty fun too. I just try to add a bit of personality to the site. I've been adding custom coded elements, and make fun little animations and things when they take stuff off the list... just so that they feel a little bit special, and it's not boring because you're working on your marketing. You know, make it fun, as much as possible."

Being able to organise content around her Roadmap was actually a key reason why Deborah was drawn to the membership model.

"I think that's why I love membership so much, and what got me... What decided me was the idea that some people simply are not working on the right things at the right time. I wanted to have the ability to have all sorts of trainings, but also to tell them, 'Hey, this one is not for you right now. Focus on this instead.'"

A Chatty Community

Deborah already ran a large free Facebook group, so she chose to create her membership community on a separate forum, to create a distinct experience, and stop her members from being distracted.

"I thought the challenge was going to be keeping active in the community. That's actually turned out to be just the easiest thing to do. I was a bit scared, I was like, 'How much time is this going to take? Will I be able, you know is it going to be overwhelming?' I just love, like I love every day checking in with my members and getting to see the progress that they're making. So that's been actually really enjoyable."

Initially, Deborah was expecting it to take some to get members engaged and talking in the forum, but that wasn't the case.

"It happened quite organically. I was waiting for those crickets, like this is going to be empty and horrible, and will people like the forums. It's not a Facebook group. But it actually worked quite well. I've added a lot in my courses…to encourage them to, 'hey, at this stage, come and upload this to this part of the forum so that we can take a look', so that people would engage and create conversations in there. So, quite rapidly, people were chatting… it was pretty much from the beginning"

Deborah no longer replies to posts as much as in the beginning, but still reads everything, although this is getting harder to keep up with.

"Since I launched, I don't think I've missed a single post that's been posted in this thing. I don't reply to everything, not as much as when I started, but I definitely read everything, and if I see something that I can add in the conversation, I'll definitely go in and comment. I still mostly reply to almost everything.

...It's already getting a little bit too sort of like chatty in there for me to do that, but I'm very engaged and very present, and I'll do surprise videos or you know sometimes instead of replying by typing, I'll record a video for something that I think is going to be helpful for more than one person, and post it instead of just a text."

Welcome Packages

When Deborah first launched she was keen to get her founder members engaged in the membership straight away, and decided to send a welcome package in the mail to help members feel part of something and more inspired to connect with the community.

"When I launched... I was scared that no one was going to be chatty in the community. I really wanted to sort of encourage them [the founder members] to feel like they were part of something. So I sent a little special welcome package through the mail, like physical things...I think all of this added up to an experience that made them feel like they were part of something bigger than just the regular membership site."

The package included a polaroid photo of Deborah holding up the recipient's name, and a card, in a handcrafted envelope, with a wax seal.

"I made it really look special. Inside, I had a map of my Roadmap, because I had that design, kind of like back in the days when we didn't have GPS and you actually had a map in your car, kind of looks like that. So I printed that.

Then, and this is what took me so long, I took a Polaroid of myself with the person's name on a piece of paper, which I was like, 'This is going to be so easy.` You know, it's not. Like with 250 of them, I had to have my partner obviously take the picture because I'm holding the paper every time. We had to write 250 names, and then match that with the envelope. It was just a lot of work, but it was so special, because each name, I was like, 'This is an actual person that I'm going to get to help.'"

A More Relaxed Life

Deborah likes to wake early (5am) and take the first few hours of the day to herself, before starting work.

"I start work at around 9:30 or 10:00, which is quite late in my head. I used to work so much more than that.

I used be at work at 6:00 or 7:00am. And I've just realised… you can't do that for more than a couple of years. So I'm much more chilled now that I've got a membership."

Deborah runs her membership with the help of just one assistant currently.

"She feels like so much more than an assistant…I could not do what I do without her. She has been amazing. She was my first hire. I got her as a virtual assistant just a few hours a week. She was just meant to help me with promoting my blog post and things like that. Now she just does so much more for me. She'll do anything from support, emails, and things like that too.

All of my content pretty much, she takes care of. I record my videos, but I am not involved at all in scheduling them, editing them, turning them into blog posts, putting them onto social media. I don't do any of that.

When I send my newsletter, I have to actually go and have a look at 'What's going out tomorrow, I don't actually know. I forgot because I did that three months ago.' So yeah, she's been fantastic. Then I also have a video editor that does all the editing for me. That's it, really. Growing slowly, but I think in the future, I'm definitely going to need to add some more, or give her more hours."

Ideally, Deborah would like to outsource metrics tracking and reporting, admin and community management in the future. She already has a system in place to make delegation easier.

"When you start delegating though, this is pretty addictive. The first time I hired Alicia, I thought 'this is scary, she's not going to be doing this the right way'. Now I'm just like this system freak. I record everything I do. It goes into an Asana system and a process because I don't know if I'm going to want to do it next month. If I don't want to, it's there and someone can take it. So I'm feeling a lot more... I love delegating. If I could afford to have a bigger team right now, I would absolutely do it because time is so precious."

What's Next For Tizzit

Being able to predict her monthly revenue has reduced stress levels for Deborah, and made it possible for her to consider retiring her partner so they can travel together more.

"The fact that I can predict revenue has just changed a lot of my personal plans and all. My goal for next year, is to retire my partner...it feels so much easier with the membership because I'm like, 'this is how much I take every month for ourselves. If I can grow that by that number, then you can quit your job, and we can go travelling

because I can work with my computer anywhere.' So that's really... it's really helped me work towards that goal....

...And then it's just made me so much more happy to work on my business, because I get up, I know the people I'm working for. The community aspect has been huge because it just creates that... You know, I can put names and faces and real stories behind the people I work with. That's really gratifying and it's really motivating.

I don't know why I didn't start a membership site earlier really."

Caylee Grey: Get Messy

Membership Details:

Name: Get Messy

Topic: Art Journalling

Launched: 2014

Website: getmessyart.com

Interview Date: May 2019

Caylee Grey is runs Get Messy, a membership site devoted to art journaling.

"We focus specifically on art journalists, because it's a different type of art technique and it's one that's very freeing, very painful...And it's called Get Messy because we kind of encourage people to get messy."

Get Messy wasn't originally started as a membership site, instead it began life as personal challenge between Caylee and her best friend, run on a public blog.

"In 2014, my internet BFF and I, were chatting online and we were talking about how we wanted to be artists, right? And how ridiculous it was that we wanted this, but we weren't making any art...

We decided to challenge each other to be accountable to making three pieces of art per week. We chose our art journal as the medium for it. I mean, we could have done anything, but when you're making a journal, it's low pressure. We have to post on our blogs. That's how we started."

The friends called the challenge LNC Get Messy and planned to take it in turns posting on their blogs. Within a week someone new had asked to join in.

"We did that on our blogs and...that lasted exactly a week before someone asked if she could join the challenge...and from there it just more and more people asked to join the challenge. We had a rotating blog hop every single week. What we would do, is we would just link everyone that was part of it. And they became 50 members and we're like, we can't link 50 people every blog post."

When the challenge grew large to be sustainable in it's existing form, Caylee and her friend turned it into a business and gave Get Messy its own site, offering lifetime access for $50.

Fifty members quickly became 500 members.

"We decided to close it there and that's when we turned it to a business and we invited everyone to join, Get Messy on a private site... Then we had a whole lot of people join. We thought it would maybe be 50 more. We had 500 people join us.

All from blogs. And then we decided we're going to stop making tutorials on there and we're going to have art prompts and all that. It became more formal over time. 2014, was when the organic thing happened and then 2015 we made it paid and people started committing.

...We were just hoping to make more art after work, or whatever. Then we eventually [in 2015] both quit our jobs and started doing this full time."

Ever Evolving

Over the last five years, Get Messy has undergone a number of changes around how the site is structured and functions.

*"I think that we have evolved a lot, Get Messy has evolved a lot, but I think that **it's really important to know what stage you should evolve, because you don't want to do it when it's too late. You don't want to have all these fancy things when you're very small.***

I feel evolution has been pretty good. And because our artists and members in our community are evolving as well, they need different things. That's the beauty about membership site, right?"

Despite changing tech platforms twice (from Blogger to Wishlist Member to MemberPress) and experimenting with different kinds of content delivery, the core of the membership has always remained the same.

"The core is just that we want people to make more art. It's a very simple thing that we want. Everything has always had that focus. It's just over time, the technology's become better. The artists that are teaching in our membership site, they've become better.... Better quality and a lot more content, because over five years you tend to get a lot of content on the membership site....

...When we changed over to MemberPress, I went through every single piece of content that we had because in the beginning we were basically outputting about four new pieces of content per week, which is quite a lot. It's insane. We honestly realised this is too much. No one can create all of it. We didn't want that to be the barrier of entry for people making art.

When I went through every single piece, they were, I think maybe 20 things that I deleted. But there's still a lot of value in some of the first things that we put out. I just figured out a better way for organising it."

On A Mission

Caylee is as passionate as ever about her membership site, and on a mission to help as many art journalists as possible.

"But the truth is that I have a mission. My mission is to get 10,000 artists nurturing their creative practice regularly. If I want to achieve a mission, I need to let other people know about it...

And I'm very lucky because our marketing is probably 80% word of mouth. It's all been members posting their artwork on Instagram, mainly Instagram. And just sharing their own excitement about what they've made. Then because of that we've seen a lot of growth."

While not something she ever imagined herself doing, the membership site has changed how Caylee looks at life and her ability to help people and make a difference.

"Someone gave me a nickname...this nickname has changed my life. She called me a fairy art mother, which is just like my favourite thing ever...

...**Being a fairy art mother to artists has just filled me with happiness that I never knew was possible. Growing up, I never had dreams to change the world.** I was totally happy with having an office job. I was fine with finding my value in doing, I don't know what, but I was fine to just lead a normal life.

I feel Get Messy has completely revolutionised the way that I feel about life, and it's made me realise that I can help people because I truly believe that art heals and it heals people in different ways. It's healed me. It heals people emotionally, maybe not physically yet. We need to figure that out.

But seeing other people changed by art as well is just amazing. It's really amazing and I just feel so grateful to be able to do that."

After 5 years of working together though, Caylee's business partner, Lauren, has decided to leave the business. A tough transition but one that allows Caylee to refocus on her mission, and hiring extra team members is making things easier.

"Lauren is moving on. She wants to do things in real life, instead of teaching through a computer. It's just me being in charge, essentially. But I've hired a few people to help me out. We've got a Community Manager, we've got someone who's going to be the person communicating with the artists. Then, I have a few other contractors."

Action & Accountability

There's no natural endpoint to art journaling, so Caylee has found that if a member enjoys the first month or so, they tend to stay for the long-term, something that Caylee encourages with her focus on action and accountability.

"I've kind of figured that people join Get Messy and they'll opt to stay for a month and then leave and realise it's not for them, it's not helping them on their journey. Or they'll stay forever, which is lovely.

We have a big focus on being action driven and we kind of try to reinforce the idea that you're an artist if you're making art....

In everything that we do, we make sure that it's practical. We're not just like, 'Hey, look at this pretty piece of art.' We are saying, 'Okay, look at this art, now you go and you do X, Y, Z.'
We make it very actionable for them.

The other thing that we do is we have strong accountability. The friendships that have been made in Get Messy are, they're incredible. People have met in real life, people have gone on to pair up and start their own businesses. They've paired up for gallery shows. The level of friendship, real, true friendship is super deep.

That is something that I'm focusing on too. To be able to harness that even more, so that more people in the community get to experience that even if they are introverted or they live in the village, or whatever.

You say 'people come for the content and stay for the community' - you're right. So nurturing that is definitely something that makes people stick around. We've got a few things that we do around that."

A 24/7 Hangout

To encourage more connections within her community Caylee has an online video chat room that's always open, something that has really deepened member connections.

"People can join in whenever they want. They can ask a bunch of people to join in and then they just have the computer open and everyone is making art and chatting…

*… I think **that's where the majority of friendships, the deep, deep friendships have been happening.** Is because they're meeting every single week…They're not only talking about art anymore. They're talking about other things, which is kind of magical."*

To help new members join in with the community, Caylee is organizing a hangout just for them at the start of each season.

"It's obviously tough for people who are new to just join in when everyone knows each other. Right?…I'm very excited about that because then we'll get new people being able to experience that magic."

Combining Facebook & Forum

The membership includes an onsite forum, which is great for creating resources and long term community content, however despite disliking Facebook herself, Caylee also has a Facebook group as well to allow for more casual conversations.

"Facebook and I have a difficult relationship… I've called it a pop-up Facebook group because I'm going to see… I'm not promising that it's going to be up there forever.

My thoughts on that is that we have the forums which are beautiful, so beautiful. And they're there for resources, right? If you're looking for the best paints you can go and search, then you'll immediately find all these recommendations. Then we're treating Facebook kind of as chatter.

And we do tend to have an audience or like our members tend to be less keen to hang out on the computer. Facebook works well for them. They don't enjoy the forum. Some of those are... they tend to like Facebook more. I'm not a fan of Facebook, but I am a fan of connection and that's why we've got Facebook."

Free Classes

Caylee uses free content to build her audience, then offers a free class to give an insight into the membership.

"We have a free class. It's called How To Start Art Journaling. That's just to get anyone that doesn't know what our training is, to get a taste and to see if they like it, to see if they like the way we teach. And we recently improved the content on that. But other than that, we've got a newsletter. We give free classes and stuff."

Sourcing Expert Teachers

Caylee provides the tools, space and encouragement to help her members create their art, but she isn't the only expert in the membership.

"The best thing about Get Messy to me is that, I'm not the best artist... but I'm very good at getting other artists to be their best selves.

And some of our guest teachers are members, which is amazing because we've seen them grow...And we've realised that there is a lot of power in that as well...Like 60 artists that have taught on the site, they've taught in different ways. They've either taught a tutorial or they've done a whole class or they've done a lot of master class..."

While Caylee releases a lot of new content into her membership, including from guest teachers, she has a very organised approach to content creation.

"We plan a year in advance, because I'm very routine driven and I like to know what's happening and I don't like the idea of doing things on the day of. But, recently my business partner left. I'm changing a few things just to make it manageable for running myself. Now, I'm working about six months in advance, which is kind of stressful for me. I think I'm very bad at it. I need to be more flexible."

Worst Case Scenario

Caylee's advice for anyone thinking about starting a membership site is not to focus too much on the perks, like the impact you can have and the time and income freedom, when making your decision. Instead think about the downsides and whether they are things you can live with.

"Make friends with other people in the industry. Really, really enjoy talking about the topic that you want to have, all the time you can. Because if you don't like it even a little bit you're going to get so sick of it and it's not going to be fun. And it needs to be fun. Because if you're choosing this route then, choose something fun... ...You don't look at the good parts, but you look at the bad parts and you think, am I willing to take on those bad parts? A membership site... I don't know, you have to be creative on demand, right? That could be a downside.

If you think about the worst possible scenario, and you're still happy with that, then that's a very good sign that this is meant to be and you should hustle towards it."

What's Next For Get Messy

Caylee is focused on her mission of helping 10,000 artists, but as a result of this mission would also like to grow from a 6 to a 7 figure business.

"My five year plan, is to empower 10,000 artists into our regular creative practice... and through that I want a million dollar company. Million Euro because it's now... it was an American company. It's now a German company, so a million Euro company."

Chris Ducker: Youpreneur

Membership Details:

Name: Youpreneur Academy

Topic: Personal Brand Businesses

Launched: September 2015

Website: youpreneuracademy.com

Interview Date: May 2019

Chris Ducker runs YouPreneur Academy, a membership that helps people build, market, monetise and grow personal brand businesses.

"It's for anybody that wants to build a business based around them, their personality and their expertise...people like coaches, consultants, podcasters, content creators, authors, public speakers, that sort of thing.

If you're selling ultimately you and your experience as either a service or if you productize in some way, then that's who the Youpreneur Academy is for.

And it is a combination of both learning material, which is everything from monthly workshops through to recordings of our live sessions from Youpreneur summit, which is our annual conference that you're well aware of. And then obviously, there's the community forums and all that sort of stuff as well."

When the membership first launched it was focused around the more general topic of online business. After the initial success of his launch however, Chris didn't see the ongoing results that he wanted, and so he decided to niche down further and focus on personal brands.

"The funny thing is, when we launched back in September 2015, it was just build an online business. And it was great. Right out of the gate, we had over 300 members within a week, it was fantastic.

And then things started just dropping off, and we couldn't quite figure out why. And then we realised that it was actually just too broad, the forums were too broad. So you have one guy talking about Amazon reselling, and another guy talking about online courses, and another person speaking about public speaking. And the conversations were just way too varied….

…we figured out the whole niching down thing, becoming the leader in your space. And that really ended up niching down even further into that personal brand business niche. And slowly but surely, now we're starting to own it, through the marketing messages that we put out, obviously, the language that we use, and all that sort of stuff as well."

Creating a Legacy

Chris already had two 7-figure businesses before starting YouPreneur and the membership began out of a desire to share his experience and knowledge with others. It has quickly become what he sees as his legacy and life's work though.

"We [Chris and his wife, Erz] have gotten very good at creating, launching and building businesses over the last 15 years, that ultimately end up not requiring us day-to-day…which are multi seven figure annual revenue businesses….

Youpreneur was kicked off really, scratching my own itch... As of 2012, I started doubling down on my own personal brand, the speaking, book deal, high paying consulting, that type of stuff.

And there was nothing really else out there that could really take me on the journey of that build, market, monetise model, which we ended up giving it the nickname of the Business of You model. And so I started scratching my own itch...

*...**I don't need Youpreneur, but I love Youpreneur. I believe that this is ultimately going to be my life's work. That's the way I look at it.** So when we launched it four years ago, I remember saying, 'This is going to be the next decade of my career. I can't wait.' But now we're four years in and I'm like, 'I'm not doing nothing else. This is it. This is all I want to do now going for the rest of the time that I'm at work.'*

So that might change and morph and pivot as the years go by. But ultimately, I'm having way too much fun working with this very particular subset of people within the world."

Experimenting with Launches

Initially the membership site was open all the time, but Chris later decided to experiment with limiting enrolment periods, something that had mixed results for him.

"We were open, all the time, when we first kicked off. And now we're open all the time...But January 2017, we closed the doors. We did one big promo at the beginning of the year, we closed the doors... And we launched again in May that

year. And it was very, very successful, extremely successful. And then we closed the doors again. And then we tried it again with another launch, I think in September of that year. And it was not as successful as the one earlier on that year.

*And when I look retrospectively back on it, I didn't like it. **I didn't like the launch model at all, particularly for a membership. Because there were definitely people that were discovering the Academy in between launches, when we were 'closed'. And we were having to turn them away because the doors weren't open, plain simple.***

…We were saying to ourselves all the time, how many people did we lose this week, I wonder? How many people went to join another one, perhaps? Or buy another course or completely disappear from our ecosystem never be seen again?

…When we looked at the numbers, ultimately, we wouldn't have or we didn't get any more members, and we would have done in that six to eight month period, post during and before those launches. So in the end, we decided to swing the doors wide open and leaving it like that."

While Chris is glad he tested the two approaches to discover which was best for him, he does also regret the time he lost on other marketing activities by closing the doors.

"I think we almost wasted a year in regards to fine tuning our marketing efforts, fine tuning our messaging, and all the rest of it. Because when the doors are closed, they're closed, you're not even talking about it, are you really? You're just busy showing up and just providing what you promised those that are on the inside already.

I think that year cost us. It cost us in a number of different ways. And I think that if I could go back and have a do over, I wouldn't have closed those doors twice in 2017, I'd left them wide open."

The Youpreneur Ecosystem

While Youpreneur began with just the membership academy, over the last 4 years more products have been added, with the Academy becoming less of a focus.

"When we launched it was the only thing that was on offer. And it was the only thing that we focused on.

But as time has gone by over the last four years, things have changed now. Things just naturally evolve and pivot. And as we get deeper and deeper into our legacy planning for the company, it really does come down to the fact that we want to be known ultimately as an education company. That's what we want to be…And so because of that, the Academy has become less of a focal point within the overall Youpreneur ecosystem, it's still a priority."

Alongside the membership Chris offers the Youpreneur summit, an annual 2-day conference, a VIP mastermind group, his book, Rise of the Youpreneur, and a soon-to-be-launched flagship course based on that book.

"It's funny how things have grown, because the book came from feedback from the Academy. And now the book is being turned into the flagship online course…there are some people that will be happy to read the book and get to work. There'll be some people that will join the academy and just love the fact that there's that virtual water cooler that they can get to, to learn and gossip and network with each other.

But they'll never come to one of our live events, for example. But then there are other people who do want to do nothing but live events, and will never touch your digital stuff.

So we're trying to build out the ecosystem as a whole, to ultimately get to the point of being able to serve anyone, no matter where they are in their personal brand business journey, but more importantly, in a way that best suits them.

And so there's other things that we're planning, mastermind groups, and things like that, which will be launched going into 2020, as well."

Organic Content Wins

Chris has spent a lot of time finding what works for the membership when it comes to attracting members, and refining his niche combined with organic content has proven to be the key factor in membership sales.

"Without a doubt, it's our organic content. We create a lot of content and going into 2020, we'll be putting our foot down on the gas even more on that.

…And so we drop three pieces of content on a weekly basis. Right now, we want to get that up to five pieces going into next year, we're about to put our foot down quite heavily on video content, which we haven't done a lot of up to this point…

…we have a weekly digest email that goes out to everybody as well, where we have that's been really chopped down from our larger mailing list, which is 10s and 10s and 10s of thousands of people. The digest comes in probably, I think there's about 18,000 or so people on that email right there, with an open rate of early 40% plus.

So we're very happy with the way that has gone. But again, it's been about a language that we're using, it's been about the fact that we're really consistent with subject lines surrounding keywords, like personal branding, or online branding and things like that.

So we've niched down a lot in the last eight to nine months, and it's certainly starting to make things a lot easier for sure."

Initially, Youpreneur didn't have its own site and free content was published on Chris's personal brand website instead, something that hindered his content plans.

"I was always hyper aware of not allowing anybody but me to publish content on my personal domain name website. So we couldn't do guest posts, we couldn't do guest contributors, we couldn't do any of that sort of stuff. With youpreneur.com, there's a blog post from me once a week, which is purely republished from other content that I've created. There is a guest contributor article once a week. And then we have Youpreneur FM, which is our weekly podcast, which obviously is published once a week as well."

Making the switch to using a separate public website for the Youpreneur brand enabled Chris and his team to see that the personal-brand focused content was what people wanted. They weren't just attracted to its affiliation with Chris.

"That's not to say that chrisducker.com is still not an incredible driver of traffic for the Youpreneur Academy. But certainly, I'll put it this way, we don't promote content on chrisducker.com anymore. We don't even create content on

chrisducker.com anymore. The website itself is being redesigned right now to be more of a positioning strategy for me, as a keynote speaker, as an author and investor and advisor, that sort of type of thing. Whereas everything we do personal brand business now, is at youpreneur.com.

And so that's been a pretty major change force, and a crap tonne of work, obviously. But I think, it's definitely early days, but I'd say it's paying off very well for us."

Focusing on Retention

Despite a churn rate of just 5-6%, Chris would still like to improve his member retention.

"Now we've got a good influx of new members every month coming in. Obviously, there's a bit of churn as well, we churn around about 5% to 6% or so a month, which is not horrific. But it's not amazing. I'd like it to be a little bit better. But I think it's just the nature of the beast, you cannot please all the people all the time. And we are very, very niched down now in regards to what we do and who we do it for.

So you might get somebody that joins for a month or two and realises it's just not for them. And that's cool, I hope that we've been able to help them or inspire them in some way, within that couple of months. But there are other people that have been with us for years, literally. So those are the people ultimately that we do everything for, you know what I mean?"

A key focus for Chris going forward is retention strategies and increasing member engagement, something he already has some plans for.

"We have not been as proactive as we could have been in regards to retention strategies…

…This [creating a member news show] was something we initially discussed actually beginning of this year, and we tabled it. And then we had another full team meeting about three weeks ago. And it was right at the top of the agenda. And what we're going to be doing actually is, we're going to be losing our monthly mastermind call, which is a live call. Because we've had increasing complaints from worldwide based members that the timezone just sucks, plain and simple….

… And then we're actually going to be doing a monthly show, we're going to call it Youpreneur TV. And it's going to be on the inside of the academy only, and it will be that news/community/submitted questions and answers. So that way, no matter where our members are in the world, they can go ahead and submit questions throughout the course of the month. And my team will also be pulling questions and hot topics from the forums as well, prior to the shooting of that episode every month. And it's going to be very relevant, we're going to be shooting about 10 days before its due to go live. It should be very relevant, very up to date, and all the rest of it…basically, it's going to be a one hour show, once a month. And yeah, I can't wait to put it together."

A 12 Week Onboarding Programme

When new members first join Youpreneur Academy, Chris has a 12 week roadmap that he takes them through in order to help them get the best results. While this is optional, he's found 80% of new members use it.

"And so what we do is, we actually focus in the first 12 weeks of their membership on onboarding them through what we call our Youpreneur Roadmap. And that, again, is based and built upon that build-market-monetize strategy. So every week, they get a different email, which they can opt in for, or not opt in for when they join....80% of the people that join, click to opt in for that 12 week programme."

Growth Records

Chris has an onsite forum as part of the membership site, where members can ask questions, form mastermind groups and create growth records.

"Every day there's people posting, and replying in there.

I'm in there a couple times each week, replying to people, linking people up together, filling in the gaps for some of our content.... me and my team are very good at connecting the dots in that regards in there...

The big section for me is the growth records section. This is the area that I enjoy visiting the most...every month, they can come back, and they update with what they did that month, whether they hit their goals, what was the struggles, what was the wins, all that kind of stuff. And it just works very very well."

There's no doubt for Chris that members who create a growth record in the community are the ones that succeed.

"Those that do it consistently, month in, they show up month in, month out, they update the group on their goals, they go ahead and set themselves new goals. They are the ones that do the best out of their membership... they're the ones that see the most advancement, the most success."

A Core Remote Team

Chris has a mostly remote team split between the Philippines, where he lived for 17 years, and the UK, where he currently lives. It's also become a family affair, with both his wife, Erz, and now his eldest daughter, Chloe, working for the business too.

"There is Sian, who's our community leader. She's actually based over in the Philippines. She's been a member of my staff for about six years now. Initially, she came on with Virtual Staff Finder, and then when we opened the doors to Youpreneur, she got promoted into that role. So she's coming in the forums every day, connecting those dots for people, welcoming people. She even shoots little welcome videos for our new members…

…And then there is Mersha, who is on the back end, she's my executive assistant/Youpreneur admin girl. She's also based over in the Philippines and she fundamentally handles anything like cancellations, or payment failures, if people want to pause the membership, all that sort of type of stuff. She'll be on the back end of all of that as well. She also handles all of the logistics for our live events as well. She's incredible with all that stuff…

… And then there is Morgan, who joined us in May last year. She's the head of our digital development as a company, as a brand. But she's also in there quite regularly, again, welcoming people, getting people into the right discussions and things like that as well.

And then there's us, my better half… she is not only my biggest fan and cheerleader and supporter, but she's also an extremely important part of our business. She's honestly the heart, I think of Youpreneur… she compliments me perfectly.

And that is the core team. We have freelancers that we work with…we've got a graphic designer in Australia, we've got a Facebook ads manager here in the UK. We've got a content creator in Canada, we got a content creator in the UK as well.

So the team is very much remote, it's very much spread out. And it is definitely growing very rapidly. In fact, actually, we are three days away from our next full time employee, which is my daughter, Chloe. Who's just graduated from University, and she's coming on board to manage all of our social media and rich media, such as the Podcast and YouTube and stuff like that."

3 Hours A Week

Now that everything is running smoothly with the membership and its more refined niche and content strategy, and because he has a core team in place, Chris can spend just 3 hours a week on the membership site.

"The forum is a little sporadic for me, because I travel a lot and things like that. But I'd say on average, I probably do about an hour a week, inside of the forums…I will reply to a ton of messages, I'll start a couple of new threads. That 30 minutes twice a week is very productive, in terms of my own personal input in there.

…other than that there's not much that I personally have to do on a regular consistent basis.

The fact is that the machine has been very nicely oiled over the time that we've been running it…I probably do around about three hours a week, all in.

But four years ago, that was 30 hours a week. So things have pivoted, things have changed slightly. It's not that it's not a priority, it's part of a bigger game plan right now..."

Working less and having more lifestyle freedom was a key reason why Chris turned to the membership model in the first place.

"...the reason why we start these types of lifestyle businesses is because we don't want to have to be sat at a desk for 10 hours a day. I mean, that doesn't interest me at all. I can't affect any change that way. That's not what I want to be doing at all. So I love the recurring nature of the revenue, I love the predictive nature of the business as a model overall. And I love the fact that I can dip in and out as I want, drop those value bombs, converse with people and move on to the bigger picture stuff."

You Have To Show Up

When it comes to achieving success with your membership site, Chris has some simple, but effective, advice.

"Show up, plain and simple. People are going to join because of you and your messaging and your vibe. I often say your vibe attracts your tribe. And it's very, very, very true. You're going to show up, you can't expect to do this and not put in the time, energy and effort particularly on the outset.

That predictable, that recurring revenue is a big, attractive point for a lot of people wanting to start something like this. But if you don't show up, particularly in the early year or two, the chances of it surviving and doing well are very, very, very small indeed.

And when you can afford it, the moment you can afford it, start building a team around you because everything becomes so much easier when you do that."

What's Next For YouPreneur Academy

Chris wants to be seen as the leading authority in the personal brand space, and the membership is a pivotal part of this plan. The most important thing for him however is to see his members doing well.

"I think we definitely want to continue fine tuning the messaging a little bit. And I don't know exactly what that will look like. At the moment, we survey our members once a year, I think that's probably going to end up going to twice a year, to really try and stay on pulse. The big defining goal here is to be seen as the leader, plain and simple, in personal brand, business, education. And again, the Academy is right there at the centre of the entire ecosystem for us.

*So certainly continuing to provide great public content to utilise that to market and obviously to grow the membership overall. But I want to try and get as many poster boys and girls out there as possible in the form of our members, who are revolutionising the way that they make money off of their experience and their personality. So the big thing for me is to see our members doing well. **I think if you can make your members the heroes ultimately of your own journey, then you've done something worthwhile."***

Thanks & Acknowledgements

This book wouldn't have been possible without our podcast guests over the last 3 years and their generosity in sharing their membership journeys. So a huge thank you to:

Stacey Harris, Colin Gray, Avalon Yarnes, John Tuggle, Julie Christie, Christopher Sutton, Holly Gillen, Shannon Rogers, Lisa League, Laura Robinson, Scott Devine, Janet Murray, Brandon Vogt, Kim Bultsma, Scott Baptie, Tim Topham, Anissa Holmes, Mark Warner, Terra Dawn, Nigel Moore, Kim Jimenez, Jared Falk, Mike Collins, Louise Brogan, Melissa West, Chris Marr, Jodie Clarke, Varvara Lyalyagina, John Hatcher, Deborah Engelmajer, Caylee Grey and Chris Ducker.

May your memberships be ever successful!

Thanks to Team TMG – the guys and girls who help us to keep everything ticking over behind *our* membership: Sam, Laura, Claire, James and Amy

Big thank you also to Laura Robinson from Worditude for her help in shaping these stories.

And thank you to all of our members inside Membership Academy. Watching your progress and seeing your membership growth is what enables us to tell stories like these, and it's truly humbling to see everything you're achieving. Thank you for trusting us with your membership sites, and thank you for showing up and doing the work.

You're the reason we do this and we couldn't be prouder to be even a small part of your journey.

And of course thank you to our podcast listeners too for tuning in and supporting us through 3 seasons of Behind The Membership.

MEMBERSHIP
ACADEMY

Ready to take your membership to the next level?

Membership Academy is Your Essential Resource For The Training, Advice, and Support you need to Grow a Profitable, Meaningful Membership Website

Membership Roadmap   **In-Depth Courses**

Expert Workshops   **Supportive Community**

Private Coaching   **Live Q&A Calls**

Exclusive Resources, Software & Discounts

"You have saved me many hours of grief, saved me from missing out on important things I need to be doing that I didn't even know about and have rescued me when I've been overwhelmed and confused. You've helped me with things that probably seem small to you, but have been huge for me. My membership paid for itself within a few hours of joining."

Kim McKenney - xcskination.com

**Join the community today at
www.membershipacademy.com**

Made in the USA
Monee, IL
15 November 2019

16875422R00215